Think on These Things

Thoughts to Ponder for Each Day of the Year

Myron D. Miller

Think on These Things
First Printing: June, 2014

Cover design: Keith Peiffer
Graphic design/layout: Keith Peiffer
Image selection: Dara Houp
Editor: Rebekah Peiffer
Printed by CreateSpace, An Amazon.com Company
ISBN: 978-1497358102 (Paperback edition)

All photography used is public domain, except for the images on the following pages:
Kate Elizabeth Photography: 132, 418
Amelia Tatnall: 282, 338, 366
Janae Rose Photography: 86, 138, 256, 316, 372
andy olsen photography: 344
Larry Bieber: 190, 302
Portrait Innovations: author photo

Dedicated to my parents Mahlon and Dorothy
Miller, who so fully and naturally followed Moses'
words of encouragement:

*Impress [God's precepts] on your children. Talk about
them when you sit at home and when you walk along
the road, when you lie down and when you get up
(Deuteronomy 6:7).*

ENDORSEMENTS

"This book of reflections is a gifted piece of writing, full of the fruit of an examined life. Dr. Miller's stories, insights, and wisdom are offered with both a physician's down-to-earth directness and the gracious delight of a wonder-filled child of God…Definitely worth reading!"

> - Jo Ann Kunz, pastor, spiritual director, Affiliate Faculty Evangelical Theological Seminary

"I think you will experience some of the same joys I have known with Myron Miller as you open this book… He telescopes decades of life experiences and scriptural ponderings into a year of reflective readings. The book navigates through the fog of controversy and pain to give refreshing biblical perspectives. I was struck with laughter, sadness, fresh thoughts and ultimately obtained a sharper view of self, God, and the intimacy Jesus desires with each of us. Here is a treasure in the way of Oswald Chambers' *My Utmost for His Highest*—applying ancient truth to 21st century issues. Followers of Jesus and those curious about the faith will find these pages filled with insights and glimpses into the inner life of a devoted Christian. Whether in full agreement or not, readers from all over the world will 'think on these things.' Draw up a chair and ask the Spirit to breathe a fresh word from God for your situation."

> - James W. Barnett, MD, Associate Clinical Professor in Family and Community Medicine, University of Illinois College of Medicine; Associate Staff, Christian Medical Association

"*Think on These Things* is a wonderful daily meditation guide. The book is relevant for those exploring Christianity and those well familiar with the faith…Dr. Miller openly, honestly and humbly shares his life experiences and the Christian lessons learned. He makes God real and offers practical advice on how to make God part of our everyday lives. The book is both humorous and poignant. It is difficult to read just one vignette at a time; I read the entire year's worth of meditations in one sitting. This is a book not to miss!"

> - Kathryn Chu, MD, MPH, FACS

"Myron Miller is thoughtful, invitational, compassionate and Christo-centric. He invites readers to join him as he probes the depth of God's unrelenting love and the practical implications of the radical new creation, the church...The author seasons his own observations and experiences with insights gained from his wide reading. These meditations are practical, inspirational, instructive, and vibrant, with an occasional dash of humor."

- John E. Sharp, history professor and author of *Orie O. Miller (1892-1977) Biography of a Servant Leader*

"Like a coach with an athlete, or a friend on the porch, Myron Miller offers encouragement to those walking the way of Jesus in this collection of daily devotions...Myron brings a warm and winsome wisdom to situations we know and face. His familiarity with a wide range of authors adds their voices to the mix, too. *Think on These Things* is full of insight, reminders, and gentle nudges for all who move along the path God marks out."

- Dan Schmidt, pastor and author of *Playa Perdida* and *Taken by Communion*

"Myron Miller draws living water from a deep well of wisdom gained through his experiences...It is a clarion call for followers of Jesus to think: to use the brilliant, beautiful, imaginative minds that God created. Myron's devotional readings will motivate you to think, to pray, and to hunger and thirst for Christ and His Kingdom."

- James L. Schwenk, PhD, pastor, teacher, and author of *Catholic Spirit: Wesley, Whitefield, and the Quest for Evangelical Unity in 18th Century British Methodism*

"Myron did not just write this book; he lives it. His words are born out of a wealth of experience...You have in your hands a book that is both very practical and highly inspirational—a must read!"

- Robert A. Haggard, MD

Contents

ACKNOWLEDGMENTS

I have been blessed to be a member of seven churches over the years, all of which have left their imprint on me. They have had positive molding influences, yet I alone am responsible for my residual imperfections, which are legion.

This book could not have been written without the help of others. When I balked at all the work of getting this book done, my family came to the rescue. My daughter Bekah has contributed her amazing editing skills to help my grammar, coherence, spelling and flow. My daughter Dara has added her photography skills so that hopefully what I lack in content won't be noticed due to her choice of artistic photos. My son-in-law Keith has done the layout and graphic design; without his computer skills, I'd have been lost. I can't say enough about my wonderful wife Doreen. Her love for God and desire to grow spiritually are contagious to all those around her, including me. My hope would be to be able to pass on some of that yearning, which lies in all our souls, to know God more fully and to experience his love and presence each day.

In *Pensées*, Blaise Pascal notes how authors often talk about *my* book, *my* insights and *my* stories, when in reality they should be saying, *our* book. Because for the most part, much more of what is found in a book belongs to other people than to the author. This is particularly true in this book, which contains many stories of my patients (who are usually disguised and have pseudonyms), my family (who have to put up with me writing about their uniquities), my friends, and fellow church members. My thanks to all of them for sharing their lives and stories with me, and now with you.

INTRODUCTION

Some years ago in an effort to have a more regular devotional life, I began to write down my meditational thoughts. Like the construction worker who discovered he was missing a finger after pouring some concrete, I felt like I had put a lot of myself in my work. It struck me that if what I was writing was helpful to me in my spiritual life, perhaps it could help others as well—this is the desire of my heart.

Reflections on life experiences, Scripture, and God are the garden soil from which my writings grow. I am a theologically conservative Christian, though my spirituality is somewhat of a mosaic. I grew up in a Mennonite home, and both my parents were raised Amish. In addition to my Anabaptist heritage, the charismatic movement and the contemplative stream have also influenced me. Nonetheless, my primary perspective is evangelical. My writings are flavored by medical mission work—three years in Zambia (with the Brethren in Christ Church) and five months in Honduras (with the Moravian Church). Some of my stories are from working over twenty-five years as a family practice doctor in rural Pennsylvania, some from being the father of four daughters, and others from serving as an elder in our local church. My meditations also reflect the fact that I have always enjoyed reading and studying on my own, and I have taken just enough seminary courses to make me theologically dangerous.

I would encourage you to read these meditations devotionally with an open mind and an open heart. Listen to what God's Holy Spirit may say to you and to what you may be invited to ponder. Remember the admonition, "Keep an open mind—but not so open that your brain falls out." Use discernment and test what is shared; take what is good and helpful, and discard the rest.

January

ACCEPTED ANYWAY

"I will set out and go back to my father and say to him: Father, I have sinned against heaven and against you. I am no longer worthy to be called your son … But while he was still a long way off, his father saw him … he ran to his son, threw his arms around him and kissed him." (Luke 15:18-20)

We all fear rejection. We know our inadequacies, yet we long for approval and acceptance in spite of them. Rejection is a painful reminder of our flaws. Most of us can vividly remember times we've been rejected. The pain associated with rejection often strengthens the memory of what might have otherwise been a trivial event.

During recess in fifth grade, I remember getting picked *last* for a dodge ball team. Not that it really mattered; it's a dumb game anyway. Then there was the time as a junior in high school, I was on a bus trip returning from a weekend football game. I was sitting next to Tina, my heartthrob, and finally got up the nerve to steal a kiss. Unfortunately, she turned her head so fast I only ended up with a mouthful of hair. I wisely deduced I was being rejected. I was able to come to that astute conclusion because it had happened to me once or twice before … okay, twenty-seven times before, but the exact number isn't what's important here.

Our souls yearn for acceptance while simultaneously being aware of our failures and inadequacies. We resemble the prodigal son, who shunned wise counsel, squandered his wealth, and lived a wild and self-absorbed life. Nonetheless, we still long for the father who will throw his arms around us, put a ring on our finger, and kill the fattened calf. It's a puzzling reality—we know we are a mess, yet we want acceptance anyway. Would God give us hunger if there were no food to satisfy it? Or would he give us thirst if there were no liquids to quench it? The longing of our souls for acceptance must also have a way for fulfillment. Our deepest desire is to feel God's arms around us, and his deepest desire is to have his arms around us. Let us turn toward home, where our father awaits us, and experience the desire of our hearts … acceptance anyway.

OUR UNCHANGING HEARTS

Woe to the city of oppressors, / rebellious and defiled! / She obeys no one, / she accepts no correction. / She does not trust in the LORD. / She does not draw near to her God. (Zephaniah 3:1-2)

In the verses above, the prophet Zephaniah personified the city of Jerusalem as a woman. He brought a scathing indictment against Jerusalem for oppressing those around her and rebelling against God above her, resulting in a defiled state. Before we collectively bend over to piously pick up stones to pelt this harlot of a city, Zephaniah goes on to enumerate her shortcomings.

In short, Jerusalem was disobedient, insubordinate, distrustful and proud. **Disobedient**: She knew right behavior but failed to act rightly. **Insubordinate**: She wouldn't accept correction since she wanted to do things her own way, not God's way. **Distrustful**: In spite of a long history of God's proving he was faithful, Jerusalem refused to trust him. **Proud**: Jerusalem's refusal to draw near to God revealed an arrogant pride: *I need no one.*

Are we any different today? Checking to see if any of these failings might pertain to me, I was embarrassed to find that they *all* pertain to me. How could Zephaniah, a man who never met me, writing 2,600 years ago in a cultural setting completely foreign to me, describe me so well? How could his words reach across the centuries and intrude on me as I sit in my usually comfortable living room recliner?

The explanation lies in the fact that Zephaniah was the mouthpiece of God, who knows people's hearts. And in spite of centuries of acquired knowledge and humanistic strivings, we are no closer to pleasing God than Jerusalem was in 630 BC. The problem (the nature of humanity) has not changed, nor has the solution; we need to draw near to God and rely on *his* goodness and *his* mercy.

DEEPER WITH JESUS

Now that same day two of them were going to a village called Emmaus ... Jesus himself came up and walked along with them; but they were kept from recognizing him ... And beginning with Moses and all the Prophets, he explained to them what was said in all the Scriptures concerning himself. As they approached the village ... they urged him strongly, "Stay with us ..." So he went in to stay with them. When he was at the table with them, he took bread, gave thanks, broke it and began to give it to them. Then their eyes were opened and they recognized him, and he disappeared from their sight. Then they asked each other, "Were not our hearts burning within us while he talked with us on the road and opened the Scriptures to us?" (Luke 24:13, 15, 16, 27-32)

I've always been intrigued by the Russian nesting dolls. You pull apart the snugly fitted pieces, and inside there's a new doll revealed and then another and another. Our knowledge of Jesus is similarly unveiled by new revelations. However, with Jesus each new revelation makes him *bigger*, not smaller than before.

As with the disciples on the road to Emmaus, we are often unaware that Jesus walks with us on life's path. As we read Scripture, we may also feel our hearts "burn within us," as the Holy Spirit reveals a new layer of Christ to us. But, like those bound for Emmaus, there is still more of Jesus that we can experience.

There's a deeper level of revelation that God desires for us. Attaining the next revelation involves both our personal responsibility and God's sovereignty. The two disciples on the road to Emmaus strongly urged Jesus to stay with them (personal responsibility). As Jesus broke bread with them and gave thanks, Jesus opened their eyes (God's sovereignty) and revealed himself to them in a very personal way while eating together.

Are we content to know in our heads that Jesus walks with us, even though we may not feel his presence in our hearts? Are we satisfied with intermittent revelations through his Word? Or does our inner spirit yearn for a deeper, more intimate fellowship with Jesus that reveals more and more of who he is? It may be a little scary, but it is also very exciting to go deeper with Jesus—and no matter how deep we go, there is *always* another layer within.

IN THE BLAZING FURNACE

[Nebuchadnezzar] commanded some of the strongest soldiers in his army to tie up Shadrach, Meshach and Abednego and throw them into the blazing furnace … Then King Nebuchadnezzar leaped to his feet in amazement … "Look! I see four men walking around in the fire, unbound and unharmed, and the fourth looks like a son of the gods." (Daniel 3:20, 24-25)

The past several years have been very difficult for me. Numerous times I've found myself asking, "Where is God, and why isn't he doing anything about all these disasters?" Last week I met with some friends to process my struggles. In preparation for the meeting, I was asked to write down anything God might have been teaching me during this trying time. I thought I could probably come up with a few ideas but was stunned when my completed list contained twenty-two items! I was amazed at what God had been doing, embarrassed by my lack of faith, and deeply moved by God's love for me.

God had not been absent or inactive. In fact, he had been intimately working in my life. Although these past few years have been painful, they have been an intense time of spiritual growth for me. Like Shadrach, Meshach and Abednego discovered, it is sometimes not until we are in the fire that we are aware of Jesus' presence. Not only is God always present with us, but he is also always doing something. We may not know God is working because he often does things we don't see, we don't understand or we don't agree with. But, as Isaiah noted, God's ways are not our ways (55:8), and his school of spiritual instruction is not always an easy one.

I've come to realize that while I've sung the song "Have Thine Own Way, Lord" many times, I didn't really mean it. What I meant was, "Have Thine Own Way, Lord… *most* of the time." I would never have asked for this blazing furnace experience, but without it I could not have experienced the all-sufficiency of Jesus: his comfort in sorrow, his hope in despair, and his provision in times of dire need. God truly is good … *all* the time.

EMBRACE THE DARKNESS

I want to know Christ and the power of his resurrection and the fellowship of sharing in his sufferings ... (Philippians 3:10)

If we touch a candle's flame or if we step on a nail, our hand or foot withdraws an instant before our brains are aware a painful contact has been made. The painful contact sends a nerve impulse to our spinal cord, where two pathways are activated—one goes toward the brain and the other toward the hand or foot, causing a withdrawal reflex. So by the time our brains are aware we've touched something painful and decide we should pull back, the spinal cord reflex has already withdrawn our limb from harm's way.

Our emotional responses often mirror our physical responses. When we encounter something painful (e.g., criticism, conflict, rejection), it is common for us to withdraw before we have consciously processed what is happening. Withdrawal may be appropriate. However, sometimes God uses pain and suffering to work out his purposes in our lives (James 1:2-3). At times, we need to allow ourselves to be vulnerable and embrace the darkness of suffering and pain as part of what God has for us.

In his book *A Grace Disguised*, Gerald Sittser, who suffered great pain and loss, chose not to turn away from his pain but to walk straight into the darkness. He discovered the best way to reach the light of the fading sunset was not to pursue it westward. Instead, he turned eastward, going *into* the darkness. In so doing, he was met by the light of the rising sun. Similarly, we sometimes need to learn to accept or even embrace the pain God has allowed in our lives. As we embrace the darkness, remaining vulnerable, a spiritual brokenness occurs. The very cracks and openings from our brokenness often allow God to infuse his love and character into us, making us uniquely his; we are met by the rising sun. We all want to know "the power of his resurrection," but do we also want to know "the fellowship of sharing in his sufferings"?

A FULL VIEW OF GOD

All Scripture is God-breathed and is useful for teaching, rebuking, correcting and training in righteousness. (II Timothy 3:16)

"We're a New Testament church," he said with a tone of pride and piety. Although I think I understood and agreed with most of the intent of his statement, I also had some concerns. In AD 140, Marcion from Rome promoted teachings that gained mild popularity. He rejected the Hebrew Bible and viewed the God of the Old Testament (OT) as different from and inferior to the God of the New Testament (NT) incarnated in Jesus. Second-century author and theologian Tertullian rightly denounced Marcion's teachings as heresy.

It is true we no longer live under the OT Law (Romans 6:14), and we now have a "superior" covenant in Christ (Hebrews 8:6). However, I fear that our relative ignoring and ignorance of the OT is our loss. When Paul said, "All Scripture is God-breathed and is useful" (II Timothy 3:16), he was referring to OT Scripture since the NT had either not yet been written or was not yet accepted as Scripture. *All* Scripture reveals God to us. The God revealed on Mount Sinai (at the giving of the Ten Commandments in Exodus 20) is the same God revealed on Mount Hermon (at Jesus' Transfiguration in Matthew 17). Different portions of Scripture come together to produce a mosaic-like image of God. OT Law reveals God's nature, his heart and his ways. In the psalms we see God's glory and in the prophetic books his justice and mercy. The NT Gospels offer a uniquely clear picture of God through his incarnate son, Jesus. Finally, in Revelation, at the end of time, we see our Lord in majestic splendor. And these are not even all the different kinds of writings in Scripture! Ignoring any portion of Scripture gives us an incomplete view of God.

The first-century church's view of God was not Jesus in a vacuum. First-century Christians had the panorama of Jewish history, revealing God in the OT as well as through Jesus. We have access to that same panorama. Ironically, therefore, if we say, "We are a New Testament church," we are *including* the OT portrait of God because the original NT church would have included it. It is only as we view both the Old and New Testaments together that we obtain a fuller view of God.

SIN HURTS US

"But God did say, 'You must not eat fruit from the tree that is in the middle of the garden, and you must not touch it, or you will die.'" (Genesis 3:3)

Our daughter Bekah has a teenage friend who recently became pregnant. In spite of prayers and discussions, this young girl had an abortion yesterday. Although we continue to pray for her well-being, we know that the very essence of what makes sin sin is that it causes harm. That is why God wants us to avoid sin; sin is not so much a proscription as it is a protection (from harm).

It is a basic unavoidable truth that sin will in some way injure us—physically, emotionally and/or spiritually. Writer Jose Narosky sagely noted, "In war there are no uninjured soldiers." It's similar when we engage in sin; we can't walk away uninjured. Ironically, it was an *unwillingness* to walk away from sin that got humanity (via Adam and Eve) in trouble in the first place.

Have you ever noticed that even today we have an uncanny attraction to the one tree that is forbidden? Why don't we just walk away from it? We quickly lose interest in the rest of the forest that God has given for our pleasure as we stare at the one tree of our desire. As we gaze at that solitary tree, we find it is pleasing to the eye, and before we know it, we are rationalizing. He couldn't have really meant we would *die.* Then like the proverbial rats mesmerized by the pied piper, we march toward the river, certain that although sin might harm other persons, we are somehow immune. Sin is harmful, and none is immune—Adam and Eve failed to heed God's warning; what about us?

A THREE-DIMENSIONAL REVELATION

... "No eye has seen, / no ear has heard, / no mind has conceived / what God has prepared for those who love him" / —but God has revealed it to us by his Spirit. (I Corinthians 2:9-10a)

Bible teacher Ed Miller has a point he repeats before each and every message he delivers. He says, "When we come to the Word of God, there is one principle that is absolutely indispensable ... total reliance on God's Holy Spirit. Only *God* can reveal *God.*" In other words, we can read the words on paper and even consult Bible dictionaries and commentaries, but without the Holy Spirit we are powerless to perceive what God wants to show us.

In the 1960s the first computer-generated 3-D images (autostereograms) were created. They became more sophisticated and took off in popularity in the early 1990s in *Magic Eye* books. At first glance, these two-dimensional pictures look like nothing more than repeated patterns of colorful lines and dots. However, if one views them in just the right way, a three-dimensional picture will almost magically emerge. One eye must view one pattern while the second eye views a second pattern, seemingly at a different focal length. By maintaining both focuses simultaneously, a new, unique 3-D picture will suddenly appear.

Scot McKnight, in *The Blue Parakeet*, says in reading the Bible we want "to turn the two-dimensional words on paper into a three-dimensional encounter with God." Just as 3-D pictures merge art with science, so reading the Scripture merges our minds and our spirits. Our minds perceive the words on the page while our spirits/hearts perceive what God wants to show us. With both Scripture and 3-D pictures, the deeper image may not be immediately apparent. Initially, one may even feel foolish trying to see a second image. However, as one learns how to do it, it becomes easier. There will always be some persons, nonetheless, who don't see a second image and therefore refuse to believe there is one. Yet when we have perceived it ourselves, it is difficult to deny the truth and reality of the spiritual message that lies beyond the words on the page.

INTRINSIC WORTH

For you created my inmost being; / you knit me together in my mother's womb. / I praise you because I am fearfully and wonderfully made ...
(Psalm 139:13-14)

It was the worst snowstorm we'd had in over ten years—twenty-four inches of snow fell in less than two days. The roads were closed, and everyone was snowed in. That was fine with me until I got a phone call from one of my patients who decided to go into labor on that not so balmy day. I called the hospital, and they dispatched someone from the emergency highway crew to transport me to the hospital. When I was done with my work, I was surprised to discover that I was stranded at the hospital. Although it was considered an emergency to get me *to* the hospital, it was not considered an emergency to get me back home. I had special transportation arrangements not because I was important but because my services were important.

Although the world around us assigns value based on what we do, God does not. When I was still being knit together in my mother's womb, I had great value to God, and that was before I had done anything. Even more amazing is that all I have done since my birth has not increased or decreased my value in God's eyes. Worth is an intrinsic quality in God's eyes; it is not based on performance. Now that I'm on the far side of fifty, it's reassuring to know that as I become less productive and my mind and body weaken, I'm not losing value in God's eyes. When my time is over, God will not leave me stranded like the emergency highway crew did. God will take me home. I am so thankful that God declares that "I am fearfully and wonderfully made," and God's love gives me value that I need not earn.

THE REAL ME

Then Saul dressed David ... He put a coat of armor on him and a bronze helmet on his head. David fastened his sword over his tunic and tried walking around ... "I cannot go in these," he said to Saul ... So he took them off. Then he ... chose five smooth stones from the stream, ... and, with his sling in his hand, approached the Philistine. (I Samuel 17:38-40)

When David went to fight the giant Goliath, David didn't get much encouragement. His brother questioned his motives, declaring David lazy, conceited and wicked (I Samuel 17:28). King Saul questioned David's ability, as a young shepherd boy, to stand against a trained, experienced warrior (17:33). Goliath taunted David, declaring his flesh would soon be animal food (17:42-44). In spite of everyone around David suggesting he was foolish to fight Goliath, David remained steadfast, confident God had called him to this task.

Observing David's resolute position, King Saul offered some protective armor and weaponry to give David *some* possible chance for success. David tried on the armor but realized it did not suit him (17:39). He knew he could not be like someone else, wearing their armor and weapons. David had to be the person God had made him and use the skills God had given him. David was a young man with a sling—and with God's help it would be enough.

Do we try to be someone we are not? The pressure to fit in, to be liked or to appear normal seduces us. We wear facades, masking who we truly are and who God wants us to be. The early Hassidic sage Rabbi Zusya noted, "In the coming world, they will not ask me: 'Why were you not Moses?' They will ask me, 'Why were you not Zusya?'" We need to take off the armor, helmet and sword; they do not suit us. Instead, let's pick up the sling and five smooth stones and be the person God created us to be.

HOW JESUS DIED

… They crucified him, along with the criminals—one on his right, the other on his left. (Luke 23:33)

A hospice nurse once told me, "People die the way they lived." This statement was certainly true regarding Jesus' death. His last words before death conveyed much about his life.

Forgiving – "Father, forgive them, for they do not know what they are doing" (Luke 23:34). This is a powerful demonstration of Jesus' deep desire that people experience forgiveness. His executioners were doing the greatest injustice imaginable, and they hadn't even asked for forgiveness, yet Jesus prayed for them to receive it.

Caring – "'Dear woman, here is your son,' and to the disciple, 'Here is your mother'" (John 19:26-27). Jesus ignored the unbelievable injustice, the excruciating pain, and his own imminent death, to show care and compassion for his mother, who would soon be losing her eldest son. Mary would need someone to look after her needs, and Jesus attended to her care with some of his last words.

Redeeming – "Today you will be with me in paradise" (Luke 23:43). Here is a first-century equivalent of a "deathbed conversion" by a common criminal. His life had been wasted in sin, and he had no chance to prove his sincerity by changing his ways. Yet a last-minute recognition of his own sinfulness, Jesus' righteousness, and the simple request, "Jesus, remember me" (23:42), was enough to secure eternity in heaven.

Trusting – "Father, into your hands I commit my spirit" (Luke 23:46). When Jesus bore the sins of the world on the cross, he felt the abandonment of his Father. Yet in spite of his Father's letting him suffer and die, and seemingly abandoning him during this most difficult time, Jesus still trusted him and committed his spirit into his Father's hands. Jesus died the way he lived—forgiving, caring, redeeming and trusting his Father to the end.

TRIALS WITH PURPOSE

Consider it pure joy, my brothers, whenever you face trials of many kinds, because you know that the testing of your faith develops perseverance.
(James 1:2-3)

There's a story about a man who found a butterfly cocoon. After guarding the cocoon for many days, the man noticed a small hole had appeared in the cocoon. For several hours the butterfly tried unsuccessfully to squeeze its body through the hole. Finally, the man could wait no longer, and he took a small scissors and cut open the cocoon. The butterfly emerged with a swollen body and shriveled wings. The man waited, expecting the wings to enlarge and the body to shrink, but the change never happened. The butterfly spent the rest of its life crawling, unable to fly.

The impatient man had acted out of kindness, but he didn't understand that the butterfly's struggle to get through the small hole was necessary to force the body fluid into its wings. The man's well-intentioned intervention with scissors doomed the butterfly to a life without flight.

Our youngest daughter, Dara, is presently going through a very difficult time at college. We are praying, worrying and advising from a distance (nine hours away by car). It's very tempting to "get out the scissors" and try to help her with her problem. We could catch a plane tomorrow and spend the weekend with her. But perhaps God is using this stressful situation to develop something in her life. Sometimes, after one prays, the best plan is to do nothing but to wait on God and trust him with the situation. "Dear Father God, please be with our beloved daughter Dara. Strengthen her through this difficult time so that she may have wings to fly. Amen."

A TASSEL REMINDER

"... You are to make tassels on the corners of your garments, with a blue cord on each tassel ... so you will remember all the commands of the LORD..."
(Numbers 15:38-39)

Decorations on garment hems were common in the Ancient Near East. The type of decoration often reflected the status of the bearer. Writer and teacher Stephen Bertman, in "Tasseled Garments in the Ancient East Mediterranean," noted that tassels were usually only worn by royalty or priests. The color blue or purple was also indicative of royalty, an association that started almost sixteen hundred years before Christ when purple dye was so expensive (it had to be extracted from certain sea snails) that only royalty could afford it.

God knew his people would be inclined to forget their identity and their calling as they were caught up in the busyness of everyday life. The command to wear tassels with blue cords on their garments was to remind them they were a special people (royalty or priests) called by God into a covenant relationship with attendant responsibilities.

It would also behoove us today to remember that we are sons and daughters of the King and therefore royalty (Galatians 4:6). We often live and act like we have completely forgotten this truth. God, however, deemed the fact that we are children of the King so important that he commanded tassels with blue cords be tied on garments, so the children of Israel would not forget. God also deemed this truth important enough to have it recorded in Scripture so *we* would not forget.

SABBATH'S PURPOSE

"The Sabbath was made for man, not man for the Sabbath." (Mark 2:27b)

When I rest on Sunday, I often have a smug feeling that I've done something worthwhile for God. Yet Jesus clearly states that the Sabbath rest is for *us*, not for him. The Sabbath was created for our physical, emotional and spiritual well-being. We need to slow down in order to rest and focus on God. The Sabbath is a yield sign on the freeway of our lives. It encourages us to ease off the accelerator of urgent activities, in order to spend time with God.

More than thirty percent of Americans say they are rushed "all the time." Apparently time is one of the few commodities God created in an insufficient quantity. Our only remedy is to go faster and rest less (which makes us restless). But what are the other costs of our refusal to slow down and rest? I believe our relationships with God and with others are the primary casualties of our hurry-up lifestyles.

In recent years, we hear a lot about spending "quality time" with each other. I fear, however, that *quality* time is nothing more than a justification for the small *quantity* of time we devote to our relationships. "I know I only spend ten minutes a week with my kids, but it's quality time." Somehow, we hope that by labeling it quality time we can magically make up for any deficiencies in the quantity of time. The truth of the matter is that we can't schedule quality time. "Listen, kids, I have ten minutes of free time. Let's quickly bond so that we can then share our greatest joys, deepest fears and hardest struggles." It just doesn't work that way. If we want *quality* time, we must invest a significant *quantity* of time to obtain it.

In our relationship with God, as well as in our relationships with others, an investment of time is an essential ingredient. The Sabbath is God's reminder to us that there is more to life than frenzied activity, and the Sabbath is also God's encouragement to experience the "more" God has to offer.

ENVY: THE ENEMY OF CONTENTMENT

"Friend, I am not being unfair to you. Didn't you agree to work for a denarius? ... I want to give the man who was hired last the same as I gave you. Don't I have the right to do what I want with my own money? Or are you envious because I am generous?" (Matthew 20:13b-15)

A busy winter season had just ended for our medical practice. Our office had done well financially, so we decided to give our staff a bonus. In the past, we had used different formulae to decide bonus allocations. However, this time one of my partners suggested a simpler plan. We had about eight thousand dollars to disburse and forty employees—let's just give each employee two hundred dollars. We all naively nodded in agreement and moved on to the next agenda item. We were happy to have made such a quick decision and felt good about being able to give a tangible thank you to our hardworking staff while having a sense of satisfaction about our own generosity.

In less than a week, however, our delusional bubbles of good decision-making and a thankful work force had been burst. Three employees had come to me, upset about the unfairness of the bonus allocations. The disbursements didn't factor in how many years persons had been working for us. In addition, some workers were only part-time, and they had gotten the same amount as full-time workers. Also, the quality of each person's work had not been taken into account.

From management's perspective, the bonus was an unearned thank you gift; it didn't need to take into account all the fairness factors that are reflected in hourly wages. Furthermore, when each person initially received the bonus checks, they had been grateful and pleased. It was only after comparison with other employees that envy told joy and contentment to take a hike. Envy is not an attractive emotion.

A SENSE OF ETERNITY

[God] has made everything beautiful in its time. He has also set eternity in the hearts of men ... (Ecclesiastes 3:11)

I remember reading about a person with terminal cancer who was pondering the future. He raised a poignant question: "How could I no longer be?" We are each the focal point of our own universe, making it difficult to imagine the world marching on without us. Why is it so hard to imagine our total absence, not just from planet Earth but also from existence *anywhere*?

C. S. Lewis says that if we were created for "time" and a finite existence, then a limited existence would seem normal and appropriate to us. Lewis says it is similar to a fish in water that doesn't complain of feeling wet because he was *made* for water. We, however, were not *made* for time or a limited existence, and for that reason it doesn't seem right to us. We feel "wet" because we were created for eternity.

The Bible tells us we are eternal beings. Matthew 25 says we will either experience eternal judgment or eternal life. God has not, however, left us clueless about this fact. Indeed, he has "set eternity in [our] hearts" so that we might seek him. We are also told that God "rewards those who earnestly seek him" (Hebrews 11:6).

Abraham Lincoln seems to have agreed with the writer of Ecclesiastes: "Surely God would not have created a being such as man to exist for only a day! No, no, man was made for immortality."

TOUCHABLE

"Look at my hands and my feet. It is I myself! Touch me and see ... "
(Luke 24:39)

Some years ago, First Lady Michelle Obama breached a centuries-old protocol when she touched (put her arm around) Queen Elizabeth II. British etiquette clearly and sternly warns persons in proximity to the Queen, "Whatever you do, don't touch the Queen!" With one accord, the entire British nation choked on their breakfast bangers and mash as they witnessed the social gaffe of the decade. Historically, the Queen was considered to be in her position by divine appointment, and the holiness of her touch was thought to heal the sick. Therefore, divine contact (i.e., touching) was to occur rarely, and it was a privilege obtained not by the subject's initiation but by the sovereign's decision.

Our King and Lord, Jesus Christ, demonstrated a different royal protocol. Jesus, whose nature was God, humbled himself to become a man (Philippians 2:6-8). Unlike earthly royalty who aspire to be *above* the commoners and thus untouchable, Jesus chose to be "God *with* us" (*Immanuel*, Matthew 1:23) and hence touchable. Moreover, Jesus reached out to touch those around him. Jesus touched the sick (Mark 1:41) and the children (Luke 18:15), and he invited his disciples to touch him (Luke 24:38-39).

My friend, Bob, is a recovering alcoholic. He tried to stop his addictive behavior on many occasions but always failed. One day about fifteen years ago, after yet another failed attempt, he cried out, "God, help me!" He was lying on his back with his hands over his head when he felt someone put their hand in his. He sat up and looked behind him to see who had taken his hand—no one was there. Bob has not had a drink since that day. Our King Jesus still reaches out to touch and heal us today, and he still invites us to reach out to touch him.

OUR NEED FOR GOD

"For all have sinned and fall short of the glory of God." (Romans 3:23)

I'm not a Greek scholar, but I've been told that if you look up the word "all" from this verse in the original Greek language, you'll find that it actually means ... "all." What's surprising to me is not so much that "all have sinned," but rather that we should need to be reminded of it! How could we be so blind or distracted that we could fail to see the depravity of our basic nature? I can barely make this statement without feeling proud at how self-effacing and perceptive I am—see what I mean?

Yet since the time of the Renaissance with its emphasis on the importance of man, we have become progressively more self-enamored and less objective in looking at ourselves. Secular humanism teaches that we have outgrown the need for religion or a god, and we need only to look within ourselves for the solutions to our problems. Our intelligence, goodness, resourcefulness and justice will prevail. The very fact that we don't rise up in arms against such undeserved self-assurance confirms our corrupt nature.

When we see ourselves as good and self-sufficient, we have no need for God. However, if we are able to wipe the egocentric mist from the mirror, we will clearly see ourselves as sinners, desperately in need of help. Augustine said, "The beginning of knowledge is to know oneself a sinner." Only as we see the problem can we realize the need for a solution. Some years back in *The Times* of London an article was entitled, "What's Wrong with the World?" One person sent a terse, insightful response, "I am. Yours truly, G.K. Chesterton."

WORSHIP IN SPIRIT AND TRUTH

"True worshipers will worship the Father in spirit and truth, for they are the kind of worshipers the Father seeks. God is spirit, and his worshipers must worship in spirit and in truth." (John 4:23-24)

This passage reveals two very important qualities for worship. We are to worship both "in spirit" and "in truth." God himself is spirit, and the Bible tells us we were created in his image. The spiritual essence of who we are has been made similar enough to God's Spirit to allow communion between the Almighty and his creation. When we worship God, a mystical fellowship occurs in which God's Spirit and our spirits make contact—wow! Whether singing, praising or lying prostrate before God, we have the same goal. Our goal is worship, in which our spirits and God's Spirit are in holy intimacy.

We are also told to worship God "in truth." The highest worship evolves from an accurate estimation (the truth) of who God is. The more clearly we see God as he actually is, the more in awe we will be, a recognition that results in spontaneous worship. To grow in our knowledge of who God truly is, is to grow in worship.

I remember a discussion I once had with an agnostic who speculated that if there was a God, he would be a more "sophisticated" God than the one presented in the Bible. Many of us would like to make our own personalized versions of God, ignoring the absurdity that our brush-strokes on canvas could actually *create* the landscape. God is who he is, quite apart from any imagery we may conjure up. He has chosen to reveal himself to us through the Bible. God seeks those who worship him as he truly is, not their own constructed view of him, and he seeks those who worship him with the very essence of their beings, their spirits. *They* "are the kind of worshipers the Father seeks." May we be them.

THE BREATH OF GOD

The LORD God formed the man from the dust of the ground and breathed into his nostrils the breath of life, and the man became a living being. (Genesis 2:7)

In the Old Testament there are different Hebrew names referring to God that emphasize different attributes of God. *El Shaddai* means "God Almighty," and *Adonai*, "The Lord." *Yahweh*, the covenantal name of God, means "the self-existing one." The Hebrew language was originally written without vowels, so *Yahweh* was actually *Yhwh*. Teacher and pastor Tom Gotwalt points out how the "h" is a very breathy sound in Hebrew, as in English. The result was that as people wrote or spoke the covenantal name of God, the breathy nature of his name reminded them that his spirit embodied his name, since "breath" and "spirit" are the same word, both in Hebrew and in Greek, the language of the New Testament.

The activity of God's breath and spirit also seems to morph together in Scripture. In Genesis, when God created man, Scripture says God "breathed into his nostrils the breath [spirit] of life." In the New Testament, when Jesus appeared to his disciples after his resurrection, Jesus "breathed on them," and they received the Holy Spirit (John 20:22). Physical life and spiritual life were both imparted by God's breath (spirit).

In Genesis 17, *Yahweh* made a covenant with Abram. When God made this covenant, he changed Abram's name to Abra*h*am, and his wife Sarai's name to Sara*h*. An "h" was added to each of their names. As *Yahweh* entered into covenant with them, Gotwalt says God gave them the breathy (spirit) part of his own covenantal name. By implanting part of his name in theirs, God was giving them part of the essence of who he was to seal the covenant.

God also implants his Spirit (breath) into us today, with the covenant of salvation through Jesus Christ. The apostle Paul tells us that as Christians we are sealed with "the promised Holy Spirit" (Ephesians 1:13-14). The breath/Spirit of God was involved in the creating of humans, in giving the Abrahamic Covenant, in empowering people with the Holy Spirit at Pentecost, and in saving people through the new covenant of salvation through Jesus. Holy God, continue to breathe your Spirit on us today!

THE GOD WHO SEES ME

The angel of the LORD found Hagar near a spring … She said, "I have now seen the One who sees me." … The well was called Beer Lahai Roi [well of the Living One who sees me]. (Genesis 16:7a, 13b-14a)

The first Old Testament appearance of the angel of the LORD (likely a pre-incarnate form of Jesus) is when he encountered Hagar at the well in Genesis 16. The similarities to the story of Jesus' encounter with the Samaritan woman at the well in John 4 are both interesting and instructive.

In both cases, the woman at the well was not someone a man would usually address. Jesus' disciples were surprised to find him talking with a woman (John 4:27). Both women were also the "wrong" ethnicity. Hagar was a pagan Egyptian, and the woman in John 4, a despised Samaritan. Both women were needy (thirsty), and our Lord initially spoke to them about the mundane, progressing to the eternally significant.

A significant insight in these two stories is revealed by the women themselves. Hagar said, "You are the God who sees me" (16:13) and even named the well with these words to commemorate the epiphany. Hagar was amazed and comforted that God noticed her. The Samaritan woman told the townspeople Jesus was "a man who told me everything I ever did" (4:29). God knew the details of her life—like Hagar, the Samaritan woman was also *noticed* by God.

To be noticed means that *we matter*; we are of significance not coincidence. God sees us, he hears our cries, he knows our circumstances, and we matter. This is what sets us apart from all the other collections of atoms across the galaxies; they *are* matter, but we *do* matter.

ARGUING WITH GOD

[God] throws me into the mud / ... "I cry out to you, O God, but you do not answer; / I stand up, but you merely look at me. / You turn on me ruthlessly; / with the might of your hand you attack me." (Job 30:19-21)

It was our first year of marriage, and my wife and I were having an animated discussion, and for some reason she failed to see how right her new husband was. I thought it was intuitively obvious that as the husband in the relationship, I was the logical one to be driving the car when we went somewhere together. She failed to see the inherent logic in my line of thinking and asked me to explain. It was at that point that I realized the "logic" behind my position was that it was the way my parents had always done it. Not wanting to lose an argument just because I was wrong, I argued on for a while, generating more heat than light. When I finally was able to admit the weak reason behind my position, we were able to have a fruitful discussion that brought us closer together.

Interestingly, many of the biblical accounts of discussions between God and humans seem more like the volatile arguments of newlyweds than mature, polite discussions between two unemotional parties. Moses argued incessantly about God's calling him into leadership (Exodus 3). Abraham haggled with God about his decision to destroy Sodom and Gomorrah (Genesis 18), and Job took God to task for his unjust punishment (Job 30). Yet in these cases and many others, God seemed to give some degree of vindication to these impertinent, argumentative upstarts.

Christian author Philip Yancey goes so far as to say, "God invites argument and struggle." In our newlywed quarrel, when I was able to be honest, we learned things about each other and about ourselves that bound us together. Perhaps this is the reason we have been given an open invitation to argue with God—to help bind us together as well.

THE JUSTICE/MERCY PARADOX

I have decided to assemble the nations, / ... and to pour out my wrath on them— / all my fierce anger. / The whole world will be consumed / by the fire of my jealous anger. (Zephaniah 3:8b)

Wrath, anger and fiery destruction—it's rather disconcerting to hear these words spoken by our God. However, God is completely holy and just and thus cannot be indifferent to evil and injustice. One of the unavoidable consequences of God's holiness and justice is his hatred for sin and the requirement for punishment or a penalty for injustice.

Most of us prefer to dwell on the fact that God is loving and merciful; it makes us feel safer. However, mercy and justice are *both* part of the inherent nature of God. As the just ruler of the cosmos, God must punish sin and evil. At the same time, however, his great mercy desires to save us from this just punishment. How can justice and mercy, which seem mutually exclusive, be present at the same time? Jesus' sacrificial death on the cross serves as the meeting place for God's justice and mercy. God's justice is realized by Jesus' death, which is payment in full for our sin. At the same time, God's mercy is demonstrated, par excellence, by allowing us to receive vicariously the pardon we could never earn. Just as two nonparallel lines find common ground at the point where they cross, so justice and mercy find common ground at the point of *the* Cross (of Jesus Christ).

We need to have a greater appreciation for God's complete holiness and his perfect justice and therefore his inherent antipathy toward sin. The more we understand this truth about God, the more we can appreciate the amazing provision of the atonement and how it demonstrates God's unsurpassed love and mercy to us as sinners.

FORGIVENESS

Bear with each other and forgive whatever grievances you may have against one another. Forgive as the Lord forgave you. (Colossians 3:13)

Both receiving and extending forgiveness are essential qualities of the Christian. Since God is holy, sin causes separation in our relationship with him and receiving his forgiveness is essential for closeness. God's forgiveness of our sin is not just a willingness to overlook the sin or a casual cancellation of our debt. Rather, forgiveness represents God's loving initiative to reconcile us to him, made possible by Christ's sacrificial death.

Scripture also stresses the importance of our forgiving others. Our unwillingness to forgive people is both proud and foolish. We are haughty-spirited Christians if we forget the huge debt that God has forgiven us and refuse to forgive the relatively small offenses of others. Refusing to forgive the sins of others is also useless since clinging to old grudges hurts only us. British pastor Charles Spurgeon said, "A man who cannot forgive is a poor fellow indeed, for he punishes himself for the sins of others."

Finally, being unable to receive God's forgiveness is saying either that God erred in extending his merciful forgiveness to me or that Christ's sacrifice was inadequate for me. It is true that we, in ourselves, are unworthy of God's love and forgiveness. Nonetheless, his loving us and the mysterious work of Christ's atonement somehow make us worthy—our job is to believe and accept this. It is a form of pride to believe that God's love, manifest through his grace and mercy and Christ's sacrifice, is somehow inadequate or insufficient in our case. How pompous can we be to believe that the significance of our sins exceeds the power of God's love and Christ's atoning death? As we humbly accept Christ's forgiveness, we are set free from the power of guilt, and God's love and compassion begin to grow in us, better enabling us to love and forgive others. For Christians, forgiveness is not an optional tenet of the faith but a commandment from God himself; yet it is he in us who enables it to happen.

CREATED WITH PURPOSE

For he chose us in him before the creation of the world ... having been pre-destined according to the plan of him who works out everything in conformity with the purpose of his will. (Ephesians 1:4, 11)

We were in the mind of God before the creation of the world. He ordained a plan and purpose for our lives from the foundation of time—a concept that is both humbling and difficult to understand. Given this truth, however, how do we discover the purpose for which we were made?

I was once looking at a book with a pen-and-ink drawing of a "unique invention." It was a very simple item, and I thought if I studied it long enough, I should be able to figure out its function. It was a six-inch long, soft rubber cord with loops on each end. Although anyone could have made the object, I couldn't even begin to guess its purpose. Giving up, I read the inventor's description. This gizmo was to help avoid the annoying, uneven tanning of the legs that occurs when one is sunbathing, lying face upward; both legs tend to turn to the outside, resulting in more tanning on the inside of the legs. By putting the cord loops over the large toe of each foot, the device prevents the sunbathers' legs from rotating externally and promotes more even tanning. How elegant—and vain, useless and trivial! The point of the matter is, however, that to find out the purpose of this invention I had to turn to its creator.

Pastor and author Rick Warren reminds us that our culture often tells us to look within ourselves to discover the meaning to our lives. Yet since we didn't create ourselves, how can we know what we were made for? Logic mandates that only by turning to our Creator, God, can we find the meaning and purpose for which we were created.

THE REAL JESUS

His head and hair were white like wool, as white as snow, and his eyes were like blazing fire. His feet were like bronze glowing in a furnace, and his voice was like the sound of rushing waters. In his right hand he held seven stars, and out of his mouth came a sharp double-edged sword. His face was like the sun shining in all its brilliance. When I saw him, I fell at his feet as though dead. (Revelation 1:14-17a)

Most of us don't envision Jesus as he is graphically depicted in the book of Revelation, even though the book is the *"revelation* of Jesus Christ" (Revelation 1:1, italics mine). We prefer to envision a Jesus walking with us through life, who looks a lot like the gentle Galilean pictured in those *Road to Emmaus* paintings. Paradoxically, both the gentle and the awesome portrayals are accurate. Nonetheless, we tend to shy away from the image with stars, a sword, blazing fire and glowing bronze. We need to remember, as C.S. Lewis said, that Aslan (symbolic of Jesus) "is not a tame lion."

Pulitzer prize-winning author Annie Dillard notes most of us have no idea the kind of amazing power we light-heartedly invoke when we pray and worship. She says we're like a group of children with our chemistry sets, naively mixing up a batch of TNT. "It is madness to wear ladies' straw hats and velvet hats to church; we should all be wearing crash helmets! Ushers should issue life preservers and signal flares; they should lash us into our pews!"

The real Jesus cannot be put in our measured boxes of tame logic. Jesus is fully human and fully divine, both transcendent (above us) and immanent (with us). He has unfathomable power, yet he is as gentle as a soft breeze; he's a roaring lion and a docile lamb. The fact that we have trouble reconciling these characteristics is simply a reflection of our own limitations. It would only stand to reason that the real Jesus would be all we can imagine and much, much more ... and that's exactly what we find.

A HUMBLE REFLECTION

Your attitude should be the same as that of Christ Jesus: / Who, being in very nature God, ... / made himself nothing, taking the very nature of a servant / ... he humbled himself ... (Philippians 2:5-8)

Humility seems such an elusive goal, for as we strive for it and note our progress, we become proud of our achievement, and all is lost. This conundrum reminds me of when a friend once instructed me, "Think of anything you like, but don't think about purple elephants!" He paused and then asked me, "What are you thinking about right now?"

The key to becoming more humble lies not in striving for humility, but in striving for greater intimacy with Christ, for he himself *is* our humility. Pastor F.B. Meyer noted, "The only hope of a decreasing self is an increasing Christ." John the Baptist learned this difficult lesson as he stated, "He [Jesus] must become greater; I must become less" (John 3:30). As created beings, it is what we were made for—to glorify our Creator. In the same way, a setting for a precious stone should show the gem in all its splendor, without the setting being memorable. Andrew Murray in *Humility* says, "Nothing is more natural and beautiful than to be nothing in order that God may be everything."

To reflect Christ truly and humbly in our lives, we need a degree of unawareness. When we begin to notice our humble reflection of Christ, we become less humble. I live near Hershey, Pennsylvania, and some of my patients work in the Hershey's chocolate factories. When they come to the office, they seem unaware that they exude the sweet fragrance of chocolate. The odor permeates their clothes, their hair and even their skin. Similarly, Christ should be such a permeating aspect of our beings that we are unaware that those around us notice the fragrance of Christ from us; when this happens, humility is present.

THE FRUIT OF MY DESIRE

But the fruit of the Spirit is love, joy, peace, **patience***, kindness, goodness, faithfulness, gentleness and self-control. (Galatians 5:22-23a, emphasis mine)*

You see it, don't you? The one fruit fails to blend in with the others, kind of like a watermelon in a bowl of cherries. *Patience* is listed fourth as if it had no special significance, but it sticks out like a sore thumb. I even tried to type it with a normal font, but it demanded bold type.

Lack of patience has been my spiritual and psychosocial nemesis for as long as I can remember. Two car accidents I've been in were due to driving too fast; I was impatient. Many of the arguments my wife and I have had over the years could have been avoided if I'd been more patient. Twenty-two years ago, I was knocked unconscious, and both bones in my leg were broken when I was hit by a car while on an unnecessary errand of impatience.

I would really like my impatience to be fixed—and *now* would be a good time for it to happen. I've made this a matter of prayer, Bible study and self-psychoanalysis, to little avail. Actually, I need to be fair by stating that God has been working on me in this area, but my progress is so slow. When plumbers and computer repairmen come to our house, they quickly fix the problem and leave, a couple hours and several hundred dollars later. But my impatience is like a football field of tall grass, and instead of God using his wide-deck riding mower, he's using a pair of tweezers to pluck the grass blades one at a time! I've become impatient about becoming more patient. Could God be trying to teach me something by not *immediately* granting the desire of my heart? Could there be some intrinsic value in my having to *wait* for patience? ... Naah.

REDEFINING OUR WORLD

[Peter] fell into a trance. He saw ... a large sheet being let down to earth by its four corners. It contained all kinds of four-footed animals, as well as reptiles of the earth and birds of the air. Then a voice told him, "Get up, Peter. Kill and eat." (Acts 10:10b-13)

This vision from God entirely changed Peter's view of the world. The animals in the vision included those considered "unclean," yet God told Peter he should eat them. Prior to this experience, Peter believed the good news of the gospel of Jesus Christ was for the Jews alone. This vision, however, revealed to Peter that the gospel was also for the Gentiles. Peter's world was suddenly redefined and was now much larger than before.

God often seems to work in our lives by changing our perspectives. My family spent three years in Zambia doing mission work at a rural hospital. During those three years we saw many short-term visits by expatriates. Seeing this parade of motivated visitors convinced us of the value of short-term mission trips. Some of the value was related to the purpose for their visits. However, the greatest value was often the changes God made in the lives of the short-term missionaries themselves. For many of these visitors, their view of the world was dramatically changed forever. It was like they had previously viewed the world through reading glasses, but now they'd been given a telescope.

Unfortunately, we suffer from myopia in many areas in our lives. Thankfully, God delights in paradigm shifts that redefine our worldviews. There's an old Yiddish saying, "To a worm in a horseradish, the whole world is a horseradish." We need God's help to see beyond our horseradishes.

UNDER-WHELMED BY HOLINESS

Moses saw that though the bush was on fire it did not burn up. So Moses thought, "I will go over and see this strange sight … " "Do not come any closer," God said. "Take off your sandals, for the place where you are standing is holy ground." (Exodus 3:2b, 3, 5)

God-things, holy things and sacred things tend to be shy. They don't assertively force themselves on us. Holy and sacred things seem to have great patience, unpretentiously waiting to be found. A holy encounter between God and humanity brings together the sovereign decision of God to reveal himself with the willingness and desire of humans to see the divine. The reserved nature of God-things honors us by giving us the choice to ignore them and do something else. Moses was tending sheep, yet he decided to "go over," or as the King James Translation says, to "turn aside" to see this thing.

God's presence, his activity and therefore his holiness are always around us. We are often blinded to God because we are preoccupied, looking in the wrong places, or looking for the wrong things. God is continually involved in our world, doing far more than we can see or imagine. His activities, however, are often without fanfare. God could have placed the burning bush in the middle of Moses' path, where he would have been unable to avoid it. Instead, Moses had to "go over" to see the sight. Similarly, we have to decide if we will take the time, invest the energy and struggle against the gravitational pull of the urgent to turn aside to see the burning bush, as Moses did. If we take the time to turn aside, we too may find ourselves standing on holy ground, unlacing our shoes in the presence of the Almighty.

LOVE BEYOND REASON

The LORD said to me, "Go, show your love to your wife again, though she is loved by another and is an adulteress. Love her as the LORD loves the Israelites, though they turn to other gods ... " (Hosea 3:1)

Hosea's marriage was a living metaphor and a living nightmare. God told Hosea he was to marry Gomer, a prostitute. In spite of Hosea's unmerited love for Gomer, she soon left him for someone else. Hosea had made himself vulnerable, only to be hurt. Adding insult to injury, God then told Hosea he should pursue his unfaithful wife. Hosea even ended up having to pay money to retrieve his ungrateful, unfaithful, and (I can only assume by now) undesirable wife.

Gomer's unfaithfulness to Hosea was symbolic of Israel's unfaithfulness to God. Israel had been chosen as the undeserving object of God's love and blessing. Yet she was unfaithful, worshiping Baal and other Canaanite gods. Hosea's mercy, jealousy and persistent pursuit of Gomer's affections all reflected God's amazing love for his chosen, beloved people Israel.

As we read about Gomer, it is easy to be critical of her behavior. Her selfish lack of gratitude and loyalty paint a portrait that is both dishonorable and disgusting. Yet as we gaze intently at this portrait, we can see the facial lines slowly morph into a familiar countenance that is our own. Paul reminds us, "While we were still sinners, Christ died for us" (Romans 5:8). In spite of God's amazing overtures to us, we continue to have affairs with our jobs, our leisure time, and our possessions. Nonetheless, God relentlessly pursues our affections—God's love, like Hosea's love, is beyond human understanding.

February

SPIRITUAL WARFARE

For our struggle is not against flesh and blood, but … against the spiritual forces of evil in the heavenly realms. Therefore put on the full armor of God…
(Ephesians 6:12-13)

Although many of us have sung "Onward, Christian Soldiers" with fervor and zeal, we've seldom really imagined ourselves involved in spiritual warfare. Nevertheless, this verse from Ephesians informs us the struggles we experience, which may seem unrelated to our faith, are often spiritual in nature. Perhaps the enemy's use of secular camouflage has lulled us into being unprepared, unarmed and therefore unengaged.

Dutch author Corrie Ten Boom notes, "The first step in the way to victory is to recognize the enemy." This recognition calls for spiritual discernment that goes beyond our five senses; we must "see" with God's eyes. When we realize the battle is spiritual, we may change our choice of weapons. Instead of using our intellect to argue with persons involved in destructive, ungodly pursuits, we pray for God's Holy Spirit to redirect them. Rather than trying to get rid of our bad habits by the force of our wills, we put ourselves in God's hands, asking him to do that which we cannot.

Engaging in spiritual warfare, however, does not come easily or naturally. We can't become spiritual Green Berets just by putting on one of those funny French caps without a brim. To prepare for battle, we need basic training in spiritual boot camp. Our mentor is Christ himself, with the Bible as our training manual. Ironically, however, the spiritual training itself will not give us success. We can only obtain victory when we give up on our own strength and are empowered by the strength of the Holy Spirit.

THOUGHTFUL CONFORMITY

Do not conform any longer to the pattern of this world ... (Romans 12:2)

Why do we need encouragement not to conform? Aren't we individuals with minds of our own who carefully weigh the pros and cons and study the data before adopting our beliefs and behaviors? The advertising world has based its existence on the assumption that the answer to this question is "No."

Alka-Seltzer commercials used to show a hand dropping an Alka-Seltzer into a glass of water. A clever advertising consultant suggested showing the hand dropping *two* Alka-Seltzers. The company followed this advice, and in a short time sales nearly doubled. There were no new studies suggesting two Seltzers were better than one. There was nothing more than a new visual prompt that redefined normalcy. Everyone seemed to forget there had ever even been a time when only one Seltzer was enough. We often assume the media reflects behavior that is representative of our society. In point of fact, however, the media often molds our society rather than reflecting it.

Conformity is not inherently wrong, but we need to be aware of our tendency to conform, and we need to be aware to what we are conforming. Being well-fitted to an ill society does not make us healthy. In contrast, the apostle Paul says we should be conformed to the image of Christ (Romans 8:29). Let's think before we imitate the world around us. Let's strive to conform to the image of Christ, not the pattern of this world. One Alka-Seltzer or two?

HONEST EMOTIONS

The floods engulf me. / I am worn out calling for help; / my throat is parched. / My eyes fail, / looking for my God. / Those who hate me ... / outnumber the hairs of my head. (Psalm 69:2b-4a)

I have a friend who became a believer as an adult. After attending our church for several months, he was startled when a church member shared some troubles in her life. "I used to think everyone in your church was perfect," he sighed with obvious relief. All too often contemporary Christianity portrays a false veneer of perfection. When greeted with "How are you?" we invariably respond with "Fine." F-i-n-e has been said actually to mean "feelings-inside-not-expressed." We Americans are subtly indoctrinated with the idea that we should conceal our anger, grief, doubts, pain and troubles. Not only is this idea unhealthy, but it's also dishonest and unbiblical.

Job cried out in deep pain, cursing the day he was born (Job 3:3-4). Jeremiah wrote an entire book of laments. Two-thirds of the Psalms are complaints, laments or expressions of anger or grief. Tremper Longman III, in *How to Read the Psalms*, says the Psalms are a type of literary sanctuary where God meets man. This divine encounter may be in praise, but it may also be in lament, anger, doubt or tragedy. We need to stop viewing difficult situations or emotions as sinful anomalies. A more scriptural view would be that these trying circumstances and feelings are normal channels or avenues that should lead us to a personal encounter with God. Jesus said that it is truth (reality) that sets us free (John 8:32), not denial or illusion. When we are dishonest and suppress our painful emotions and situations, we deny God the opportunity to answer our prayers with healing, blessings and joy. We also miss out on the chance for a personal encounter with the God of comfort.

SPIRITUAL EYES

... An army with horses and chariots had surrounded the city. "Oh, my lord, what shall we do?" the servant asked. "Don't be afraid," the prophet answered. "Those who are with us are more than those who are with them." And Elisha prayed, "O LORD, open his eyes so he may see." Then the LORD opened the servant's eyes, and he looked and saw the fields full of horses and chariots of fire all around Elisha. (II Kings 6:15-17)

Our Western culture has been strongly influenced by the Enlightenment period of the eighteenth century. The idea that reason and the use of our senses are the best way to learn truth still permeates our society. The English journalist Malcolm Muggeridge once said, "We have educated ourselves into imbecility." I believe we have also enlightened ourselves into darkness. It is so tempting to think, like Elisha's servant, that what we see is all there is.

Yet Scripture reminds us time and again that complete reality includes much more than our limited eyes perceive. The Apostle Paul tells us our struggle is against the "spiritual forces of evil in the heavenly realms" (Ephesians 6:12). In Daniel 10 we see that angels may be commissioned in answer to our prayers. Jesus tells us in John 14 that even now he is preparing our eternal home for us. All of these realities lie beyond the threshold of our feeble vision, hearing, and tactile awareness. It is ironic that all that seems so real, sturdy, and tangible now is as fleeting as a rose in bloom in the context of eternity. Meanwhile, the spiritual world that now largely avoids detection by our senses will soon be our eternal experience. May we pray, as the prophet Elisha did, that God would open our eyes to see true reality.

A THEOLOGY OF ACTION

*"I hate, I despise your religious feasts; I cannot stand your assemblies. ...
Away with the noise of your songs! ... But let justice roll on like a river, righteousness like a never-failing stream!" (Amos 5:21, 23-24)*

As Western Christians we tend to have a fairly well thought out theology.
Each Sunday we discuss morality and Christian principles in Sunday
school, followed by hearing the preacher present a sermon illustrating orthodox doctrines. We read Christian books and even watch video series
on how to be better Christians. We are strong on theory but often weak
on action. We look so long that we often fail to leap.

Some years ago my teenage daughter Amaris went on a short-
term mission trip with me to Latin America. We had been instructed that
we shouldn't give money to beggars: "It only encourages them to remain
beggars, instead of helping them to find honest work." One evening as
a group of us were returning to our hotel, a small, disheveled child with
palms up implored us for money. Having a well-regimented doctrinal
position in place, we politely said "no" and passed by on the other side
(any resemblance to the story of "The Good Samaritan" is purely coinci-
dental). Amaris pulled me aside, pleading with me to let her give the boy
some of her money. Her child-like theology put mine to shame. What
kind of lofty, impractical theology do we have when it *stops* us from doing
good deeds?

The prophet Amos said justice should "roll on like a river." A
river is flowing and active, not inactive and stagnant like a pond. If we as
Christians don't have an active, practical theology to care for and stand
up for the oppressed, who will? To do nothing means we let suffering
and oppression continue. Anglican bishop Desmond Tutu from South
Africa said, "If you are neutral in a situation of injustice, you have chosen
the side of the oppressor. If an elephant has his foot on the tail of the
mouse, and you say you are neutral, the mouse will not appreciate your
neutrality."

WRESTLING WITH GOD

... A man wrestled with [Jacob] till daybreak. ... He touched the socket of Jacob's hip so that his hip was wrenched ... Jacob [said], "I will not let you go unless you bless me." ... Then he blessed him there. So Jacob called the place Peniel, saying, "It is because I saw God face to face, and yet my life was spared." ... He was limping because of his hip. (Genesis 32:24-26, 29-31)

This is a very unusual story. God condescended to a wrestling match with Jacob, and it appeared to be a stalemate, a *tie*, mind you, in a contest between a mere mortal and the Creator of the universe! Perhaps it wasn't really God with whom he wrestled. Notice, however, that Jacob was disabled by just a touch from his opponent (v. 25). We also read that Jacob says he "saw God face to face" (v. 30). It seems that God was willing to humble himself, as he did with the Incarnation, in order to connect with his feeble creation.

Jacob was a self-sufficient man who needed to become God-dependent. Jacob was accustomed to getting what he wanted through his own efforts, so God met him where he was, in an all-night, effort-intensive struggle, to move him where he needed to be—dependent on God. God was not actually fighting against Jacob but for him. God wanted Jacob to find strength in weakness, to win by losing.

In this God-man struggle, God's touch had results beyond the physical injury. Jacob was apparently physically dependent for the rest of his life; he limped and needed to use a staff to walk. His physical handicap was a living metaphor, however, that pointed to a more important truth. He became spiritually dependent and realized his need to lean on God. Finally, God's touch also conferred a blessing on Jacob. To receive God's caring touch may not always be something that is easy. It is, however, always something that is a blessing.

Jacob's limp was a lifelong reminder of God's grace and Jacob's need to depend on God. Many years later, the writer of Hebrews tells us when Jacob died, he persevered in faith, blessed others, worshiped God and "leaned on the top of his staff" (11:21).

HONORED NAMES

The king of Egypt said to the Hebrew midwives, whose names were Shiphrah and Puah, "When you help the Hebrew women in childbirth ..., if it is a boy, kill him ..." The midwives, however, feared God and ... let the boys live.
(Exodus 1:15-17)

Scripture clearly teaches us to submit to our government (Romans 13:1), yet we are also clearly told to "obey God rather than men" (Acts 5:29). Jesus' statement to, "Give to Caesar what is Caesar's, and to God what is God's" (Matthew 22:21) indicates there will be times when we need to discriminate between these two authorities. When God and Caesar are in disagreement, God's authority must be paramount.

The king of Egypt's edict was clear, yet the two Hebrew midwives refused to obey him. Although the king could have imprisoned or executed them, Scripture says the midwives disobeyed the king because it was *God* they feared.

By the way, what was the name of the mighty king of Egypt who ordered the babies killed? No one knows. The Scripture leaves him nameless, and while archaeologists and historians have proposed six possible persons it could have been, his name remains unknown. While the powerful king's name is unknown, God honored the two lowly midwives who chose to obey God by having their names recorded for all time. Three thousand five hundred years later, we still read their names ... Shiphrah and Puah. God honors those who honor him (I Samuel 2:30).

REDEEMED CATASTROPHE

"For whoever wants to save his life will lose it, but whoever loses his life for me and for the gospel will save it." (Mark 8:35)

On January 8, 1956, five young missionary men excitedly awaited contact with the Auca Indians (now known as the Waodani). They were anxious to share the gospel of Jesus with these stone-age warriors in the jungles of Ecuador. The meeting ended tragically, however, as all five missionaries were speared to death.

One of the five men killed, Jim Elliot, had once written in his journal, "He is no fool who gives up what he cannot keep to gain what he cannot lose." Elliot's prayer journal revealed that he was praying "not for a long life but a full life." God answered Jim Elliot's prayer beyond what he could have ever imagined.

In the summer of 2000, in Amsterdam, there was an international conference with evangelists from 209 countries. Mincaye, one of the Waodani warriors who killed those five missionaries, was a speaker at that conference. He shared how the love of God had transformed his life. Translating for Mincaye was Steve Saint, son of Nate Saint, one of those Mincaye had killed. After Mincaye shared his testimony, Steve wanted Mincaye to understand that God can even use an Amazon warrior's evil intent to bring good. So he asked the huge crowd of evangelists from all around the globe how many of them had been spiritually impacted by the "Auca Story." He hoped at least a small group of persons would stand, but he was overwhelmed to see almost the entire crowd on its feet. In his book *The Great Omission*, Steve Saint says, "It was the most humbling and gratifying demonstration of God's sovereignty that I have ever witnessed."

THE INCARNATION

Who, being in very nature God, / did not consider equality with God some-thing to be grasped, / but made himself nothing, / taking the very nature of a servant, / being made in human likeness. / And being found in appearance as a man, / he humbled himself / and became obedient to death— / even death on a cross! (Philippians 2:6-8)

The incarnation seems to be the preeminent example of paradox. In Christ, we see one person who is fully human and fully divine. We also see omnipotence strong enough to become weak and a veiling of God's glory (in human form) in order to reveal his glory more fully. We see a king who becomes a servant, and finally, we find victory through defeat on the cross.

While the incarnation itself is a great theological mystery, it also unveils some of the mysteries of God. I have recently been impressed by two revelations of God that the incarnation provides. Jesus coming as God's son was an entirely new disclosure of the intimate relationship that is available between God and humans—a father/child relationship. We can even presume on the intimacy between us by calling him "Abba," an Aramaic word for "Daddy" (Galatians 4:6).

A second revelation is regarding the questions about pain, suf-fering and death. Best-selling Christian author Philip Yancey points out that while the incarnation does not answer the question of *why* God allows his children to experience these hardships, it does clearly reveal *how* God feels about them. When Jesus was confronted with sickness, there was never a sense of "You got what you deserved" or a fatalism that said, "Such is life." He cared deeply and reached out to heal the ill, restore the isolated, and even raise the dead. Looking at Jesus gives us a surpris-ingly intimate view of how much God really cares about us. Yancey says, "Jesus gives God a face, and that face is streaked with tears."

God became flesh and made his dwelling among us (John 1:14). He did this to reveal himself more clearly to us. Jesus' life and teach-ings serve to give us a much richer and clearer picture of God than was present in the Old Testament. And since we were created in the image of God, we know what our response should be to the suffering in our world—we should begin by having faces streaked with tears.

TRACKS IN THE SNOW

For since the creation of the world God's invisible qualities—his eternal power and divine nature—have been clearly seen, being understood from what has been made, so that [people] are without excuse. (Romans 1:20)

It's as though God walked through the woods after a snowfall, consciously aware of the tracks he made yet with no attempt to hide the signs of his presence. Timothy Keller, in his book *The Reason for God*, says God left us "clues" or "fingerprints" that he exists. The Apostle Paul declared those clues to be so clearly seen that we are "without excuse."

Even scientists who believe in the Big Bang Theory and an undirected evolution admit how highly unlikely it is that we should be here. Calculations of the probability that human life could have evolved by chance alone usually fall somewhere between one in a Godzilla-trillion and zero. Atheistic scientists defend their belief in something so statistically indefensible by saying: "Since we are here, no matter how improbable it seems, we know it had to have happened." What this argument lacks in force of logic, it makes up for with presumption. Rather than being open-minded to the possibility of God, these scientists start with the premise that there is no God.

It seems provocative that there are any clues for God at all. After all, if there were no God, it would seem unlikely that we would find evidence for someone who didn't exist. On the other hand, if there was a God, we might have expected him to leave clues suggesting his existence, which is exactly what we find. The smoking gun evidence for the existence of God is Jesus—his life, teachings, death and resurrection. Yet most atheists, who would call themselves objective and open-minded, refuse even to examine this evidence.

It's a cold winter morning, and there's fresh-fallen snow on the ground. The window pane is covered with frost, yet you can clearly see some tracks in the snow outside. Put on your boots, gloves and a warm winter coat. A compelling adventure awaits the brave; be courageous, follow the tracks and see where they lead.

KOINONIA

And our fellowship is with the Father and with his Son, Jesus Christ ... But if we walk in the light, as he is in the light, we have fellowship with one another... (I John 1:3b, 7)

Koinonia is the Greek word for fellowship. It can also be translated "sharing," "partnering" or "contributing." It goes beyond friendship, as it applies to both our vertical relationships with God and our horizontal relationships with other believers.

The Bible has numerous metaphors illustrating our relationship to God. We are variously described as "the vine and the branches" (John 15:5), "children of our Father" (John 1:12), "the bride and the bridegroom" (Revelation 21), and a "body, with Christ as the head" (Colossians 1:18). It may surprise us to find the American ideal of self-sufficient individualism is not portrayed by any of these metaphors; each image has our true identity being in affiliation with others. The reality of the matter is that we were created to be in relationships (*koinonia*). The fullness of what God asks us to do and be is impossible outside the context of our relationship with God and others.

When Jesus was asked what the most important commandment was, his answer was all about relationships. Our most important relationship is *upward*, with God. Jesus said, "Love the Lord your God with all your heart and with all your soul and with all your mind" (Matthew 22:37). However, Jesus said our *outward* relationships with others are also very important: "Love your neighbor as yourself" (Matthew 22:39).

While God stresses the importance of meaningful, loving relationships in our lives, our busy culture often does not. My mother-in-law recently died. As she lay dying, she surrounded herself with people, not things, just as she had throughout her life. Her relationship with God gave her hope and peace; her relationships with those she loved gave her comfort and joy. In one's final hours of life, priorities suddenly become crystal clear—relationships are what life is all about.

PLACING TRUST

Some trust in chariots and some in horses, / but we trust in the name of the LORD our God. (Psalm 20:7)

As Christians we have put our trust in God. Nonetheless, we have health insurance, car insurance, life insurance and retirement plans just to hedge our bets a bit. We think, "Certainly God wants us to be prepared for the unforeseen!" All too often, living in an affluent industrialized society, we seem not to need God. We have many "chariots" and "horses" on which we can depend. It is easy to become deluded into believing we are self-sufficient, with all our preparations for every conceivable difficulty in the future. Occasionally, however, harsh life events may reveal our self-reliant illusion for what it is—smoke and mirrors.

There's a story told about boxing legend Mohammed Ali when he was in his prime. He was a passenger on a jet airliner. The plane encountered some turbulence, and the pilot announced that everyone should fasten their seat belt. The flight attendant noted that Ali's seat belt was unfastened and asked him to please fasten his belt. Ali informed her, "Superman doesn't need a seat belt." The flight attendant retorted, "Superman doesn't need an airplane either."

Like Ali we too often forget that we are not Superman. Trusting in our own strength is egocentric and foolish. The validity of our trust is not dependent on either the intensity or sincerity of our belief, but rather the *object* of our trust. Are we trusting in horses and chariots that rot and rust or the eternal God of the universe who creates and sustains?

THE NATURE OF SIN

"… I have come that they may have life, and have it to the full."
(John 10:10)

I remember that as an adolescent, it seemed Christianity had a canonized list of restrictions (no sex, no drugs and no R-rated movies) constructed to minimize our enjoyment of life. The prohibitions seemed designed to stifle curiosities, desires and self-actualization. It never occurred to me that my unconstrained attempts to satisfy selfish desires could actually harm me or cause me to feel unhappy and unfulfilled. The only idea I might have considered more incredible would have been that restraint and restriction would somehow allow me to enjoy life more completely. However, what appeared to me as nonsense at that time was actually a profound truth that God's Holy Spirit slowly revealed to me. "Sin" is just the name for things God wants us to avoid *for our own good.*

When God created us, he realized that some choices we could make would ultimately be self-destructive. He called these choices "sin" and warned us to avoid them. But being the wise, all-knowing creatures that we are, we are often able to out-think God and thwart the universal principles and consequences he established from the dawn of time … or maybe not.

Jesus said he came not to condemn and restrict us but to allow us to experience abundant life, full of joy, peace and purpose. Do we really believe him, or do we know better?

THE NATURE OF GRACE

And if by grace, then it is no longer by works; if it were, grace would no longer be grace. (Romans 11:6)

One night we received a phone call from our eighteen-year-old daughter, Dara, who was in Hungary. She was in eastern Europe with two of her friends on an exciting adventure. I guess part of what made it so exciting was that it was minus her parents. Her unexpected phone call was to let us know that her wallet, containing her money, credit cards and driver's license, had just been stolen. My empathetic wife seemed very quick to forgive any laxity of due diligence that may have allowed the theft. I, on the other hand, found myself wondering how she could have allowed this to happen. We had told her numerous times to keep her wallet in her money belt and to be on vigilant guard for potential thieves. "Try not to look like three naïve American teenagers on a vacation in Europe," I told her. Although, of course, that's exactly what they were.

As I struggled with my thoughts and feelings, my wife wisely encouraged me to extend grace to our daughter. Well sure, that sounds nice and noble, but it would have been a lot easier for me to forgive her if she had done the things I had told her to do. If I were truly to extend grace, however, it could not depend on Dara's actions, for if based on works, then "grace would no longer be grace."

Fortunately, my wife's words helped me pause long enough to reflect: "How often have I sinned, disregarding the clear instruction of God's word?" And even though God had lavishly bestowed grace on me, I was withholding that same grace from my daughter. I realized what an ungrateful person I was. On my knees yet again, I asked God's forgiveness. I will always be desperately in need of that which I do not merit and cannot earn—grace. Although I'm embarrassed to admit it, I find myself asking God, on an almost daily basis, to extend to me the same grace I find so difficult to give others.

February 15

BORN AGAIN

"You should not be surprised at my saying, 'You must be born again.'"
(John 3:7)

The sign along the highway stated its message clearly and perhaps bluntly: "You must be born again." I'd read it before, but the birth imagery impressed me more that morning, as I had spent the previous night sleepless, helping one of my patients go through the difficult process of giving birth to her child.

The first task of motherhood, however, starts nine months before the birth—the task of waiting for the unborn baby. This tends to be a thankless job, often associated with nausea, vomiting, feeling fat and the inability to get out of an armchair without the aid of a small crane. Our spiritual births also have a waiting period. God's expectant waiting for us is graphically portrayed in the story of the Prodigal Son (Luke 15:11-31). As we struggled through our period of rebellion and/or unbelief, our expectant father waited with love and outstretched arms for our homecoming (our spiritual birth).

While an unborn baby cannot make himself be born, he/she is part of the birth process. Nonetheless, it is the mother who must actually give birth. Similarly, we cannot birth ourselves spiritually. There is no special knowledge, force of will or act of service that can cause or even expedite our salvation. God, through the work of Christ on the cross, did the work required for our spiritual birth. If we accept it, we are born again by the work of Christ. Unfortunately, many reject this offer of new life.

Imagine how silly it would seem for a baby in his mother's womb to decide he doesn't want to be born. He's decided to stay in the only world he's sure exists, the inside of his mother's uterus. "Birth looks like a painful process, and what if there's really no other world out there at all? It's better to stay here where it's safe and warm than to risk the unknown." Little does he know that his "safe" choice to remain where he is will ultimately lead to death—for the womb is only created to house him for a short time. How silly to imagine such a scenario ... silly and sad.

WHAT PLEASES GOD

And without faith it is impossible to please God, because anyone who comes to him must believe that he exists and that he rewards those who earnestly seek him. (Hebrews 11:6)

If I were to poll a group of Christians about what is needed to please God, I would probably get a variety of responses. "Love," "kindness," "holiness," "good works," and "a life of sacrifice to God" might be on the list of responses. While these are all good things and even things God calls us to display, God doesn't say it is impossible to please him without them. Jesus commended those with great faith (Matthew 15:28), and he criticized those with little faith (Mark 16:14). Why does faith seem to stand alone on a pedestal above other worthy attributes?

The author of Hebrews gives two reasons why faith is so important. First, without faith we can't even believe God exists. And yes, God does care about this, and it displeases him if we don't believe he exists. But the passage goes on to say that just believing in the reality of God is inadequate. He also wants those who "earnestly seek him." The reward for our seeking God is that *we are found by him*. Ultimately, therefore, faith pleases God because it is through faith alone that we can come into a relationship with him and be saved by him (Ephesians 2:8-9).

The almighty God is pleased when we, part of his lowly creation, are in right relationship with him. It is humbling to be so exalted. Faith is the means to this relationship, and this relationship is the primary purpose of creation and redemption. This perspective makes it easier to understand why "without faith it is impossible to please God."

THE RIGHT RITE

"I baptize you with water, but he will baptize you with the Holy Spirit."
(Mark 1:8)

I clearly remember when my youngest daughter, Dara, received water baptism and joined the church. It was a meaningful service. She and several others professed their faith in Christ and their desire to join our local body of believers to live out that faith. As I sat through that service, the importance of baptism as a symbol was reinforced in my mind.

Baptism is an outward expression of an internal reality. Dara had already committed her life to Christ several years earlier. So why should one have the ceremony at all? A similar argument against marriage was made popular when I was in high school: "If you're really in love, the piece of paper is unimportant."

Whether with baptism or marriage, there are several reasons I believe a visible ceremony is important. First, it requires one to make a *clear commitment.* One has to have thought through some basic questions: "Do I know what I'm doing?" "Am I ready to make this pledge?" As my former pastor, John Landis, would say, "I'm driving in a stake" of certainty by receiving baptism. Second, the visible sign provides a *rite to remember.* A vague mental assent is much easier to forget than a special ceremony. C.S. Lewis, cognizant of the phenomenon of spiritual dementia, said that we frequently need to be "reminded more than instructed." Third, a public ceremony provides a sense of *obligation to others.* I have made this promise in the full view of others, implicitly and perhaps explicitly asking them to help me keep it. Finally, a visible observance is a *witness to the world.* We are declaring that what has been instituted by God is important enough to us to formalize and proclaim with a public ceremony. Official services can serve as more than just ritual formalities—I believe they are right rites.

NARROW-MINDED TRUTH

Jesus answered, "I am the way and the truth and the life. No one comes to the Father except through me." (John 14:6)

"All roads lead to the same God," she replied with a note of finality. Clearly she thought this should end our discussion. Her reasoning was, "You believe your way, and I'll believe mine, and we need not argue since we can *both* be right." The only problem is that Christianity brazenly asserts that Christ is the *only* way to God. The apostle Paul, not realizing how politically incorrect he would be, said Jesus is the only mediator between God and man (I Timothy 2:5).

One day while I was working in a Zambian mission hospital, a 28-year-old diabetic man came in with ketoacidosis, a severe, life-threatening complication of diabetes. He had first gone to the local witchdoctor for treatment but continued to worsen. He desperately needed insulin. Unfortunately, I discovered our pharmacy had used the last insulin vials several days earlier. We gave him IV fluids and diabetic pills, but he died two days later. To say that insulin was his only chance for survival was "narrow-minded." However, it also happened to be true.

Although it might seem tolerant and nonjudgmental to say, "All roads lead to the same God," that doesn't make it true. The gospel writer Matthew says there is a "broad road that leads to destruction" (Matthew 7:13); we don't want to choose that one. Truth by its very nature is exclusive of all that is false. Christianity's exclusive claims don't leave room for other paths to God. Christianity is either true (and the only way), or it's false. I believe it to be true. Like the 28-year-old diabetic man, there is only one cure for our condition—the remedy for the sickness of our souls is Jesus Christ. Other attempts at treatment are destined to fail.

DON'T GREENHOUSE YOUR CHILDREN

A deacon must be the husband of but one wife and must manage his children and his household well. (1 Timothy 3:12)

While it's been relatively easy to have "but one wife," managing my children well has been more challenging. My youngest daughter is now in college, so our years of greatest parental influence are behind us. When I consider some of the parenting mistakes I've made, I cringe and blush. Nonetheless, our daughters seem to be emerging as four wonderful young women, which must be more *in spite of* me than *because of* me. Fortunately, God gave me an amazing wife whose mothering skills and spousal encouragements have helped offset my shortcomings, and God's grace has shown itself, once again, in a very tangible way.

Three of our four girls are now out of college and increasingly independent of us. Although we raised them to take on more and more responsibilities and decision-making with age, it's still difficult not to worry about them as adults. We know there will be difficult times, disappointments and perhaps even heartbreaks that lie ahead for them. The world seems a harsh place when viewed from the eyes of a concerned/worried parent.

I have a friend, Les, who owns several greenhouses. He once explained to me how plants that grow in the protected, environmentally controlled conditions of the greenhouse grow fast and look pretty, but they won't be hardy. To develop strength and vigor, they need to be placed outside, to experience the sometimes harsh effects of the weather. He called it "hardening off" the plants.

As parents, we want to protect our children from the harsh experiences the world may throw at them. But will our children develop a steadfast faith in God if they've never gone through difficult times when their faith was tried and tested? We want our children to experience the "peace of God, which transcends all understanding" (Philippians 4:7), but we don't want them to go through difficult times to get there. Do we love our children enough to let them out of the greenhouse? Do we really trust the Master Gardener?

THE PRIORITY OF JESUS

Mary ... sat at the Lord's feet listening to what he said. But Martha was distracted by all the preparations that had to be made. She came to him and asked, "Lord, don't you care that my sister has left me to do the work by myself? Tell her to help me!" "Martha, Martha," the Lord answered, "you are worried and upset about many things, but only one thing is needed. Mary has chosen what is better ... " (Luke 10:39-42)

How do I evaluate my success as a Christian? Does spending time at Jesus' feet seem worthwhile? Luke says Martha was "distracted." Distracted from what? She was doing good "things" but was distracted from the one most important thing ... Jesus. One of the more subtle yet devastating sins of the church is doing good things. Jesus reminds us the greatest commandment is to "love the Lord your God with all your heart and with all your soul and with all your mind," which takes priority even over "love your neighbor as yourself" (Matthew 22:37-39).

My daily prayer needs to be, "Lord, help me not to be worried and distracted by many 'things,' but give me the desire to sit at your feet and focus on you alone, for this is better." It's better not because the work of the church is unimportant, but because Jesus desires our time together—he loves us and desires a close relationship with us. Also, it is only *after* we sit at Jesus' feet that we can effectively do his work, enabled and empowered by our time together.

SHARING CHRIST

When I came to you, brothers, I did not come with eloquence or superior wisdom as I proclaimed to you the testimony about God. For I resolved to know nothing while I was with you except Jesus Christ and him crucified.
(I Corinthians 2:1-2)

Focusing on the wrong things sometimes hampers sharing our Christian faith. We worry we'll say the wrong words or say the right words in the wrong way. We worry about whether we'll be able to answer questions about our faith. We fear our imperfections will invalidate our witness since we know all too well our own obvious shortcomings. The net effect is that we worry ourselves into an anxious state of inactivity.

Concerning our imperfections, Tolstoy says, "Don't judge God's holy ideals by my inability to meet them. If I know the way home and am walking along it drunkenly, is it any less the right way because I am staggering from side to side?" A flawed messenger does not invalidate the message.

While it is wrong to focus on our imperfections, the apostle Paul, in his letter to the church at Corinth, also gives instructions not to focus on our words, elocution or wisdom. Our focus is to be on presenting Christ and him alone. Bible teacher Dana Congdon says the Church's witness is like a lake, in which Jesus is the water and we are the unsightly underwater debris. When the water (Jesus) is low, the dead stumps, rocks, and branches are evident. But when the water (Jesus) is high, a beautiful, clear, shimmering lake is all that is seen. This is our goal—to be full of Christ. With time the underwater debris that is part of us is slowly and gradually broken down and taken away by our Lord.

We want to speak words of truth, and we want to deliver those words clearly, with love and conviction. We also want to lead godly lives that are a reflection of God's grace. Nevertheless, the focus of our faith sharing has to be more than holiness in our lives and truth in our doctrine. In fact, good doctrine is inadequate, for the essence of Christianity is not theology but a relationship with Jesus Christ. Our message is a person—Jesus of Nazareth.

GREED

Give me neither poverty nor riches, / but give me only my daily bread.
(Proverbs 30:8b)

Greed can be defined as an excessive or inordinate desire for wealth. Of course each person's definition of excessive is different, making this definition of greed somewhat impractical.

A study was once done in which people were divided into different groups based on their income. The persons in each group were then asked if they were content with their income, and if not, how much more they would need to feel satisfied. As one might expect, there were very few people content with their present income. Interestingly, almost every group from the poorest to the wealthiest, thought they would be satisfied if they made just a little more (i.e., if they made enough to put them in the group just ahead of them).

This study reveals a key aspect of greed. Greed is not dependent on how much one has, for greed is present in both the poor and the wealthy. Greed is an inherent part of our nature and cannot be satisfied by getting what we desire, for we will just desire more.

Although we're hesitant to admit it, greed is also an integral part of our Western culture. Greed is why capitalism works so well and communism so poorly. Most people are willing to work harder if they will get more for themselves, while they are unlikely to work harder if they won't receive additional fruits from their extra labor.

Being generous rather than greedy goes against the inclination of our nature and the influence of our culture. For generosity to overpower greed requires a renewal of our hearts and minds by God. The words of St. Francis of Assisi demonstrate that he had experienced this transforming renewal: "Remember that when you leave this earth, you can take nothing that you have received … but only what you have given." The elusive goal of contentment is realized not by getting more but by wanting less. It is only when God transforms our desires that we find ourselves satisfied with our daily bread.

THE LUKEWARM "NORM"

[To the Church in Laodicea] "So, because you are lukewarm—neither hot nor cold—I am about to spit you out of my mouth. ... You do not realize that you are wretched, pitiful, poor, blind and naked. ... So be earnest and repent." (Revelation 3:16-17, 19)

It seems there is an epidemic of the "Laodicean Syndrome" in American churches. I fear lukewarmness has become more the rule than the exception. Pastor Jim Cymbala says, "We have so institutionalized Laodiceanism that we think lukewarm is normal."

But certainly just *barely* being a Christian is still adequate. There's no sense overdoing it; God can't really want a bunch of fanatics. And God can't really mean he'll "spit us out" either, just because we're lukewarm. After all, it must be better to be lukewarm than ice-cold. And what about other Scriptures, certainly they don't imply that God really expects such a radical commitment from us, do they? Unfortunately, it's hard to find Scripture that supports our rationalization for half-heartedness. The Bible says to "offer your bodies as a living sacrifice" (Romans 12:1), and it commands, "Love the Lord your God with all your heart and with all your soul and with all your mind and with all your strength" (Mark 12:30) and "Never be lacking in zeal, but keep your spiritual fervor, serving the Lord" (Romans 12:11).

But what would the church look like if everyone was a wholehearted fanatic?—pretty amazing! Okay, so how do we begin? Scripture tells us we need to begin by realizing we are "wretched, pitiful, poor, blind and naked," and then we need to "repent." Confessing our inadequacy puts us in a position for God to empower us and use us—much preferred to becoming divine spittle.

LIVING WATER

... His delight is in the law of the LORD, / and on his law he meditates day and night. / He is like a tree planted by streams of water, / which yields its fruit in season / and whose leaf does not wither. / Whatever he does prospers.
(Psalm 1:2-3)

Even as we delight in the existence of God, how much more do we delight that he has spoken and revealed himself to us through his Word, the Bible! The psalmist reminds us that we should not just read the Bible as we might read a textbook, with the goal of gaining knowledge. Rather, we should ponder and reflect on God's Word. We want it to affect not only our minds but also our hearts and inner spirits.

A tree planted distant from a stream is dependent for moisture on the uncertainty of rain. But when planted near a stream, that tree can count on the steady nourishment provided by a continuous and bountiful supply of water. A tree is incapable of producing fruit by the force of its own will. However, as trees absorb nutrients and water, they naturally and effortlessly realize a plentiful harvest of fruit.

In our own lives, regular meditation on God's Word can likewise be counted on to provide nourishment to our spiritual beings and yield "its fruit in season." This is true not because the Bible innately has any mystical powers, but because its inspired message points us toward and puts us in touch with Jesus, the "living water" (John 4:10). Jesus is as vital to our well-being as water is to a tree. As we meditate on God's Word, we are hooked into a conduit to Christ. As we allow him to nourish our souls, we also will begin to bear fruit in season.

JARS OF CLAY

"Certainly this fellow was with him, for he is a Galilean." Peter replied, "Man, I don't know what you're talking about!" Just as he was speaking, the rooster crowed. The Lord turned and looked straight at Peter. Then Peter remembered the word the Lord had spoken to him: "Before the rooster crows today, you will disown me three times." And he went outside and wept bitterly. (Luke 22:59-62)

It's that moment in time we all have felt or feared—that instant when the rooster crows. We somehow imagine that if we succeed in hiding our depravity long enough, perhaps it really doesn't exist ... then the rooster crows. Like Peter, we hope against all odds that perhaps Jesus didn't notice that cock-a-doodle-doo piercing the night air. He certainly has more important matters to consider than our relatively unimportant peccadilloes. And even if he does see them, why would he care?

But then as we dare to glance toward Jesus, we see what our hearts have already known. He is looking straight at us. If only it were a look of anger or even hatred, it would be deserved penance. But his countenance is far more distressing. We see disappointment framed in love. Our best defensive arguments melt in the warmth of his unconditional love. As we ponder our response, we find ourselves sobbing, lamenting that his perfect love is directed at such unworthy recipients.

Yet the good news goes beyond his amazing mercy. Not only is our punishment withheld, but Jesus also entrusts us, as he did Peter who denied him and the other disciples who deserted him, with the precious gospel message. As rough earthen vessels, we are such unlikely receptacles. Nonetheless, a treasure (the gospel message) has been placed in us, diamonds displayed in "jars of clay" (II Corinthians 4:7). We are unworthy, flawed earthen vessels glorified beyond reason!

A TRIVIAL ROLE

From him [Christ] the whole body, joined and held together by every support-
ing ligament, grows and builds itself up in love, as each part does its work.
(Ephesians 4:16)

Our church is presently going through some difficult times. Last week
one of my friends said she fears our church is going to "melt down."
As I considered her apocalyptic words, I remembered the near nuclear
disaster that occurred in March 1979 at the Three Mile Island (TMI)
nuclear power plant. I recently read how an investigation into the cause
of that event revealed a series of five errors that came together to create
the near disaster. Each of the errors in itself would have been considered
trivial, but as a part of the whole picture, each ended up having ominous
significance. What I found encouraging, however, was that if even one of
those five errors could have been avoided, the near meltdown would also
have been averted.

One of the "trivial" mistakes was an indicator that would have
alerted the workers to the evolving problem had it not been covered up
by a repair tag hanging down from the switch above it. If there had been
a TMI worker who made transparent repair tags (so they wouldn't block
warning lights), I'm sure he would have considered his job insignificant.
Nevertheless, his job could have prevented the $975 million disaster.

In Ephesians, the Apostle Paul says that as members of the Body
of Christ, we are to build each other up in love "as each part does its
work." Like my imaginary TMI worker, however, some of us may think
our parts are insignificant, which is misinformation contrary to God's
word. We should never underestimate the significance of what God calls
us to do. With our present church difficulties, I believe that if each of us
does our part in supporting each other and building each other up with
God's love, we too can avoid a meltdown. And we can "grow to become
in every respect the mature body of him who is the head, that is, Christ"
(4:15).

THE ETERNAL "I AM"

"I tell you the truth," Jesus answered, "before Abraham was born, I am!"
(John 8:58)

We tend to think of Christ's existence as having begun with the birth of Jesus in Bethlehem. However, there's nothing like Scripture to enlighten our misunderstandings. Jesus said, "Before Abraham was born, I AM." This was more than a declaration that his existence antedated Abraham. Jesus was also echoing Yahweh's words to Moses from the burning bush. When Moses asked God who he should say was sending him to the Israelites, God said to tell them, "I AM has sent me to you" (Exodus 3:14).

The name "I AM" comes from the Hebrew verb "to be." When Yahweh responded to Moses, his self-given name was declaring, "I exist," which lies in stark contrast to all the other gods of the day who actually did *not* exist. The Hebrew verb "to be" in this context can also be translated "I am actually present." For Moses, knowing God was actually present must have been a bit frightening yet also reassuring, since Moses was about to step outside his comfort zone.

When Jesus said he was the "I AM," he was declaring his oneness with Yahweh of the burning bush. The meaning was not lost on his Jewish audience. They knew the penalty for blasphemy was death, and the Jews picked up stones to carry out the punishment. The Jews' assessment was accurate: Jesus had committed blasphemy, claiming to be God, ... or alternatively, Jesus was and is God in flesh, the Christ, the Messiah, the Son of the living God.

PEACEMAKERS

"... Do not resist an evil person. If someone strikes you on the right cheek, turn to him the other also. ... Love your enemies and pray for those who persecute you."
(Matthew 5:39, 44)

Jesus' teachings in Matthew 5-7 are often referred to as "The Sermon on the Mount." Understanding and applying these teachings have divided sincere Christians since the fourth century. Prior to the conversion of the warrior Constantine in AD 313, most Christians interpreted this passage literally and believed *all* war was wrong. With Constantine's conversion came an unexpected melding together of church and state. Following on Constantine's heels, fourth-century theologian Augustine developed the concept of a "just war," and since that time most of Christendom has conceded the necessity of going to war, at least in certain situations.

There are three main objections to a literal interpretation of the Sermon on the Mount. The first states that the sermon is a noble theoretical ideal to strive toward but not something we are actually expected to attain. This line of thinking would allow us to ignore a lot of inconvenient biblical passages that seem difficult. Furthermore, Jesus doesn't leave the "theoretical" option open to us as he states that persons putting these words into practice are wise (Matthew 7:24).

The next objection claims these words apply to individuals but not nations. Nations, however, are made up of individuals. If these commands suddenly no longer apply to individuals who become soldiers of the state, then it would appear the law of man takes precedence over the law of God. The final objection is that these instructions are not for us today but for the future perfect Kingdom of God. This makes little sense, however, since in a future perfect world there would be no hatred and no enemies to love.

The apostle Paul said we are to resist evil by overcoming it with good (Romans 12:21). Pacifism is not passivism. In fact, the word "pacifism" means "peace*maker*." Peacemakers should take initiatives to help prevent situations that can foment anger, resentment, and ultimately conflict. Since suffering and injustice are major causes of war, alleviating suffering and promoting justice can help *prevent* potential conflicts. Mennonite author and theologian Myron Augsburger once said, "We lay aside guns and bombs because they are too weak to achieve His goals. As Christians, we are armed with love, believing that love is the one valid way to conquer our enemies."

CHRISTIAN MAKE-UP

Peter asked [Sapphira], "Tell me, is this the price you and Ananias got for the land?" "Yes," she said, "that is the price." Peter said to her, "How could you agree to test the Spirit of the Lord? Look! The feet of the men who buried your husband are at the door, and they will carry you out also." At that moment she fell down at his feet and died. (Acts 5:8-10a)

Ananias and Sapphira sold some land. They kept some of the money they received from the sale but pretended to give it all to the church. Although they demonstrated generosity, they tried to make themselves look better by stretching the truth a bit. Our human nature makes us all prone to put on a bit of Christian make-up to help us look more holy than we are.

When we present ourselves to the world, we may need a little mascara to mask our envy, some lipstick to legitimate our motives, a bit of powder to produce humility and a touch of rouge to radiate holiness. Is this how we show the world Christ? The most frequent criticism I hear from non-Christians about the church is that we are hypocrites. Perhaps they noticed the heavy make-up.

It may not have been accidental that the first recorded sin in the life of the church was one of pretended holiness, since we are still doing the same thing today. Jesus, however, calls us to a different attitude of the heart. Jesus says it is the "poor in spirit" and "those who hunger and thirst for righteousness" who are blessed (Matthew 5:3, 6). Let's admit we are dirty rags in need of cleaning. It behooves us to be honest, lest the feet of the men who carried out Ananias and Sapphira carry us out also.

March

THE MYSTERY OF GOD

Can you fathom the mysteries of God? / Can you probe the limits of the Almighty? / They are higher than the heavens—what can you do? / They are deeper than the depths of the grave—what can you know? / Their measure is longer than the earth and wider than the sea. (Job 11:7-9)

Mysteries can be very intriguing, yet mysteries without a solution can also be frustrating. The satisfying part of a mystery novel is the revelation of an elegant solution. The satisfaction of doing scientific research lies in *solving* the mysteries of nature. Working on a jigsaw puzzle gives little gratification if one can't find the last piece to set in place. So how do we keep from becoming frustrated with our less-than-complete understanding of the mystery of God?

God has revealed some of his mystery through the Bible and through Christ's incarnation (I Timothy 3:16). Nonetheless, there are elements of God and his ways that we do not and cannot know. Writer and pastor Frederick Beuchner says that God is so far above us that trying to explain his ways to us is like "trying to explain Einstein to a clam."

Do we really want a God we can fully understand? If we seek a God we feel comfortable with and can fully understand, that may be exactly what we get. Poet and author Kathleen Norris describes such a reduced God as "a God suspiciously like ourselves, the wideness of whose mercy we've cut down to size." The fact that we cannot fully fathom our God is not so much a testimony of our inadequacy as it is a testimony of his awesome greatness! The alternative to a God with mystery is a god we have diminished and simplified so we can wrap our minds around him but who is totally lacking awe and wonder.

LIKE A CHILD

"Let the little children come to me … I tell you the truth, anyone who will not receive the kingdom of God like a little child will never enter it."
(Mark 10:14b-15)

Those of us who grew up in the church have had years to dress up and polish our prayers. We've borrowed holy-sounding phrases from others over the years and incorporated them as our own. Warren Harding's speeches were once described as "an army of pompous phrases moving over the landscape in search of an idea." Similarly, our prayers are too often an army of pious platitudes flowing from our mouths in search of sincerity. We are like the hypocritical Pharisees who prayed to be seen by men, babbling with many words (Matthew 6:5-8). We come to God with prayers that are bleached, smooth-sounding and sophisticated. We have forgotten to come to God as a child, without pretense, guile or make-up.

One of my friends, who didn't grow up in the church, recently became a believer. I asked her if she would pray in our Bible study group, but she declined. She was embarrassed but explained that she had heard me pray and knew she could never pray like that. Initially, I was flattered at how eloquently I was apparently praying, but I later realized her comment was really an indictment, not a compliment. I'd forgotten the simplicity and transparency that should be present in our prayers. The fact that she wasn't like me was actually a cause for rejoicing—one of us was coming humbly like a child.

Like children, we are to come just as we are, with runny noses, skinned up knees, untied shoelaces and messes in our pants. The very things we try to hide from God are the things he wants us to bring him. We aren't supposed to fix ourselves first. Jesus entreats us: "Come to me, all you who are weary and burdened, and I will give you rest" (Matthew 11:28). The burdens, the messes and the problems in our lives are the things Jesus died for. Come as a child—come.

BREAD OF HEAVEN

Then Jesus declared, "I am the bread of life. He who comes to me will never go hungry, and he who believes in me will never be thirsty." (John 6:35)

In the ancient Hebrew culture, bread was the staple of their diet. The Jewish people universally understood the importance of bread for their very existence. The unfolding revelation of Scripture develops a metaphoric significance to "bread" that is ultimately embodied by Christ. Bread represents God's provision, his presence, and his plan.

During the Hebrews' exodus from slavery in Egypt, God met their need for food with manna, which showed up on the ground each morning except the Sabbath. In the Psalms this manna was referred to as the "bread of heaven" (105:40). This was God's *provision* for his people.

The tabernacle was the center of worship for the children of Israel as they wandered in the wilderness. In the Holy Place of the tabernacle was the "bread of the Presence" (Exodus 25:30). This bread represented the *presence* of God among his people.

At the Last Supper, Jesus took bread and broke it, saying, "This is my body, which is for you" (I Corinthians 11:24). In doing this, Jesus was symbolically tying together the past (God's provision), the present (God's presence) and the future (God's *plan* for humanity's salvation) in a way that would not be understood until after Jesus' death.

On the road to Emmaus, we are again reminded of bread's important symbolism as the resurrected Jesus appeared to two of his followers. Jesus walked with them, talked with them and even prayed with them, but the Scripture says they did not recognize him until "he broke the bread" (Luke 24:35). Today as we eat our daily bread, let us remember God our provider and Christ our provision.

PRAYERS: FRAGRANT AND POWERFUL

The smoke of the incense, together with the prayers of the saints, went up before God from the angel's hand. Then the angel took the censer, filled it with fire from the altar, and hurled it on the earth; and there came peals of thunder, rumblings, flashes of lightning and an earthquake.
(Revelation 8:4-5)

Pastor and biblical scholar Eugene Peterson says the book of Revelation does not provide much new information about the Christian life that hasn't already been taught elsewhere in Scripture. Peterson believes, however, that the book of Revelation states known truth in a unique way that stimulates one's imagination and evokes an emotional response.

The symbolism seen in the images described here is dramatic and vivid. An angel of God (possibly Jesus himself, sometimes referred to as "the angel of the LORD") takes the prayers of God's people and mixes them with incense on the altar and presents this as a sacrifice to God. Our prayers are a fragrant sacrificial offering to God! The picture of smoke rising to heaven and being smelled by God leaves little doubt that our prayers are heard.

So God hears our prayers, but do they have any effect on our earth? Yes! John, the author of Revelation, reports the fragrant prayer incense was hurled down to earth. The results were lightning, thunder and an earthquake—a picturesque reassurance that the effects of our prayers may be seen, heard and felt in very powerful ways.

THE REST OF THE STORY

So when Joseph came to his brothers, they stripped him of his robe ... and threw him into the cistern. ... So when the Midianite merchants came by, his brothers pulled Joseph up out of the cistern and sold him for twenty shekels of silver to the Ishmaelites, who took him to Egypt. (Genesis 37:23-24, 28)

Joseph had more than his share of difficulties in life. His brothers beat him and sold him off into slavery in Egypt. There he then found himself imprisoned for an offense he hadn't committed (Genesis 39). Joseph must have wondered what he had done to deserve such a litany of misfortune.

It wouldn't be until many years later that Joseph would understand his story in its fuller context. It would eventually become clear that Joseph was only one part of a bigger plan God was orchestrating. Joseph's string of calamities would one day save not only his family but also the entire land from the ravages of a seven-year famine (Genesis 41-47). What appeared to be a tragic story about Joseph was really just a subplot to a grander story God was writing about his provision for his people. Fortunately, Joseph ultimately got to see the bigger story that put his own story in perspective.

Sometimes we puzzle over how God could allow disasters to occur. The adversities seem unfair, and we can't imagine how any good could ever come from them. We need to remember that it's not all about us. We are only minor characters in a very long drama, and often it's about the bigger drama, not us. One day in heaven we'll be able to talk with God, and we can ask him, "Why did you let that happen?" God will lovingly look at us and say, "Have a seat, my son/daughter." Then, like Paul Harvey, God will proceed to tell us "the rest of the story."

THE ADVENTURE OF YOUR LIFE

The LORD had said to Abram, "Leave your country, your people and your father's household and go to the land I will show you …" So Abram left, as the LORD had told him. (Genesis 12:1, 4a)

The Christian life is often portrayed by popular culture as a boring one, stripped of all elements of excitement and adventure, a life best suited for the feeble, straight-laced, and elderly. Yet as we read the Bible, we find stories rife with risk, excitement and adventure.

Christian author and speaker John Eldredge says God has made us with a deep longing in our hearts for adventure: men long to experience adventure and women long to share adventure. Eldredge says that adventure, with all its danger and wildness, is a deep spiritual longing written into our very souls. God even created the world we live in with inherent risks. Eldredge says that life is not just an existence to be endured but rather an adventure to be experienced and shared. As we embrace the risks and dangers of life, we learn to live by faith.

I recently spoke to a group of Christian pre-med students about doing medical mission work in a country in the developing world. I didn't want to gloss over the hardships and dangers that could be involved, so I listed some of the ones we experienced while in Zambia. "Our house had no TV, radio, telephone, heat or air conditioning. We had frequent encounters with poisonous snakes. We all had recurrent parasitic infections, and each of us had malaria at least once. One daughter had malaria for five weeks that failed to respond to all our conventional drugs. We had frequent exposure to AIDS (thirty percent of our surgical patients were HIV-positive), and my wife developed a dangerous blood clot in her leg. I contracted hepatitis and broke my leg, requiring two surgeries and crutches or a cane for a year thereafter." After listing all these hardships, I paused, noting their unease, and felt compelled to add: "Honestly, those were the three best years of my life."

Thoreau once said, "The mass of men lead lives of quiet desperation." This, however, is not what Christ calls us to. He is inviting us into an exciting adventure (whether in primitive Africa or rural Pennsylvania). God himself placed the longing in our hearts, and by answering his invitation, we can bravely join an eternal adventure that satisfies that desire.

THE WRONG FOCAL LENGTH

For I desire mercy, not sacrifice, / and acknowledgment of God rather than burnt offerings. (Hosea 6:6)

Last Sunday we had an amazing worship experience! The song choices were excellent, the worship band didn't miss a note, and the four-part harmony was awesome. It was surely a sacrifice of praise that was pleasing to God ... or not?

Sometimes we focus on the wrong things, like the worship itself, instead of the object of our worship—God. We stand in awe of the sophisticated telescope when we should be focused on the distant galaxies. Transfixed by an advertiser's slick billboard ad, we drive right by the historic site itself. We aren't that different from the ancient Hebrews, who also got distracted. They focused on the sacrifices and offerings and failed to practice "mercy" (loving kindness) and an "acknowledgment of God," for whom the sacrifices and offerings were made.

We need to beware when we have a misguided focus. Worshiping, praying and reading God's Word are all to be a *means* to experience the reality of God himself; they dare not be ends in themselves. The goal is not to enjoy worship; we are to enjoy *God*. Worship is just a means to that end—worship brings us into God's presence. When the means become the ends, we are staring at the smudged windshield in the foreground and ignoring the scenic vista in the background. At the least, our myopic focus will cause us to miss out on things. More significantly, however, if we are focused on worship or Scripture rather than the God to whom they point, we are practicing a subtle form of idolatry (misplaced adoration or devotion). It would behoove us to remember that God never minced words regarding his feelings about idolatry (Exodus 20:3-6).

NONCONFORMITY

*Do not conform any longer to the pattern of this world, but be transformed
by the renewing of your mind. (Romans 12:2a)*

It seems a simple enough admonition—don't be conformed to the world.
Yet our culture gives us the opposite mandate—be like everyone else, or
we'll ridicule and embarrass you. The pressure for conformity starts at an
early age. If we are too tall or too short, too skinny or too fat, too smart
or too dumb, anyone differing by more than two standard deviations
from the norm is just asking to be made fun of or shunned. Although not
written down in any book of rules, the guidelines for suitable behavior
and appearance seem to be known by almost all, as if branded into the
DNA of our brains.

As Christians, we are asked to be different from the world, yet
most of us are inclined to want to be the same. The problem with being
the same is that with which we are aligning ourselves. Writer and peace
activist Art Gish, in his book *Beyond the Rat Race*, noted, "To be well
adjusted to a sick society is really to be sick." In other words our world is
fallen, sinful and separated from God, and when we strive to be like the
world around us, we are setting our sights too low.

Our call is not to be conformed but rather to be transformed.
The Greek word used here is the same word used when Jesus was trans-
figured on Mount Hermon (Matthew 17:2-8). At the Transfiguration,
Jesus' face shone like the sun, and his clothes became as white as light.
Our being different is not so we will stick out like a sore thumb, but
rather, so we will stick out like a light in the darkness. We do this by not
aligning ourselves with the world around us but by aligning ourselves
with Christ, who alone can renew our minds and transform our hearts.

CONSIDER THE HEAVENS

When I consider your heavens, / the work of your fingers, / the moon and the stars, / which you have set in place, / what is man that you are mindful of him, / the son of man that you care for him? (Psalm 8:3-4)

David, the author of this psalm, was the youngest of Jesse's eight sons. He grew up tending the family's sheep in the Judean countryside. There were probably many nights when David was alone lying under the star-studded sky, pondering God's vast creation and his place in it. The vastness of the universe can make us feel small and insignificant. Yet David's awe did not stop with the enormity of space and the greatness of its Creator. He went on to realize how special we humans are to God and how much he cares for us. As we view the night sky, realizing there are over ten billion trillion stars, most of which are larger than our sun, our existence can seem trivial and petty. Yet another insight from viewing that same night sky is realizing that God made over one thousand billion stars for the enjoyment of every single person he created—this is cause for rejoicing at our *significance* in God's eyes.

While the immensity of the nocturnal sky might leave us feeling trivial and unimportant, it has the opposite effect on our view of our Creator-God. We are awe-struck by him. W.E. Barnes said, "God provided the sky like a curtain so that man may not be blinded by the blaze of His glory." He's saying God's glory so far *surpasses* that of the sky that the sky is like a common curtain in comparison—wow! Consider the heavens … then consider God.

EAT MY WORDS

Then he said to me, "Son of man, eat this scroll I am giving you and fill your stomach with it." So I ate it, and it tasted as sweet as honey in my mouth.
(Ezekiel 3:3)

The scroll God gave Ezekiel to eat did not contain soothing, palatable words. It had "words of lament and mourning and woe" (2:10). They were distasteful, bitter words. God was giving these words to Ezekiel to prophesy to Israel. But before Ezekiel could proclaim the message, he had to accept the words himself. He had to swallow them, digest them and let the words assimilate into his entire being; they had to become a part of Ezekiel himself. Interestingly, when Ezekiel accepted God's bitter words, they became "as sweet as honey" in his mouth.

When our children were young, they would look at a new food and declare their dislike for it. We would remind them that they cannot taste with their eyes. In the same way, God's words and God's ways may sometimes look distasteful, restrictive and cumbersome. However, when we submit to God and accept what he has for us, we find what previously appeared distasteful and bad actually to be savory and good.

The psalmist David encourages us, "Taste and see that the LORD is good" (Psalm 34:8). As we grow in the Lord, we can echo Jeremiah, "When your words came, I ate them; / they were my joy and my heart's delight" (Jeremiah 15:16).

A FULLY FUNDED MANDATE

For I have the desire to do what is good, but I cannot carry it out. For what I do is not the good I want to do; no, the evil I do not want to do—this I keep on doing. (Romans 7:18b-19)

Several years ago, Congress passed the No Child Left Behind initiative. It was a well-intentioned plan attempting to make sure students learned what they should at each level of the educational process. However, one of the major criticisms of the measure was that although schools had new requirements they needed to meet, no financial appropriations were given to accomplish the task. The schools had been given an unfunded mandate.

In some sense the Old Testament Law was also an unfunded mandate. No one had what was needed to carry out the requirements of the Law. In fact, Paul said that rather than keeping him from sin, the Law served to reveal what sin was and its presence and power in his life (Romans 7:7-8).

However, the Old Testament Law was not the end of the story. Paul goes on to say that with the coming of Jesus and the Holy Spirit we have been rescued from the power of sin. We now have the power to meet the righteous requirements of the Law (Romans 7:24-8:4). That doesn't mean we will no longer sin, but it does mean that we have the resources (the power of the Holy Spirit) so that we *need not* sin. When we knowingly sin, we have either failed to appropriate that power or have just chosen to sin. The scriptural mandate is a call to holiness (I Corinthians 1:2). Fortunately, we have not been left to our own meager devices—the call to holiness is a fully funded mandate through the power of God's Holy Spirit.

MEMORIAL ALTARS

*Remember that you were slaves in Egypt and that the LORD your God
brought you out of there with a mighty hand and an outstretched arm.
(Deuteronomy 5:15a)*

How could the children of Israel need a reminder of their years in slavery?
How could they forget the miraculous plagues and the parting of the
Red Sea to secure their freedom? It's very easy to feel a sense of superiority as we read the scriptural account of the never-ending forgetfulness
of the children of Israel. But do we really remember what God's done
for us any better than they did? There have been numerous times when
I prayed in desperation that if God would somehow get me through a
problem, I would be eternally grateful. And although he got me through
each of those situations, I remember very few of them—my "eternal"
gratitude was somewhat shorter-lived than anticipated. Charles Spurgeon
said, "Memory is very treacherous, by a strange perversity–it treasures
up the refuse of the past and permits priceless treasures to lie neglected."

What can we do to remember those priceless treasures? In the
Old Testament there was a long tradition of building memorial altars as
reminders of some act of God or significant spiritual event. When Noah
got off the ark, he had a multitude of things that urgently needed to be
done. Yet the first thing he did was to build an altar to the Lord (Genesis
8:20). Abraham, Isaac and Jacob each built an altar after meeting with
the Lord. While contemporary "altars" might include a pile of stones as
they did in the Old Testament, other options like planting a tree, buying
a special plaque or picture, or starting a new family tradition can all serve
the same purpose.

More than twenty-five years ago God worked in a miraculous
way through the birth of our twin daughters. When they were still living
at home, each year on their birthday, we sat down with them and retold
their birth story. Eventually, this yearly storytelling about births also extended to our younger daughters, whose deliveries were less frightening
but still innately miraculous. This tradition became an altar of remembrance for our family. When God acts, speaks or moves in a special way,
it is indeed a priceless treasure to remember and to share. Let's build
memorial altars to honor God and to encourage each other.

A LIFELINE

[Jesus] said to them, "Come with me by yourselves to a quiet place and get some rest." So they went away by themselves in a boat to a solitary place.
(Mark 6:31b-32)

The twenty-first century is not unique in having distractions that divert our attention from God. Even first-century Christians had to be called away to silence and solitude to regain their peace and perspective in the presence of Jesus.

In his book *A Hidden Wholeness*, Parker J. Palmer tells a story about farmers in the Great Plains who prepare for blizzards by tying a rope from their house's back door to their barn. When a severe snowstorm comes, whiteout conditions can decrease visibility to zero. Without the rope, a farmer can lose sight of his house, become disoriented and freeze to death just a few yards from the safety of his home.

Palmer says we need a rope that binds us to God when life's distractions blind and disorient us. One of the ropes God extends to us is solitude. Solitude serves to enhance two critical devotional goals: presence *with* God and hearing *from* God. In solitude we are away from people; this makes it easier to be present with God. Teresa of Avila said, "Settle yourself in solitude and you will come upon Him ..." It's also no surprise that we can better hear God's "gentle whisper" (I Kings 19:12) if we first withdraw from the cacophony around us.

As Palmer suggests, life without deliberate spiritual structure puts us in a blinding blizzard. To avoid getting lost, we need to hold tightly to the lifelines God has provided us—one of those is solitude. If the rope accidentally drops in the snow, we need to pounce on it with a fervor reflecting the importance solitude has to our spiritual lives. Solitude is not an end in itself, however, but a beginning. When we've been alone with God in solitude, we are better able to be with others in fellowship.

GOD SEEKS WORSHIPERS

"Yet a time is coming and has now come when the true worshipers will worship the Father in spirit and truth, for they are the kind of worshipers the Father seeks." (John 4:23)

Best-selling Christian author Philip Yancey says, "We are profoundly different, God and I, which explains why friendship is not the primary model used in the Bible to describe our relationship. Worship is." God doesn't want our worship due to some egocentric need he has but rather because of our need. We were created as beings who worship. Indeed, we cannot choose whether or not to worship but only whom or what we will worship.

I believe many Western Christians today are suffering from spiritual malaise, burdened with the distractions of the world. Worship provides a wonderful antidote to this ailment. When we praise and worship God, we are renewed in body, mind and spirit. When we spend time with God and experience a taste of his glory in his very presence in the "Holy of Holies," we cannot help but be changed. From time to time, we've all gone to church distracted by the stresses at work or the squabbles at home. We may appear calm on the outside, but inside we feel like an inflated balloon, released and darting around the room before collapsing in a motionless heap. However, as we enter into God's presence through worship, we suddenly realize that our burden has been lifted. Our circumstances are unchanged, but after being with God, we are different.

God seeks worshipers not for his benefit but for ours. When our central focus is worshiping God, service, evangelism, giving and the other activities of the church will flow out from this. True worship enhances our spiritual lives. It rekindles our passion, deepens our peace and clarifies our purpose. It is for this reason that God seeks true worshipers.

PRIDE

"I am the vine; you are the branches. If a man remains in me and I in him, he will bear much fruit; apart from me you can do nothing." (John 15:5)

Lay theologian C.S. Lewis called pride "the great sin." Considering all the other contenders for this infamous title, I find his bold statement worthy of consideration. Lewis points out that God is immeasurably superior to us in every way, and we are nothing in comparison. Clearly, great pride would have difficulty conceiving of such a God and certainly no desire to search for him. So perhaps the haughty person is unable to find God for the same reason the truant student is unable to find the principal—they are not looking for him. Since the sin of pride by its very nature disinclines us from finding God, it may indeed deserve the title "the great sin."

While pride exalts self and thus displaces God from his rightful position, it also belittles others. Lewis says we derive enjoyment not so much from having something nice or doing something well, but rather we are happy because we have *more* of something than others and perform *better* than they do. The satisfaction of pride comes from comparing ourselves to others and coming out on top.

However, when we truly come to know God for who he is, we are necessarily humbled. Humility is not an artificial self-effacement, nor does it require a poor self-image. Instead, it is a true picture of us in relationship to God. Humility is simply agreeing with the truth of God and his Word: "I am the vine; you are the branches … apart from me you can do nothing."

A GRAND ETERNAL PLAN

... Magi from the east came ... and the star they had seen in the east went ahead of them until it stopped over the place where the child was. ... Then they opened their treasures and presented him [Jesus] with gifts of gold and of incense and of myrrh. (Matthew 2:1, 9b, 11b)

How opportune that Jesus' poor parents would have received expensive, easily transportable gifts from the magi right before they had to flee to Egypt to escape Herod's death warrant. What a helpful coincidence that the Magi studied the heavens and happened upon this unique star and decided to follow it. Their interest in the heavens may have started years earlier due to something as simple as a hole in the roof of one of their houses that happened to be above the lad's bed. Even today, what we see as chance and vagary in the world around us may be the result of divine coordination of events that began generations ago. Our lifetimes are very short snippets of time in the time line of history. It makes sense that for many present events we will never see their ultimate purpose.

My daughter Dara called in tears. She had not gotten the role she tried out for in the college musical. She was just getting over another disappointment and now this. Why couldn't God have let her have this small thing? I had to remember the words from Tevye in *Fiddler on the Roof,* when he wondered if it would really mess up some grand eternal plan to let him be rich, or in this case for Dara to have gotten the role? Although Tevye saw it as a rhetorical question, the actual answer is probably "yes."

God, who created and sustains the universe, who sees the past, present and future simultaneously, who is infinitely wise and powerful, is coordinating an infinite number of variables. He is like a master conductor whose orchestral players include DNA permutations, the weather, the flight of the sparrow, the orbit of planets, the free will of humanity and roles in college musicals. Giving Dara that role actually *might* spoil some grand eternal plan. If I can trust that the orbit of Neptune is as it should be, where is my faith on lesser issues?

THE QUANDARY OF QUARRELS

What causes fights and quarrels among you? Don't they come from your desires that battle within you? (James 4:1)

As family practice residents in training, one of the biggest fears we had was the dreaded "Code Blue." When a patient has a cardiac and/or respiratory arrest, the emergency resuscitation that follows is called a "Code Blue." The doctor has to coordinate this complex task that includes interpreting the heart rhythm, giving a wide array of medications, monitoring CPR efforts, giving heart shocks, starting IV lines and much more. The patient's life is on the line, and one has to make split-second decisions—hence the stress factor. One of our mentors once told us the first thing we should always do in a Code Blue situation is to check our *own* pulse. Although tongue-in-cheek, he was making the point that we can't manage the problem well without first monitoring our own reactions and avoiding panic.

James gives us similar advice. When we find ourselves quarreling and fighting with others, we should first do a *self*-assessment. Where is our emotion coming from? What internal struggles and motivations are in play? I verified this wisdom last week when my wife and I had an argument. As we were discussing the disputed issue, I suddenly realized the real underlying problem was my own selfishness, which was not even on the table. It wasn't until sometime later in the argument when I was finally able to admit my selfish motivations that conflict resolution occurred.

Perhaps we should check our own pulses more often. When we find ourselves quarreling, we need to remember James' words, step back and look at *ourselves*. If we can do that with honest candor, we may discover insights that reframe the issue and resolve the conflict.

STILL WASHING OUR NETS

[Jesus] saw at the water's edge two boats, left there by the fishermen, who were washing their nets. (Luke 5:2)

I suppose washing their fishing nets had value. Cleaning off the lake bottom scum, bits of seaweed and the odd twig probably made for more successful fishing. However, what if washing their nets was the only thing the fishermen ever did with them? Many of our churches today seem to specialize in washing nets or preparations for being "fishers of men." We talk about fishing, we watch training videos about fishing, and we even buy the latest fishing gear—yet unfortunately, we rarely actually go fishing.

I was recently reading *Back to Jerusalem*, about the Chinese evangelistic movement. The Chinese church, in the crucible of persecution, is growing at the amazing annual rate of fifteen percent. They have few Bibles, and other spiritual resources are almost nonexistent. Nonetheless, their growth rate is phenomenal. Meanwhile, we gorge ourselves with numerous Bible translations, concordances, commentaries, CDs, DVDs and seminars, yet we are not reaching out to those around us who have not yet found a relationship with God. We are bloated with information in our zeal for preparation, but to what end? The means has become the end in itself.

The bottom line is that we are selfish. We are hoarding fellowship in a lonely world. We are hiding the only map with the route to our eternal home. We are beggars who have found a loaf of bread that never diminishes, yet we refuse to share it with others. Furthermore, our selfish overindulgence is making us spiritually ill, like one stuffed with too much food who continues to hoard.

Satan is cunning. Rather than trying to take away our nets or convince us that we shouldn't fish, he is content to have us continually washing our nets. It's like we're trapped in a cruel *Groundhog Day* time warp. Every day we are once again destined to wash our nets, but we never get to the next day when we actually go fishing. Jesus told his disciples to follow him and he would make them "fishers of men" (Matthew 4:19). Let's stop washing our nets and start casting them. Let's start offering the bread of life to those who are starving.

March 19

GOD KNOWS OUR HEARTS

The heart is deceitful above all things / and beyond cure. / Who can understand it? (Jeremiah 17:9)

Humanism tells us our basic nature is good and we are continually improving the world around us. It's an attractive theory, but unfortunately it doesn't explain the observed reality around us or within us. I am *not* naturally altruistic and generous, and all too often my life experiences remind me of that sad truth.

Our family spent three years working at a rural mission hospital in the hinterlands of Zambia. We were located smack in the middle of nowhere, or as we used to say, "fifty miles beyond the Great Commission." One of the dangers of living there was the presence of several poisonous snakes: puff adders, cobras and boomslangs. It was not unusual to have a snake encounter, even on our front porch. Although our family suffered no snakebites, we frequently treated snakebite victims at the hospital. The mainstay of treatment was the use of snake antivenin, which was very expensive and hard to obtain.

One year, soon after using up the last of our antivenin, another snakebite victim showed up at our clinic. I remembered we actually did have one extra treatment course of antivenin. It had been provided by our mission board but was designated "for missionary use only" and stored separately from our general supplies for patients. I found myself in an ethical dilemma. If I used that last dose on this patient and one of my daughters were bitten tomorrow, could I live with that? Or what if one of the other missionaries' children were bitten? How would those parents feel about my decision to use up *their* antivenin? Is the life of an American missionary more valuable than the life of a Zambian? In the end, I asked for (and received) permission from the other missionaries to use the last of the antivenin on the bitten patient—and none of the missionaries were bitten before a new shipment of antivenin arrived.

It's easy to criticize ethnocentrism in others, but I should be willing to turn a critical eye on myself. Reinhold Niebuhr said, "We must fight their falsehood with our truth, but we must also fight the falsehood in our truth." This experience illuminated the "falsehood" that I was without prejudice. The truth is, however, that my heart is not only prejudiced and deceitful but also self-centered, proud, lustful, and impatient. God knows our hearts, a fact which makes his love for us that much more amazing.

MAKE A DIFFERENCE

There was a rich man ... At his gate was laid a beggar named Lazarus ...
(Luke 16:19-20)

Jesus told a parable about a rich man and a beggar. Both men died. Lazarus, the beggar, went to heaven, and the rich man went to hell. Although there were undoubtedly many poor persons the rich man could have helped during his life, we only know he was held accountable for Lazarus, who was laid "at his gate."

Sometimes the needs of our world seem overwhelming. The things we can do to help seem to amount to nothing more than the proverbial drop in the bucket. Yet that is what God calls us to. We cannot help everyone, but for those who are laid at our gate, we are accountable. For those at our gate, our faithfulness may make a huge difference.

There is a story about a man who was walking along a beach in Mexico. There had been a big storm the previous night, and thousands of starfish had been swept up on the beach. As the beach walker considered this unfortunate sight, he noticed a young boy who walked over to the stranded starfish, picked one up, carried it over to the ocean and threw it in. He then repeated the process. The man approached the lad, who was carrying a starfish, and spoke to him. "Young man, thousands of starfish are going to die from this storm. What you are doing can't even begin to make a difference." The boy looked at the starfish in his hand, and then he looked at the thousands still stranded on the beach. He then threw the starfish into the ocean and said, "It makes a difference for *that* one."

And so it is with us. The fact that we can't meet all the needs in the world cannot discourage us into inactivity so that no one's needs are met. We are responsible for those who have been laid at our gate, and for them, our faithfulness could make all the difference in the world.

ATTAINING HOLINESS

For God did not call us to be impure, but to live a holy life.
(I Thessalonians 4:7)

Bible teacher Ed Miller says the Christian life isn't hard; it's impossible! We are called to be holy, pure and Christ-like. If we honestly assess our lives, however, we see an embarrassing shortfall. What reaction do we have to persistent sin in our lives? Our natural response is to launch a frontal attack. We rely on willpower and determination to effect a change. Whether the problem is anger, impatience, jealousy or pride, we engage our wills and promise to do better. However, we soon discover our total inability to become holy by the force of will. Paul, on the other hand, tells us that righteousness is a *gift* from God (Romans 5:17). Should we then just sit back and wait for God to zap us with holiness?

According to Quaker theologian and author Richard Foster, God has given us the spiritual disciplines as a means of receiving God's righteousness. Some of these disciplines include prayer, worship, Bible study, fasting and meditation. The spiritual disciplines do not in and of themselves make us holy, but they put us in God's presence so that he can transform us. Being in the presence of infinite love and holiness cannot leave us unchanged. Anger, impatience, jealousy and pride lose their intensity when we are in God's *shekinah* (dwelling presence) glory. As we spend time with God, we will find an increased love, patience, compassion and humility growing in us. The call to holiness, therefore, is not a call to exert our willpower but a call to draw near to God.

A SURE HOPE

Jesus said to her, "I am the resurrection and the life. He who believes in me will live even though he dies; and whoever lives and believes in me will never die." (John 11:25-26a)

My mother-in-law died last week. On Thursday she went to the doctor feeling weak and achy; the following Tuesday she was in eternity. As her family, we were blessed to be able to be with her during her final hours. We were able to say our good-byes and tell her how much we loved her.

Historically, many cultures have believed the time right before death may be the most significant time of one's life. Persons often listened carefully to hear any words of transcendent wisdom from dying lips. Our hospice nurse said, "People often die the way they lived." This was certainly true for Mary Beth (Nana). She had lived a life of amazing love and service for others, and she died the same way.

In her last hours, Nana was so short of breath that just speaking was a struggle. She had every reason to be self-absorbed, angry, depressed and questioning, but she was more concerned about others than herself. She reminded a nephew not to forget to take some cross-stitch pieces she had recently finished for him. She asked a granddaughter how her injured hand was holding up at her field hockey camp. She knew Doreen and I were car shopping and told us she'd noticed a Toyota sale in the morning newspaper. A few days after her death we discovered she had written out gift checks for the grandkids' upcoming birthdays. Nana died as she lived, giving us a legacy of caring more for others than herself.

This experience has reminded me again that there is a "wrongness" about death that points to something more. We intuitively sense that our significance is such that at death we cannot just "cease to be." Jesus tells us that what seems to be the harsh reality of death is really an illusion, for those who believe in him "will never die." Our sure hope is now Nana's eternal reality.

THE PROCESS TO UNITY

May the God who gives endurance and encouragement give you a spirit of unity among yourselves as you follow Christ Jesus. (Romans 15:5)

I recently drove by a field of sunflowers and was impressed by their unity of focus; all the flower heads were facing the rising sun. Although it was only 9 AM, none of them had overslept or were distracted by other matters. They were directing their full attention to their source of life and energy. As they each turned toward the sun, their overall unity was readily apparent and impressive. These amazing plants have an unusual ability called phototropism that allows the flower heads to move and follow the sun as it migrates across the sky each day.

That field of sunflowers could be a metaphor for the church. If we Christians all keep our focus on the *Son* (Jesus), we will automatically be in unity with each other ... right? Although the metaphor demonstrates some truth, it breaks down in several fundamental ways. First of all, each of us hears God imperfectly; if we are hearing different pitches, we can't be singing in unison. Secondly, even if we were to hear the same message, we are not automatons that mechanically respond in a uniform way—God gave us the ability to choose our responses. And while sunflowers exhibit this neat trait called phototropism, we exhibit these not so neat traits like pride, envy, malice, greed and general depravity, all of which make following God in perfect unity very difficult.

So why didn't God make us like the sunflowers? Although there may be many reasons, I believe one of them is that God has a different goal for us than the sunflowers. God's desire for us is not perfect uniformity of actions or even uniformity of beliefs. Instead, he wants us to have a *spirit* of unity marked by love, patience, and bearing with one another. And what makes that unity of Spirit so amazing and special is that it occurs *in spite of* our many differences.

THE WITNESS OF NATURE

For since the creation of the world God's invisible qualities—his eternal power and divine nature—have been clearly seen, being understood from what has been made, so that men are without excuse. (Romans 1:20)

We Westerners too seldom notice the natural world we live in. When we contemplate our environment, it is often in terms of natural resources and what raw material it has to offer us rather than its inherent beauty or what we might learn from it. Science tells us the world we live in is just a snapshot of an ongoing evolutionary process, implying no need for a creator. Yet science is unable to answer the hard questions of origins: 1) What caused the Big Bang? 2) Where did matter and energy come from in the first place? and even more basic 3) Why is there *something* rather than nothing?

As Christians we appropriately thank God for the beauty of his creation. Nature could easily have been functional yet boring and mundane, lacking any aesthetic attraction. The grandeur of a sunset and the fragile beauty of a butterfly are impressive but unnecessary from a practical standpoint. Our appreciation for the aesthetic aspects of the natural world challenges modern-day science's assumptions with the question, "If we are just a natural part of this universe, why is there awe or beauty?"

In Romans, Paul reminds us that nature has a very important role beyond providing us with raw materials and beauty; nature is a revelation of God. Nature not only reveals that there is a God but also displays his "eternal power and divine nature." Author Annie Dillard views nature as God's book and states, "For many of my readers, it's the only book of God they will ever read." Nature is a book that reveals God; it is written in every language and dialect and sits on each person's bookshelf. It is for this reason that Paul states, all "are without excuse."

Nature, therefore, is a two-sided coin. The one side demonstrates God's love reaching out to reveal himself to us through his creation. The other side of the coin, however, holds us accountable. No one can say, "But I never knew."

GOD'S OPEN HAND

The eyes of all look to you, / and you give them their food at the proper time. / You open your hand / and satisfy the desires of every living thing. / The Lord is righteous in all his ways / and loving toward all he has made. / The Lord is near to all who call on him … / He fulfills the desires of those who fear him; / he hears their cry and saves them. (Psalm 145:15-19)

When my children were young, I used to play a game with them. I would conceal a piece of candy in my closed hand, and they would have to pry my fingers open one by one to get the prize inside. I made them work a bit for it but of course in the end was delighted to be overpowered and give up the treat. While I would like to think there are some similarities between God and me as fathers, the differences are far more glaring.

As a father, despite my best efforts, I am unable to give anything that is totally good. Candy, though delicious for the moment, can result in cavities, obesity, and poor nutritional habits. Also, am I willing to open my hand when the contents are painful yet ultimately beneficial for my child? This psalm reminds us that God gives us all we need, and he gives it in its "proper time." He alone can truly satisfy the needs and desires of our inner being. The void inside each of us is indeed "God-shaped" and therefore can only be filled completely by God himself.

As God's child, I find it reassuring to know he is near me when I call on him. God hears my cry when I recurrently find myself in trouble's way. And like the child on his lap, I need not fear what comes from his open hand, for he is "loving toward all he has made."

PASSING THE BATON

You then, my son, be strong in the grace that is in Christ Jesus. And the things you have heard me say in the presence of many witnesses entrust to reliable men who will also be qualified to teach others. (II Timothy 2:1-2)

Written while he was imprisoned in Rome, II Timothy was Paul's last letter. As he faced imminent death, Paul was concerned for the church's well-being after his death. Timothy was a young leader in the church, who Paul had mentored for many years. Paul knew it was time to pass on the mantle of leadership to Timothy, and Paul reminded Timothy that he would one day need to do the same thing—pass the baton.

In the 2008 Beijing Olympics, the United States track team had a vivid reminder of the importance of passing the baton. Three of the US relay teams, all of whom were gold medal contenders, dropped the baton on the handoff and failed to win any medals.

Similarly, the church often has trouble passing the baton of leadership. Sometimes, the present leader is doing such a good job with the baton that we fail to develop new leaders to receive the baton when the inevitable time for handoff arrives. In some cases, the present leader may want to keep the baton beyond the time when it needs to be passed. Occasionally, one leader may try to take the baton before the appropriate time for transition has arrived.

The apostle Paul demonstrated a graceful passing of the leadership baton. He had humility (a willingness to give up the baton), spiritual sensitivity (a knowledge of the right time for transition), and an encouraging heart (a supportive spirit for the next runner). We would do well to emulate Paul.

WHY EVANGELISM IS GOOD FOR US

*I pray that you may be active in sharing your faith, so that you will have a
full understanding of every good thing we have in Christ. (Philemon 1:6)*

A quick read of the above verse reveals a rather mundane statement of
obvious orthodox thought, and it probably evokes little more than a pious
yawn. However, on closer inspection, this verse mutates from a common
spiritual platitude to a rather cryptic statement.

Clearly, we should be "sharing [our] faith," and it is important to
understand "every good thing we have in Christ." But, this verse states
that the former is somehow necessary for, or at least enhances, the latter.
How does witnessing to others about our faith in Christ provide us with
a deeper understanding of what we have in Christ?

I was initially at a loss to explain how evangelism could enhance
understanding. However, if one broadens the definition of "understanding" to be more than a cerebral process, the intent of this verse may be
clearer. In addition to being a process of the mind, understanding the
good things we have in Christ can be an experiential process that instructs our hearts.

I may know in my mind that Christ can set one free from anxiety,
greed, addictions, pride or whatever, but to see it happen in a new believer's life is different. It creates a more complete understanding of these
truths. They become known through concrete examples that touch our
hearts, not just abstract principles that instruct our minds.

We all would agree that God reveals himself to us through Scripture. Most of us would also acknowledge that he reveals himself through
prayer, meditation, worship, the community of believers and even nature
itself. However, I think few of us have considered the truth recognized
by the apostle Paul in this text. When we share our faith with others, not
only is God revealed to them, but he is also revealed to us.

RECOGNIZING JESUS

Early in the morning, Jesus stood on the shore, but the disciples did not realize that it was Jesus. (John 21:4)

This Easter season as I've heard the familiar Easter passages read I've been impressed with the scriptural accounts of several persons who didn't initially recognize the resurrected Jesus. Mary Magdalene, who first found the empty tomb, was confused and overcome with sorrow. Jesus, always empathetic, appeared to Mary and spoke with her. Surprisingly, however, she didn't realize it was Jesus until he called her by name (John 20:16). She may have been too overwhelmed by grief to recognize anyone.

Later the same day, Jesus appeared to two disciples on the road to Emmaus, but they also failed to recognize him. The travelers were discussing Jesus' death and the rumors that he had been seen alive, but they were unable to understand what it all meant. Jesus, always a teacher, explained the Scriptures to them and the significance of what had happened. Nonetheless, they only recognized Jesus "when he broke the bread" (Luke 24:35).

Some days later at daybreak, Jesus appeared to several disciples including Peter, James and John, who were out fishing in their boat. Jesus called to them from the shore, but they did not know it was Jesus. Always ready to meet their needs, Jesus told them to throw their nets on the other side of the boat. When they followed his instructions, they were unable to pull in their nets due to the weight of fish. John suddenly remembered once before when he'd had this same extraordinary fishing experience, and he turned to Peter, exclaiming, "It is the Lord!" (John 21:7).

What about us? Are we so overcome by our sorrows, our journeys or our jobs that we risk missing the risen Lord among us? Has Jesus been calling us by name, giving us our daily bread and even working miracles among us, and we are still unaware? Our prayers should echo the words of the song by Robert Cull, "Open my eyes, Lord; I want to see Jesus."

THE MATTER OF PRAYER--DOES IT?

... You do not have because you do not ask God. (James 4:2)

Some would say that since God is all-knowing and all-powerful, everything that happens has been ordained by him. So what kind of arrogant beings are we to presume to change God's plans through our ill-informed, egocentric, feeble prayers? Since our prayers are incapable of altering God or events, we must be called to pray as a spiritual discipline for our own edification and nothing more.

While this line of thinking has a thread of logic, it flies against the strong winds of Scripture. There is a litany of biblical stories demonstrating God *answering* persons' prayers. There are also explicit statements—"Ask and it will be given you" (Matthew 7:7) and "He answered their prayers, because they trusted in him" (I Chronicles 5:20)—indicating that prayers do effect a change.

While it is true that God does not change (Malachi 3:6), one of the things about him that is unchanging is that he is affected (changed) by prayer. Throughout all Scripture, prayer affected God, and there's no reason to assume that has changed today. Paul tells us that God has chosen to be co-laborers with us (I Corinthians 3:9). It seems God has ordained times he may act or not act *only* in response to our prayers. God has woven our volitional prayers into his sovereign will to form a complex tapestry that has resulted in all the events of our world—past, present and future.

While God knows our needs before we ask him (Matthew 6:8), he still wants us to ask. God's decision to work together with us through the avenue of prayer grows out of his desire to be in a loving relationship with us. God's love is so huge that he has relinquished some of his power, allowing himself to be affected by man, so that his love can find fuller expression in the relationship prayer affords. Prayer matters.

FITTING SPEECH

He who guards his mouth and his tongue / keeps himself from calamity.
(Proverbs 21:23)

All of us can remember times when we would have given anything to retract some hastily spoken words. Reclaiming an utterance, however, is as about as easy as pushing toothpaste back into the tube.

As a senior family practice resident, I did some moonlighting in a local emergency room. After working there for several months, I learned that a new physician had joined the staff. Although I'd not yet met him, his reputation as a joker preceded him. Our work shifts eventually overlapped one star-crossed night. Spotting me by the chart rack, he came over to introduce himself. "I'm D-D-D-D-Doctor Henry," he said with an obviously exaggerated stutter. Not wanting to be outdone, I replied, "And I'm D-D-D-D-D-Doctor Miller." His face turned bright red as he spoke again, "I have a speech imp-p-p-p-pediment," he managed. There was an awkward pause as my facial color matched and then surpassed his. I eventually managed to mumble some incoherent apology as I tried to find a black hole into which I could escape.

Words are a powerful, double-edged sword. We can speak a word of encouragement or criticism. When angry we sometimes utter hurtful words that may be remembered verbatim decades later. It would behoove us to remember James' admonition to be "quick to listen and slow to speak" (James 1:19).

At times the best response may be no words at all. Scottish pastor and writer W.G. Scroggie said, "When we answer back, we may win a battle and lose the campaign; but when we are silent we may lose a battle but win the campaign." But then why is it so hard for us to remain prudently silent? Let me say more about that...

FEELINGS HAVE PURPOSE

"... A Jewish man ... was attacked by bandits. They stripped him ... beat him up, and left him half dead ... Then a despised Samaritan came along, and when he saw the man, he felt compassion for him."
(Luke 10:30, 33 [NLT])

As children, most of us were either directly or indirectly taught that many of our feelings were misleading, unreliable or wrong. As a result we've learned to suppress or hide the more "unacceptable" feelings, such as anger, hurt, fear, sadness, pride and jealousy. In fact, we may have them so well hidden that we can't even find them ourselves. It makes no sense, however, that God would give us all these feelings only to confuse us or to irritate others.

There are at least three reasons God gave us feelings: 1) *to see* our inner selves, 2) *to hear* God's voice and 3) *to act*, not just think. First, feelings can be windows into our inner hearts and souls. If we don't know our true selves, our relationship with God is hindered. Augustine said, "Grant, Lord, that I may know myself that I may know thee." Secondly, our emotions can be a tool for us to hear God. They may be his voice of guidance, conviction or that still small voice of reassurance that we are on the right path. Finally, our emotions can motivate us to act. Thoughts tend to be short-lived. Feelings, however, linger; they affect us and spur us to action. The Good Samaritan story shows us how one person was moved to action by the emotion of "compassion."

Needless to say, feelings should be our servants and not our masters. Some feelings are too strong or overwhelming to use immediately. They need to be given time to mellow, like a fine wine. Other feelings are nothing more than garbage and need to be trashed. Nonetheless, with time God may transform even useless rubbish thrown on the compost pile into something useful. Feelings may be a boon or a bane. If, however, we allow God to use and redeem them, our feelings can be a blessing from his hand.

April

TO WHOM SHALL WE GO?

From this time many of his disciples turned back and no longer followed him. "You do not want to leave too, do you?" Jesus asked the Twelve. Simon Peter answered him, "Lord, to whom shall we go? You have the words of eternal life." (John 6:66-68)

My daughter Amaris recently graduated from a Christian college. The husband of one of her professors was diagnosed with cancer. He was in his mid-thirties and had several young children at home. Over a period of months, the whole college community joined the professor in praying for healing. Her husband died. Amaris called home in tears. The whole college shared the professor's grief.

It is difficult to imagine what emotions and questions this Bible professor must have experienced. As I write these words, I have tried to put myself in her shoes. The vicarious experience was like a huge ocean wave of pain and sorrow, threatening to knock me down and pull me under. Fortunately, I could step back from the mother of all waves to the beach of reality—since it didn't really happen to me. Amaris' professor, however, had no such option. My brief daydream was her constant nightmare, from which there was no awakening.

The professor took some time off to grieve and be with her family. In chapel, she shared some of her grief journey with the students. One of the Scriptures that resonated with her contained the words spoken by Peter, "Lord, to whom shall we go? You have the words of eternal life." American author and publishing executive Joseph Bayly said we need to "remember in the darkness, what [we] have learned in the light." We *know* that God is good; he is faithful and loving. When circumstances are so difficult that they defy understanding, we need to remember that what is true has not changed. Lord, to whom shall we go? *You* have the words of eternal life.

WHEN GOD SEEMS DISTANT

Why, O LORD, do you stand far off? / Why do you hide yourself in times of trouble? (Psalm 10:1)

God is not only invisible; he is completely undetectable by any of our senses. Yet as Christians, we have a relationship with him. We hear his inaudible voice, and we see his invisible hands working in our lives. At times we can sense his presence in an almost palpable way. The fact that there are times when an invisible, transcendent God seems distant should not surprise us as much as the fact that there are times when he seems so close.

Twentieth-century Swiss theologian Karl Barth reminds us that God is free to reveal himself or conceal himself, to intervene or not to intervene in our lives. God demonstrates how much he values freedom by giving it to us. If he were to show himself to us in an unquestionable way, he would overwhelm our freedom to choose to believe in him, for there would no longer be a need for faith.

Our interpersonal relationships go through easy times, hard times, and indifferent times. The same thing can happen in our relationships with God. It's easy to love and worship God when things are going well, and we feel his presence enveloping us like steam in a sauna. But what if we lose our job, or we're diagnosed with cancer, or we have a child born with Down syndrome? Our closeness to God cannot be based on whimsical feelings that change with circumstances; it must be based on faith. Ironically, it is often through the trying times, when God seems most distant, that our faith is stretched and grows. Knowing with assurance that God is real even when we feel absolutely nothing is what faith is all about.

So there should be no surprise when our relationship with God goes through periods of doubt, frustration, apathy or anger, when God seems distant or even absent. These are feelings, and feelings are just that … feelings. Feelings do not, however, change the reality of who God is and his love for us. When circumstances and feelings fail us, we must trust in the clear promises of God's Word: "I will never leave you or forsake you" (Joshua 1:5). Feeling God's absence does not make it so. True reality trumps fickle fear every time.

April 3

GOD WILL SUPPLY OUR NEEDS

And my God will meet all your needs according to his glorious riches in Christ Jesus. (Philippians 4:19)

As a child, I remember paging through the book *Martyrs Mirror*. It contains pictures and stories about Christians through the centuries who were killed for their faith in Christ. They were imprisoned, tortured, starved, beheaded, drowned and burned at the stake. I admired those saints who refused to recant their faith to save their own lives. Many of them with their last breath gave words of encouragement to their onlooking families to remain steadfast in their faith or thanked God for the privilege of suffering and dying for him. I remember wondering if there was any way I could ever do that. Did I have the strength, the courage and the faith to hold up under such severe testing? Borrowing the title from the 1983 movie about the Mercury 7 astronauts, did I have *The Right Stuff*? I feared I did not.

My perspective has changed, however, as I've grown through my Christian life. I've seen individuals and families go through circumstances and experiences that far surpassed the limits of human endurance. These were simple Christians, mere mortals like you and me. A basic truth was impressed on me. When we are not in special need (e.g., suffering, being tortured, dying), we don't have the special grace and strength those circumstances require. However, when we find ourselves in those situations, God supplies our needs as they arise. The question is not "Do we have *what* it takes?"—we don't. But we do have *who* it takes, and he is faithful to meet all our needs out of his riches in glory.

SPIRITUAL SPATS

But avoid foolish controversies ... arguments and quarrels about the law, because these are unprofitable and useless. Warn a divisive person ... such people are warped and sinful; they are self-condemned. (Titus 3:9-11)

As a boy I remember my dad telling me about a nearby church that had split into two separate groups. They couldn't agree whether they should read the minutes of the church's yearly business meeting while standing (too proud) or seated (suitably humble). I thought it was a pretty funny story at the time. However, the longer I'm in the church, the less humorous the story becomes. It's often easy to believe the issue at hand is of fundamental importance. And if the issue is decided wrongly, we fear God's work will grind to a screeching halt!

The time, energy, and emotion we invest in these petty questions may be ponderous. The associated discussions often generate more heat than light. We forget to listen well and to speak in love, assuming the fact that "we're right" is adequate in itself.

The direct effects of spiritual spats are easily noted (anger, hurt feelings, defensiveness, etc.). The indirect effects, however, may be more significant. When our lives are tangled with trifles, we may lose the vision God is calling us to. We may also lack the time to do it. While I *want* to pursue holiness and I want to follow God's call in my life, I am often waylaid by thorny decisions like deciding the color for the new church carpet. It is for this reason that Paul warns so strongly about "foolish controversies" and calls them "unprofitable and useless." Charles Swindoll's words serve as a useful reflection: On the final judgment day as we stand before God, many of us will "wish we'd played a lot more *Risk* and a lot less *Trivial Pursuit.*"

RESURRECTION SUNDAY

Praise be to God … In his great mercy he has given us new birth into a living hope through the resurrection of Jesus Christ from the dead, and into an inheritance that can never perish, spoil or fade—kept in heaven for you.
(I Peter 1:3-4)

Death is as certain as birth yet less highly anticipated. Exercise, healthy eating and modern medicine can only minimally postpone the appointment that none of us has made, but each of us will keep. Friends, birthdays, gray hair and wrinkles serve as unsolicited reminders of our appointment. Part of the solemnity at funerals we attend is the "in-our-face" reminder of our own mortality.

As Christians, the doctrine of the resurrection is pivotal. Paul tells us that the dead in Christ will rise to be with the Lord forever, but do we believe this claim? There's a story about a missionary in Brazil who struggled to get members of a primitive indigenous tribe to cross a certain river. They badly needed the medical care on the other side but were convinced evil spirits inhabited the river. The missionary told them they had nothing to fear and even put his hand in the water to prove his point. The tribal people remained unconvinced. Finally the missionary dove into the water; emerging on the far side, he pumped his fist triumphantly in the air. The whole tribe cheered and followed him into the river, finally reassured by seeing *his* safe passage.

On Easter morning the angels must also have pumped their fists in the air. Jesus dove into the frightening waters of death and emerged on the other side, unharmed and victorious. Jesus was triumphant over death! The ramifications of Jesus' resurrection define our faith, our lives and our destinies. The resurrection is not only a vindication of Christ's life and teachings but also our guarantee that the death that grips humanity has been conquered. Our hope for eternal life has a solid foundation, based on the one who went before us and emerged on the other side fully alive.

WHAT THE LORD REQUIRES

With what shall I come before the LORD / and bow down before the exalted God? / ... He has showed you, O man, what is good. / And what does the LORD require of you? / To act justly and to love mercy / and to walk humbly with your God. (Micah 6:6, 8)

This passage is one of the most loved and often quoted descriptions of Old Testament religion. The standards are repeated in the New Testament when Jesus makes a statement similar to Micah's. Jesus said we should practice "justice, mercy and faithfulness" (Matthew 23:23).

These prophetic words from Micah answer the important question of what God wants from us. The first requirement is that we "act justly," or as the NAS version says, we are to "do justice." We should be working for personal and social justice in the world in which we live (*physical* actions). Secondly, we are to "love mercy." We are to have a heart of compassion for others that comes not from duty but from love (an *emotional* influence). Finally, we are to "walk humbly with [our] God" (*spiritual* fellowship). While Micah shows us what God wants from us, in Amos we see what God *doesn't* want from us—our empty worship, offerings and sacrifices (5:21-23). God doesn't want our things; he does want *us* (physically, emotionally and spiritually). Jesus echoes this sentiment when he says the most important commandment is to love God with all our heart, mind, soul and strength (Mark 12:28-30).

It's actually arrogant to assume that our things (e.g., money and possessions) are needed by the God who spoke our world into existence. Instead, God wants us. He wants us as co-laborers, he wants us to share his love with the world, and he wants us in fellowship with him.

God's love that wants us is the same love that calls out for justice, and he wants us to join him in bringing that to pass. God's love shows mercy and compassion, and he wants us to share this with others. Finally, God's love finds expression in fellowship with us. As we walk humbly with God, he is redeeming something that goes back to the dawn of time. God is restoring the amazing fellowship between him and us, as it was in the Garden of Eden when man and woman first walked with God, unashamed (Genesis 2:25).

PARENTAL WISDOM

... Keep your father's commands / and do not forsake your mother's teaching. / Bind them upon your heart forever; / fasten them around your neck. / When you walk, they will guide you; / when you sleep, they will watch over you ... / For these commands are a lamp, / this teaching is a light ... (Proverbs 6:20-23)

Proverbs is a collection of wise sayings, many authored by Solomon. Proverbs has often been described as more practical than theological, although I would like to think these two descriptors are not mutually exclusive. It was once said of the brilliant German philosopher Hegel that he "explained everything in life, except how to get through one normal day." The practical information in Proverbs, on the other hand, tells us just that—how to get through that one normal day. The importance of this sensible advice should not be undervalued.

At first glance, the words of wisdom in Proverbs 6 seem like good counsel for our *children*. However, closer consideration causes us to note there's something more here that may be disconcerting to those of us who are parents. This passage parallels the *shema*, the Jewish confession of faith from Deuteronomy 6:4-9. The many shared words and phrasings between the two passages make the importance of parents' instruction to their children similar to the importance of the law (the Torah) itself. As if anticipating our incredulity, the comparison between parents' instructions and God's own commands is repeated in verse 23. In this verse, parents' instructions are called a "lamp" and a "light," mimicking David's vivid metaphors for God's Word in Psalm 119:105.

The importance this proverb places on parental instruction is both challenging and humbling for those of us who are parents. We realize the only way parental wisdom can be as important as God's wisdom is when they are one and the same. The practical and the theological are not only *not exclusive* but should also be *completely inclusive*. In other words, the only way our teachings can be wise and significant is if they are completely in line with God's Word.

The gauntlet has been thrown down. The challenge to be godly parents is not an easy one. As parents we need to be willing to take up the gauntlet, to accept the challenge, and to allow God's Holy Spirit to enable us for the task that we alone are unable to accomplish.

April 8

IN THE FULLNESS OF TIME

There is a time for everything ... (Ecclesiastes 3:1)

Some have said the greatest discovery of the second millennium happened by accident. The world's first antibiotic, penicillin, was discovered by biologist Alexander Fleming in September of 1928. Fleming was gone on vacation, and when he returned to his untidy lab, he found one of his bacterial cultures was contaminated by a mold. He keenly noted that in the area surrounding the mold, the bacteria were not growing. The mold was later identified as the *Penicillium* mold. If Fleming had not gone on vacation, or if he'd kept a cleaner work area, or if a different mold had contaminated his experiment, he would never have made the earth-shaking discovery of penicillin ... but he did.

Five years later, in 1933, Nora Nissley, a sixteen-year-old girl in northern Indiana, developed peritonitis and sepsis from a ruptured appendix and was near death. Although Fleming's penicillin would not be on the market for another eight years, Nora's doctor had somehow heard about the experimental drug and was fortunate enough to get his hands on some for her. Nora Nissley was one of the first persons treated with penicillin, and she survived to later become my aunt.

In 1942, my future mother and father were dating each other, but Dad ended the relationship because my mother wasn't a Christian at the time. My aunt Nora's influence and witness to my mother were instrumental in her becoming a Christian, which led to Mom's reuniting with my father. If Alexander Fleming had not gone on vacation in September of 1928, this domino cascade of events would not have happened, and you would not presently be reading this meditational thought—for neither I nor this book would exist.

Were these accidents and coincidences the result of cosmic chance, or was a master conductor coordinating events? Scripture speaks of events and times as though they are not capricious: "at the appointed time" (Romans 9:9) and "when the time had fully come" (Galatians 4:4). I believe Fleming discovered penicillin "at the appointed time," and my aunt's survival and my mother's conversion were not due to random chance but due to a sovereign God. There is *indeed* a time for everything.

HE'S ALREADY HERE

When Jacob awoke from his sleep, he thought, "Surely the LORD is in this place, and I was not aware of it." (Genesis 28:16)

When God spoke to Jacob in a dream, Jacob had an epiphany. Jacob suddenly realized that God had been there all the time, but he had just been unaware of his presence. God's holy presence and holy activity were all around Jacob, but he was oblivious.

Our post-Enlightenment culture is also often unaware of God's presence. We tend to think "light" (i.e., knowledge) can only come from information provided by our five senses. The result, unfortunately, is that we close many doors through which God wants to reveal himself to us. As enlightened modernists, we are too "cultured" to perceive God's presence in the world around us or even in our own thoughts, emotions and dreams. If God were to speak to us in a dream, as he did to Jacob, we could think of a half-dozen ways to explain it as something else. We would explain away the voice of the Creator of the universe as some subconscious misfiring of neurons.

We've all experienced moments that glare with supernatural significance: my daughter and I sitting outside a restaurant, spellbound by the most intense rainbow we'd ever seen; our family all clustered around my mother-in-law as she passed peacefully into eternity; my wife, children and I snorkeling at the spellbindingly beautiful coral reefs of St. John Island. In those moments we were standing on holy ground. We knew what we were experiencing was due to more than the random collision of subatomic particles. Nonetheless, we tend to analyze and discount the idea that sensing a rainbow's beauty points to a Creator. We then pat ourselves on the back for being so smart—when in actuality we are just being oblivious. Our sophisticated thought processes muffle the voice of God, who is yelling, "I'm here!" We "wisely" reason things out and become like Jacob, unaware of the presence of God.

CRUSHED

Surely he took up our infirmities / and carried our sorrows / … he was crushed for our iniquities; / … and the LORD has laid on him / the iniquity of us all. (Isaiah 53:4-6)

The prophet Isaiah foretold the Messiah's suffering death 700 years before Jesus was born. Jesus himself was acutely aware of the road that lay before him. In the Garden of Gethsemane, Jesus offered an anguished prayer to his father. Jesus asked if there was a way he could avoid the agonizing death—being crushed by the sins of the world (Mark 14:32-36). Ironically, Jesus asked to avoid this crushing death while in Gethsemane, where a press was used to crush olives to extract oil ("Gethsemane" is Aramaic for "oil press"). Like the olives, Jesus would have to be crushed to produce the healing oil (his blood) for the sins of mankind.

The bread and wine Jesus used at the Last Supper (Mark 14:22-25) also seemed to have been pre-ordained to show what must happen to Jesus. Jesus took the bread and broke it, telling the disciples it was his body. He then took the wine and told them it was his blood, poured out for them. The bread had been made from grains of wheat, *crushed* to produce flour. Similarly, the wine came from grapes, *crushed* in the wine press.

Perhaps it was all some grand coincidence. Or perhaps, from the dawn of Creation, God created an oil (from crushed olives), a drink (from crushed grapes) and a food (from crushed grain). He then also inspired an eighth-century BC prophet to describe the crucifixion, in which Jesus would be "crushed." Finally, God arranged a place called "oil press" (Gethsemane), where olives were crushed, as the place where Jesus would ask if he also had to be pressed (crushed). Even more amazing than orchestrating all this, however, is the fact that because of God's great love for us, Jesus was voluntarily crushed for our sin.

April II

COMMON GROUND

"Come now, let us reason together," says the LORD. (Isaiah 1:18a)

Perhaps on no other issue are Americans more divided than they are on the issue of abortion. The landmark 1973 Roe vs. Wade Supreme Court decision legalizing abortion did little to stop the raging debate. It seems impossible to find common ground between pro-choice and pro-life advocates. The line of divide is decisive.

I remember when my first grade teacher sent me out to the parking lot to get a book from her car, a gray Karmann Ghia. There were two problems with my teacher's plan. First of all, I wouldn't have known a Volkswagen Karmann Ghia from a Ford pickup truck. Secondly, she had unwittingly sent a student who saw everything in black and white to find a car that was gray.

I believe there is, nonetheless, some gray, common ground on the divisive issue of abortion. Even staunch pro-choice advocates have said they want to minimize the number of abortions. As a pro-life advocate, I can certainly agree with this stated desire.

The Alan Guttmacher Institute estimates seven percent of abortions are for rape, incest, fetal anomalies and risk to maternal health. That means 93 percent of abortions are "elective," and 30 percent of these are for primarily economic reasons. Last year 1.2 million abortions occurred in the US. Without changing any laws or anyone's mind, by just getting rid of economic obstacles, there could be 335,000 fewer abortions each year. If this happened, a multitude of voices (335,000) would one day thank us for doing more than piously arguing about black and white. They would thank us for being able to see the color gray and for doing something about it.

ON TSUNAMIS AND SUFFERING

Then the LORD answered Job out of the storm. He said: "… Where were you when I laid the earth's foundation? Tell me, if you understand." (Job 38:1, 4)

Some years ago, planet Earth experienced one of the deadliest natural disasters in recorded history. On December 26, 2004, a 9.2 magnitude earthquake, in the depths of a Southeast Asian sea, created a tsunami that took the lives of more than 230,000 people and left another 5 million people without clean water, food and shelter.

As Christians, how do we respond to the age-old question of pain, evil and suffering? Depending on our theological bent, God either *caused* this horrific calamity or at least *allowed* it to happen. The following suggested answers, while true, seem inadequate: 1) Pain and suffering are inherent consequences of a world granted the free will to disobey God and choose evil. 2) We are all sinners deserving death and therefore deadly disasters are not unjust but actually a merciful call for the rest of us to repent. 3) God uses all things, whether good or evil, for his unseen purposes. 4) While we tend to think of how good must be better than evil, perhaps evil *redeemed* to good is the best state of all. Augustine said, "God judged it better to bring good out of evil than to suffer no evil at all." And 5) Swiss author and physician Paul Tournier said that good and evil don't reside in happenings, but in people. Events are morally neutral; what matters is the way we react to them.

In the story of Job, we note that God does not answer Job's question about the reason for his suffering. As the readers, we can see "backstage." This omniscient viewpoint makes me want to yell to Job through a time-warp megaphone: "It was all a test from the devil, Job. You didn't do anything wrong." God's refusal to answer Job, however, leads me to believe that knowing "Why?" is not what's most important.

Perhaps the important thing *is* our response to suffering. As we look at how Jesus responded to suffering, we see that he joined those who suffered and offered sympathy, healing, and hope. We are called to follow in his steps. Jesus also took on the suffering and sin of mankind through his death that atoned for our sin. Because of Jesus, we can look forward to a time when pain, suffering, and even death will be no more. This sure hope is a definite comfort.

WALK IN THE LIGHT

God is light; in him there is no darkness at all. If we claim to have fellowship with him yet walk in the darkness, we lie and do not live by the truth.
(I John 1:5b-6)

If we walk in darkness, we cannot be in fellowship with God because God is light. The Greek word used here for fellowship, *koinonia*, indicates a relationship of communion and sharing. Walking in darkness, therefore, is not necessarily walking in sin; it is walking out of communion with God. While we usually think of sin as causing separation from God (and it does), John may also be saying that separation from God causes sin.

New Testament Christians would have been well acquainted with the perils of walking on dark, starless nights—stepping on snakes, running into trees, being attacked by bandits, and wandering off the path and losing their way. When we are in intimate fellowship with God, however, we are walking in the light. God's light illuminates not only our path but also our thoughts and desires.

Just as physical light shows us the truth about the world around us, spiritual light shows us the truth about sin. Would we choose to step on a snake if we clearly saw it and knew the pain it would cause us? Neither would we choose to sin if we truly saw sin with God's light and understood how it hurts us and others. Therefore, rather than just a focused effort to prevent sin (stepping on snakes and walking into trees), we should also strive to be in intimate fellowship with God since the light of that fellowship will help us avoid sin.

GOD DESIRES TO BLESS

"Blessed are the poor in spirit, / for theirs is the kingdom of heaven. / Blessed are those who mourn, / for they will be comforted. / Blessed are the meek, / for they will inherit the earth. / Blessed are those who hunger and thirst for righteousness, / for they will be filled." (Matthew 5:3-6)

It seems that God's blessings are often doled out when we are in situations of need. The first four beatitudes all describe persons lacking something. The "poor in spirit" lack spiritual treasure; "those who mourn" have lost something or someone; the "meek" lack power, position, or prestige; and those "who hunger and thirst for righteousness" lack holiness. A situation of *need* puts us in a position to receive—empty hands are available to receive something. The opposite, however, is also true—hands that are full can receive nothing new.

My home church has recently had several difficult years. It's sometimes hard for us not to hold on to anger, resentment, mistrust and fear, even though clinging to them hurts us. I'm reminded of the proverbial baboon with his hand stuck in the pumpkin. If he'd let go of the pumpkin seeds, he'd be able to withdraw his hand, but he feels entitled to the seeds and won't let go. Some of us have been hurt, and we feel entitled to our feelings, so we cling to them. Jesus stands before us, wanting to bless us, yet here we are, unable to receive his blessings because our hands are stuck inside pumpkins, tightly fisted.

It's been said that when people are near death, when they are about to leave this world for the next, their last actions and words are often reflective of their inner hearts. It is instructive to look at Jesus' ascension from this perspective. Luke says, "[Jesus] lifted up his hands and blessed them. While he was blessing them, he left them and was taken up into heaven" (Luke 24:50-51). Jesus' last thoughts and actions were to bless those he loved, and the desire of Jesus' heart is still to bless us today. Are we willing to let go of our pumpkin seeds so we can receive his blessings with open, empty hands?

PREPARED AT ALL TIMES

Therefore put on the full armor of God, so that when the day of evil comes, you may be able to stand your ground ... (Ephesians 6:13)

No good soldier would go off to battle, forgetting to put on his armor. So why does Paul think it is necessary to remind us to put on our spiritual armor? The above verse provides a clue when it states that evil comes to us. We don't decide on one particular day to go marching into battle against evil, in which case we would certainly remember to don our armor. Instead, evil comes to us. We don't know when (or how) evil will strike. Consequently, we need to be ready (i.e., have our armor on) every day. It's hard to maintain a high degree of vigilance on a daily basis; but when our guard is down, we are vulnerable.

In medicine, we are taught the importance of practicing "universal precautions." These are a set of precautions designed to prevent transmission of HIV and other serious contagious diseases when medical staff are involved in patient-care activities where we might be exposed. Basically, taking universal precautions means assuming every patient could be carrying one of these illnesses (since they might) and taking appropriate protective measures. If we assume some patients don't have a contagious disease, we will be less careful and therefore more vulnerable to accidental exposure.

I recently read a study that showed more pedestrians are killed crossing the street at crosswalks than when jaywalking. It's not that crosswalks are more dangerous than unmarked areas. People are just more careful crossing the street at unmarked areas and less cautious at crosswalks, where they assume they'll be safe.

The stakes are high in spiritual warfare, and our vigilance cannot waver. We can't afford naïve assumptions and end up being an HIV or crosswalk casualty. Our spiritual armor must be on at all times. When our armor is on, we are prepared for surprise attacks, and we can stand our ground.

A DOUBTING FAITH

"Teacher, I brought you my son, who is possessed by a spirit that has robbed him of speech. … But if you can do anything, take pity on us and help us." "If you can?" said Jesus. "Everything is possible for him who believes." Immediately the boy's father exclaimed, "I do believe; help me overcome my unbelief!"
(Mark 9:17b, 22b-24)

Few can read this story without feeling a sense of kinship with the father. He has anguished over his son's suffering for many years. He wants to believe more than anything that his son can be healed, but doubts linger. We admire his honest statement of uncertainty. And although we may be reluctant to admit it, we also identify with his doubting faith.

While a strong, unwavering faith is often idealized, it is more often the exception than the rule. Scripture is replete with examples of those who were uncertain and questioned God or what he was doing. What seems more important than their questioning is the fact that in the end they chose to believe in spite of their doubts.

Philip Yancey says, "Doubt always coexists with faith, for in the presence of certainty who would need faith at all?" Perhaps if we are honest, a doubting faith is not an oxymoron but an honest, common reality.

God knows we will have times when our faith is weak, yet we cannot bolster our own faith. We can, however, do what the demon-possessed boy's father did. He came to Jesus and honestly admitted his feeble faith. Jesus met this frantic father where he was and answered his desperate plea for help. Like this father, we can come to Jesus with our persistent doubts and still ask for the desires of our hearts.

WHY ME?

The Egyptians ... pursued the Israelites and overtook them as they camped by the sea ... [The Israelites] were terrified and cried out to the LORD. They said to Moses, "Was it because there were no graves in Egypt that you brought us to the desert to die?" ... Then the LORD said to Moses, "... Tell the Israelites to move on. Raise your staff and stretch out your hand over the sea to divide the water so that the Israelites can go through the sea on dry ground."
(Exodus 14:9-11a, 15-16)

The memories of our air-conditioned home in Indiana seemed surreal. We were now in Sub-Saharan Africa with daily temperatures over 105°F. I had broken both bones in my left leg six months earlier, and after eight different casts, there was still no sign of healing. Why had God been so unfair to me?

We were driving to Chikankata Mission Hospital to see an orthopedic surgeon from England. The three-hour trip gave me plenty of time to review my plight and the gross injustice of it all. Immersed in self-pity, I emerged from our truck to find a queue of patients thirty yards long waiting to see the overwhelmed surgeon. Although the local patients had walked many miles and slept there overnight to get a good spot in line, they insisted the white doctor (that's me) go to the front of the line.

As I reluctantly crutched past a sea of black faces, I saw some of the worst orthopedic nightmares one could imagine. I saw people with grossly deformed limbs from improperly set broken bones and neglected bone infections with festering pus tracts draining to the skin. I also saw a man with congenital deformities of the legs that forced him to pull his body forward by using his hands on the ground. During that thirty-yard walk, God changed my thoughts and my emotions. I went from self-pity and depression to repentance and thanksgiving. God changed my focus from sulking self-absorption to caring compassion. I remember feeling the tears trickle into my beard.

Some things haven't changed much from Old Testament times. When circumstances are difficult, we still feel sorry for ourselves and wonder how God could let this happen. God's response is also much the same: "Why are you grumbling in self-pity? Move on, for I am with you." God spoke to the Israelites through Moses. He spoke to me through a thirty-yard walk.

THE CROSS AND THE EMPTY TOMB

You were taught, with regard to your former way of life, to put off your old self, which is being corrupted by its deceitful desires; to be made new in the attitudes of your minds; and to put on the new self, created to be like God in true righteousness and holiness. (Ephesians 4:22-24)

The provision for salvation is the story of what Jesus has done for us. It has two essential parts: 1) Christ's death on the cross and 2) His resurrection from the grave. Neither part can stand alone nor has preeminence over the other. While the cross has come to be the primary symbol of Christianity, writer John Eldredge reminds us that for the first four hundred years after Christ, this primacy was not the case. In fact, the apostles' preaching had a stronger emphasis on Christ's resurrection than on the cross (Acts 4:33, 17:18).

Scripture tells us that our sinful self has been crucified with Christ (Romans 6:6). We acquired our sinful nature by birth, and therefore deliverance from that sinful nature must come by death; this death happens at the cross. Thankfully, however, the story does not end there. Just as Christ died for us, so he also was raised for us (Romans 6:4). Watchman Nee in *The Normal Christian Life* says that at the cross the emphasis is on "I in Christ," while at the resurrection the emphasis is on "Christ in me." As new beings, we receive the gift of life from Christ in us.

To become a new creation in Christ, we first have to "put off [the] old self." This requires dying on the cross with Christ. We then "put on the new self." This involves being made alive by Christ's resurrection power and presence. The cross and the empty tomb form a complete package. This package is a gift freely offered to us all.

THE RIGHT TIME

But when the fullness of time had come [God] sent forth his Son, born of woman ... (Galatians 4:4, ESV)

As I reflect on my fifty-odd years of life (some odder than others), I'm impressed by this elusive thing we call time and the events that punctuate and define it. One event I vividly remember was when one of my patients, a sixteen-year-old teen, died with pus constricting his lungs—I still wonder if I had been able to put in the chest tube to drain that fluid just a few minutes earlier, whether he might have lived. Then there was the time my friend was in labor, and her baby's heartbeat suddenly stopped. We did an emergency C-section, but the baby died—if only we'd had five more minutes of that evanescent substance called time.

There have been other situations in which there was adequate time, but I missed opportunities due to hesitation or fear; I failed to adhere to the blacksmiths' proverb: "Strike while the iron is hot." There were also times, however, when I acted when I should have waited: "Haste makes waste." We can second-guess hundreds of decisions and wonder, but never know, what might have been different. It's been said, "Timing is everything." In relationships: what if I hadn't looked across the room and seen that cute brunette (my future wife) thirty-six years ago? Timing is also crucial in the stock market: buy low and sell high. In cooking hamburgers: stop too early and they're bloody, too late and they're charcoal. Life would be simpler if everything were like a Thanksgiving turkey with a red pop-up indicator to let us know when the time is right.

It's comforting to know that while our timing often misses the mark, God's does not. While we have free will (i.e., we can choose to act wrongly), God is also sovereign (i.e., our dumb choices cannot thwart God's ultimate purposes). God is never too late and never too early. He always acts in "the fullness of time."

FREEDOM FROM OUR PAST

Then Joseph said to his brothers, "… I am your brother Joseph, the one you sold into Egypt! Do not be distressed and do not be angry with yourselves for selling me here, because it was to save lives that God sent me ahead of you."
(Genesis 45:4-5)

We all know persons (perhaps us) who have had difficult or painful experiences in our past that now intrude on our present. Perhaps we were hurt or taken advantage of. We may harbor anger, hatred or resentment that saps our joy and hinders our ability for healthy relationships. These past experiences continue to wield power as long as they are allowed to affect things that are occurring now, in the present.

Rick Warren says that although "we are products of our past, we don't have to be prisoners of it. God's purpose is not limited by [our] past." Joseph is a prime example of someone with a dysfunctional childhood. He was coddled by his father Jacob, made fun of by his brothers and finally sold off as a slave. If anyone had a right to be angry and turn out badly, Joseph did. Yet by forgiving his family, he released the hold those experiences had on him.

Although we are unable to change our past, we *can* be set free from the hold it has on us. Initially, Joseph must have felt anger and a desire for revenge against his brothers. If Joseph had held on to these feelings, they would have enslaved him.

The Greek word for repentance, *metanoia*, literally means to "change [one's] mind," and I believe that's exactly what Joseph did. He "changed his mind" about a self-centered, it's-not-fair view of his situation. Joseph's changed mind helped change his heart, which enabled him to see God's sovereign hand bringing about his purposes. By forgiving his brothers, Joseph gave up his anger and resentment, which would only have been self-destructive anyway. His reward was renewed fellowship with his father and brothers. What rewards might we be forfeiting by nursing old hurts and grudges?

RECIPROCAL FORGIVENESS

"If you hold anything against anyone, forgive him, so that your Father in heaven may forgive you your sins." (Mark 11:25b)

There are numerous Scriptures that seem to indicate God's forgiveness is contingent on our forgiving others. Matthew clearly says that if we do not forgive others, God will not forgive us (Matthew 6:14-15). Jesus tells a rather startling story demonstrating this idea. A debtor owed a huge debt that was forgiven him. However, this forgiveness was later withdrawn when he failed to forgive *his* debtor (Matthew 18:21-35). While God's forgiving us is in some way dependent on our forgiving others, our ability to forgive others also relies on God's having forgiven us. The paradoxical dependency of these two provisional statements would seem to preclude any solution—a theological Catch-22, if you will. God won't forgive us until we forgive others, and we lack the spiritual power to forgive others truly until God has forgiven us.

With no apparent solution for this conundrum of corruption, God intervened with grace to provide the solution. Paul says, "While we were still sinners, Christ died for us" (Romans 5:8). Jesus' sacrificial death allowed God to forgive us unconditionally at the time of our salvation. It is because of Jesus in us that we are now truly able to forgive others. We may still *decide* not to forgive others, but the choice is a matter of our attitude, not our aptitude. Now that we are enabled to forgive others by God's having first forgiven us, we will be held accountable if we withhold that forgiveness.

Scottish author and pastor George MacDonald says God still loves us when we don't forgive others; we are held in his hand of love, but his face is turned away. When we decide to forgive our neighbor, God's face turns toward us, and a right relationship is restored.

PREGNANT FROM THE HOLY SPIRIT

Joseph son of David, do not be afraid to take Mary home as your wife, because what is conceived in her is from the Holy Spirit. (Matthew 1:20b)

Scripture demonstrates that the work of the Holy Spirit is versatile. He is a counselor, teacher, advocate, guide, and comforter, to name only a few descriptors. The word for *spirit* in both Greek and Hebrew has a broader definition that includes "breath" and "wind." This adds the connotation of the Holy Spirit as the unseen essence of God. In general terms, the Holy Spirit is the *presence* of God in us (Romans 8:9-11) and the *revealer* of God to us (John 16:14-15).

Scripture states that Mary's pregnancy was conceived "from the Holy Spirit." However, in view of the fact that Jesus is God's Son, wouldn't it have made more sense if God, the Father, had conceived Jesus, the Son? When we see the role of the Holy Spirit, however, as the *presence* of God in us and the *revelation* of God to us, then Mary's pregnancy from the Holy Spirit makes perfect sense. Jesus was Immanuel, meaning God with us (presence). Jesus was also God incarnate, the clearest and most complete disclosure of God to man (revelation).

In a spiritual sense, Christians are also pregnant from the Holy Spirit, since we have the actual presence of God/Jesus in us—like a pregnancy. The Holy Spirit in us not only reveals God/Jesus to us but also reveals him to others. Mary was pregnant and physically "showing" that Jesus was in her. Do we spiritually "show" Jesus' presence in our lives? If we aren't really "showing" Jesus to others, perhaps our pregnancy is not growing as it should. The angel's words echo: We need not be afraid of what God is growing and changing in us, for what is conceived in us is from his Holy Spirit.

April 23

HUMAN GUIDEPOSTS

Set an example for the believers in speech, in life, in love, in faith and in purity. (I Timothy 4:12b)

American culture views the world through the eyes of individualism. When an individual chooses wisely, a reward is expected for him or her. On the other hand, when one makes poor choices, he or she expects punishment or at least negative consequences if found out. Many cultures, however, do not view an individual as standing alone with their choices and consequences. Instead, each person is seen in the context of a family and a community and as part of an ongoing narrative story. The decisions one makes are perceived to affect the people around them and even descendent generations yet unborn. This cultural perspective tends to promote more restraint and less impulsivity in one's choices since one is more aware of the long-term and widespread consequences of decisions.

John Donne famously stated, "No man is an island." We are all connected to each other. Our decisions are not made, nor are our lives lived, in a vacuum. Our lives and decisions affect and communicate to others. Theologian and author Marva Dawn in her book *Joy in Divine Wisdom*, talks about how the Inuit of northern Canada and Alaska make human-appearing stone landmarks or cairns called *inukshuks*. These soundless signposts serve as directional guides for travelers and may indicate where to find food or shelter. Each of our lives is also an *inukshuk*. We can't choose whether or not we will be a directional guide to others but only what *kind* of guide we will be. Will those who follow the example of our lives find faith, hope, love and joy, or will they find fear, disappointment, lack of fulfillment and sadness? When our grandchildren tell their grandchildren stories and memories about us, what they say will be determined by how we live our lives today and tomorrow.

SHEEP OR GOATS?

When the Son of Man comes in his glory, ... he will separate the people one from another ... the sheep on his right and the goats on his left.
(Matthew 25:31-33)

It shouldn't be too hard to separate sheep from goats, especially if the sheep are all white with short, curly fur, and the goats are all brown with long, straight fur. But what if some of the sheep are brown, and some of the goats are white? Or what if some of the goats have short, curly fur, and some of the sheep have longer, straight fur? Or what if there were some that were the result of genetically engineered crossbreeding? Yeah, then what?

Our small group Bible study recently met, and Helen was sharing how her mother had just passed away. Helen's mother had lived a fairly loose, immoral life and never had much use for God or religion. The last few years of her life, she had developed dementia and was only occasionally lucid. Helen told us how the night of her mother's death, she had been babbling incoherently when suddenly she very clearly called out, "Jesus, help me!" She passed away later that night.

Our whole group would have loved to believe those words were sincere and not demented ramblings, but we hesitated to give Helen any definite words of assurance. Our sharing time soon ended, and we turned to the Scripture for the evening and read the following: "Everyone who calls on the name of the Lord will be saved" (Romans 10:13). Although I was supposed to be leading the group, I was at a loss for words. No orthodox exegesis came to mind. Sheep or goats? I'm sure glad that's God's job to decide and not mine.

BREAD FROM HEAVEN

When the dew was gone, thin flakes like frost on the ground appeared on the desert floor. When the Israelites saw it, they said to each other, "What is it?" ... Moses said to them, "It is the bread the LORD has given you to eat." ... [They] called the bread manna. (Exodus 16:14-15, 31a)

God delivered the Israelites from slavery in Egypt. As they trekked through the desert, they began to grumble that God had delivered them from slavery only to let them die of starvation (Exodus 16:3). Responding to their need, God miraculously provided bread from heaven (*manna*). It's interesting to note that they did not understand God's provision. When they saw the frost-like substance on the ground, they said, *"Manna?"*— which probably translates to "What is it?" Ironically, their perplexed question became the name for the substance.

Some years ago our family practice group lost three health care providers in a six-month period. We had been praying for God to provide for our group, but this did not seem like provision. Our response was similar to the Israelites': *"Manna?* (What is it?)" But then the recession of 2008 hit our country. Patients lost their jobs and then their health insurance. They no longer came in for their well adult check-ups and even missed a lot of appointments for their chronic medical problems. If we hadn't lost those providers, we wouldn't have had enough work for everyone.

The "surprise" economic recession, of course, did not catch God off guard. Just as God had provided for the Israelites in the wilderness, he provided for us. We are often like the Israelites, however, seeing only frost on the ground when we have actually been given bread from heaven.

CURSING MY ENEMIES

May his days be few / … May his children be fatherless / and his wife a widow.
/ … May a creditor seize all he has; / … May no one extend kindness to him…
(Psalm 109:8-9, 11-12)

Benedictions and blessings seem so much more spiritual than maledictions and curses. Nonetheless, there is a group of psalms called the imprecatory psalms, which are just that—curses. One might be prone to wonder why such expletives were not deleted from Holy Scripture.

A helpful approach to understanding all Scripture begins with the realization that there are many different genres (types) of writings. The categories include historical narrative, proverbs, letters, prophecies and poetry. We do not read and interpret them all in the same way. The psalms are neither didactic theology nor narrative prose. Instead, they are sometimes happy, sometimes distressed letters to God, written by people like us. Philip Yancey commented that the Psalms "do not so much represent God to the people as the people representing themselves to God."

In the psalms of imprecation, the psalmist has apparently experienced unjust injury and has feelings of resentment and anger. He also has a desire for vengeance—and he tells God all about it. Should we really voice such distasteful feelings to God? Perhaps we could deny the existence of such unsavory feelings, or possibly we could let our angry, vengeful feelings justify a plan for retaliation. On further thought, maybe the best option is to acknowledge our nasty feelings and present them to God. Miroslav Volf, a Croatian theologian, spoke from experience when he stated, "By placing unattended rage before God we place both our unjust enemy and our own vengeful self face to face with a God who loves and does justice." If there is justice to be meted out, God is the one to do it, not us (Romans 12:19). And if our feelings need to be healed or transformed, God alone can make this happen. In either event, we are at the right place in God's presence.

While the psalms can teach us much about the nature of God, the nature of man, and the nature of the interactions between the two (worship and prayer), there is something more that has endeared the psalms to me. As I read the psalms, it is clear that no matter what I am feeling (anger, joy, hatred, love, self-pity, praise, awe or doubt), I can openly bring it into God's presence—and this is a precious privilege.

THOUGHTS ON AGING

I was young and now I am old ... (Psalm 37:25)

I often tell my patients that getting old isn't so bad when one considers the alternative. Nonetheless, as I begin to experience the inexorable changes of aging in my own body, the abstract becomes concrete, and it becomes harder to wax philosophical.

Aging seems to be marked by a series of uninvited and undesirable losses. We lose our strength, eyesight and hearing. We lose our teeth, our good (or not so good) looks, our memory and our health. If we live long enough, we lose our friends and family. We also, inevitably, lose our independence.

One of my elderly patients recently reminded me how important independence is to us when I told him he was no longer able to drive his car safely. "If I can't drive, I'll have to depend on others for everything—that's a fate worse than death," he argued. "I've been driving for seventy-five years," he continued. "I know I can't see, or hear, or move very well, but thank goodness I can still drive my car!" His denial of losing the ability to drive was based more on fear than on fact.

Tielhard de Chardin in *Divine Milieu* says that instead of fearing and despising our diminishments (losses), we should embrace them and even consider our diminishments to be "hallowed." Our losses are made holy when we realize that each diminishment we experience as we age is a gradual losing hold on ourselves, leading up to the final diminishment of death. As we lose hold of that last remnant of our *own* power, we find ourselves helpless in the hands of God. Speaking of death, Quaker author John Yungblut says that at that moment, when we have finally let go of the last diminishment, we are aware that nothing has really been lost, for we are now in the hands of God, and all is well. Our diminishments have finally and completely been hallowed.

CALLED BY NAME

... She turned around and saw Jesus standing there, but she did not realize that it was Jesus. "Woman," he said, "why are you crying? Who is it you are looking for?" Thinking he was the gardener, she said, "Sir, if you have carried him away, tell me where you have put him, and I will get him." Jesus said to her, "Mary." She turned toward him and cried out in Aramaic, "Rabboni!" which means teacher. (John 20:14-16)

Why did Mary Magdalene not recognize the resurrected Jesus? Jesus may have intentionally prevented recognition. Or it may have been Mary's own tears that obscured her vision. Perhaps her total lack of expectation to see him ever again delayed his identification. Jesus asked her two questions: "Why are you crying?" and "Who is it you are looking for?" The answer to both her sorrow and her search stood before her, yet she could not see it. Then Jesus called her *by name* and suddenly, she was able to see that the person in front of her was Jesus.

How often have we been upset by some new life stress, wondering why God has abandoned us? Later we discover he was there all along, standing before us asking, "Why are you troubled, and whom do you seek?" Do our own tears of self-pity obscure our vision? Does our lack of anticipating his presence make it harder to see him? Thanks be to God that in spite of our shortcomings, he reveals himself to us. He breaks through the mist, the camouflage and our blinders, and he reveals himself to us in the most personal of ways ... he calls us by name.

KINGS AND KINGDOMS WILL ALL PASS AWAY

All people are like grass, and all their glory is like the flowers of the field. …
The grass withers and the flowers fall, but the word of our God stands forever.
(Isaiah 40:6b-8)

Who are the persons most admired in our culture? Those with money, power and prestige seem to top our totem poles of envy. Their fame and influence seem so desirable. Yet Scripture reminds us their glory is fleeting. Like a blooming flower, their splendor is brief.

The famous philosopher Friedrich Nietzsche promoted the nihilistic idea that there is no God. Graffiti of the time translated this as, "God is dead … Nietzsche." After Nietzsche's death in 1900, new graffiti appeared, "Nietzsche is dead … God." These words serve as a poignant reminder to all of us that, "The grass withers and the flowers fall."

When evil seems to be rewarded and persons with wealth, power and fame spurn God's ways, we should not despair. We *know* the end of the story—God and his justice will triumph. We are living in a small wisp of time with a very myopic perspective while God's perspective is eternal. French Enlightenment writer Voltaire said, "The burning of a little straw may hide the stars, but the stars outlast the smoke." Let's not illuminate our paths by those brightly burning clumps of straw that have a moment of fame and are gone. Instead, let's look to God's Word, which like the stars, stands forever.

AN ENCOUNTER WITH SCRIPTURE

They told Ezra the scribe to bring out the Book of the Law of Moses ... He read it aloud from daybreak till noon ... And all the people listened attentively ... and as he opened [the book], the people all stood up. ... all the people [were] weeping as they listened to the words of the Law. (Nehemiah 8:1b, 3, 5, 9)

One thing lost with the passing prominence of the eloquent King James Version of the Bible was the sense of awe once held for Scripture. We now have over a dozen very readable and accurate translations of the Bible, not to mention all the commentaries, Bible dictionaries and other helps that we can access on the Internet. Yet we take these resources for granted and seldom use them. Many of us are more prone to read Christian books than the Bible itself. We want pre-digested food, perhaps because we feel inadequate to interpret the Bible ourselves. Or maybe we just dislike the effort and time involved in reading from the original source.

An encounter with Scripture, however, is more than just an intellectual exercise. Paul calls Scripture "God-breathed" (i.e., inspired) (II Timothy 3:16). If God's breath or spirit is intrinsically connected to Scripture, then reading the Bible is an actual encounter with the Author. If we limit ourselves to reading only books *about* the Bible, we may miss personal encounters with God's Holy Spirit. The Holy Spirit not only inspired the words of Scripture but also makes them alive to us today in personal and unique ways. As the Israelites heard Ezra read the Scripture, they stood and listened with awe and respect. The experience was not limited to their minds, however, for they wept as the clear meaning of the words dawned on their hearts.

Bible scholars today often look at Scripture in its historical context and thereby interpret its meaning. This approach is an appropriate exercise in exegesis (the process of determining what the text meant when it was first written), but there's more. Liberation theology, a movement that emerged from the impoverished people of Latin America, worries very little about historical context and original intent. Instead, it views Scripture as the conduit for the Holy Spirit to speak directly to the reader in his or her present situation. While this personal application is also an important aspect of Bible study, a holistic hermeneutic approach integrates both academic exegesis *and* personal application. An encounter with Scripture that involves either aspect alone is lacking completeness. It's like a peanut butter and jelly sandwich—if you take only one part, you'll find it is too sweet or too sticky.

May

May 1

PARADIGM SHIFTS

For by him all things were created: things in heaven and on earth, visible and invisible, whether thrones or powers or rulers or authorities; all things were created by him and for him. (Colossians 1:16)

One doesn't need to watch infants or toddlers playing together for long to realize that they all believe themselves to be the center of the universe. Teenagers at a party aren't much different (although there is less slobbering). And although adults at a social gathering may demonstrate some degree of external perspective, a self-oriented worldview is still all too prevalent. It seems that a large part of our social maturation in society is based on trying (while routinely failing) to learn that the world does *not* revolve around us. *Spiritual* maturation, however, goes one step further. Not only do we need to learn that the spiritual world does not revolve around us, we need to learn that the spiritual world *does* revolve around someone else.

For fourteen hundred years, the Greek astronomer Ptolemy's view of the universe prevailed. The Earth was believed to be central and stationary, and all the other heavenly bodies revolved around it. However, in the 1500's, a Polish astronomer, Copernicus, developed the idea that the Sun was at the center of the solar system, and the Earth and other planets revolved around the Sun. Galileo later advanced Copernicus' theory with mathematical and experimental data. This Sun-centered idea had ramifications affecting other fields of science, and because it was true, it allowed scientists to explain and predict additional truths. With Copernicus' Sun-centered theory as an accepted assumption, the rest of the world suddenly made more sense. This paradigm shift is often referred to as the "Copernican Revolution."

An even more revolutionary truth, however, is that spiritually, our world is also Son-centered—it revolves around God's Son, Jesus Christ. The apostle Paul says that all things in heaven and on earth were created by him and for him. When we accept this Son-centered premise, other truths will fall in place, and the rest of our world and our lives will suddenly begin to make more sense.

NEEDY CRIPPLES

May your mercy come quickly to meet us, for we are in desperate need.
(Psalm 79:8b)

He had first noticed a small rough area on his skin more than a year earlier. Since then it had slowly grown to its present golf ball size. The skin had begun to ulcerate, causing intermittent bleeding. Although a biopsy was needed, there was little doubt we were dealing with skin cancer. It was hard not to be upset with the patient for delaying so long. If he'd come in earlier, it could have easily been removed and cured. Now it may have spread to other parts of his body and could be incurable. But, seeing the look of fear in his eyes, I realized he needed support, not criticism. He had probably known for some time that this was something bad. The powerful forces of fear and denial, however, had kept him from seeking help.

In the spiritual realm, there are similar forces at work. These forces try to keep us from turning to God for our spiritual needs. We've all heard people say, "I don't need God. I'm doing fine on my own." Denying our need, however, does not change reality. The truth of the matter is that we are all in desperate need, whether we realize it or not.

I used to get defensive and upset when people maligned Christianity, saying we just used faith as a crutch. Over time, I've come to realize that their statements were actually true. Author Philip Yancey illustrated this truth when he said that we are all crippled, and "For a crippled person, there is one thing worse than a crutch, after all—no crutch." So what keeps us from calling out for help in our crippled state? Are we in denial, or perhaps too proud or ignorant to admit our need? Regardless of the reason for our reluctance, God's mercy is more than sufficient to meet these needs. How unfortunate that many continue to refuse help that is so readily available! They hide the skin lump, letting the cancer (our spiritual need) grow undiagnosed and untreated.

LOVING THE UNLOVABLE

But God demonstrates his own love for us in this: While we were still sinners, Christ died for us. (Romans 5:8)

Our nephew Michael used to have a favorite blanket. That blanket was his constant companion, prized above all other toys. His mundane choice for a favorite toy was difficult to understand since we thought some of his other toys were much more interesting. Some were bright and shiny, others educational, yet none made the grade against that worn and tattered "blankey." While his criteria for "most valued possession" were a mystery to us, there was no doubt in his mind.

There is a saying, "Some things are loved because they are worthy while others are worthy because they are loved." Michael's blanket (as well as you and I in God's eyes) fall into the latter category. We are proud, impatient, unforgiving, lustful, angry, lazy and unloving—disgusting old blankets that by any reasonable standards ought to be thrown in the trash. Yet it's at this very point that God says, "I love that ragged old blanket. It's worth so much to me that I'll do whatever I can to make it mine." Suddenly, though no less soiled and tattered, we have great value!

St. Augustine succinctly said it best, "By loving the unlovable you made me lovable." Only after we have realized the humbling truth of this statement are we able to pass on that same unconditional love to others. It may not only make someone's day but also change someone's life. Loving the unlovable is not humanly possible, so when it happens through us, it's a "God-thing" that causes wonder. The impact of God-things is very unpredictable because the power of God's Holy Spirit has been unleashed—stand back and watch.

THE GREAT BANQUET

Jesus replied: "A certain man was preparing a great banquet and invited many guests ... But they all alike began to make excuses. ... 'I can't come.'"
(Luke 14:16, 18, 20)

One of our dearest friends was getting married in South Africa. We made the nineteen-hour plane ride to celebrate with her. It was an idyllic site for a wedding. There were lush flower gardens with verdant archways, sweet-smelling flora and cascading waterways. This was all surrounded by rolling hills covered with meticulously groomed vineyards. There was an ethereal otherworldliness about the location, and I half expected to see Frodo or a leprechaun step out from the bushes at any moment. I gazed intensely and breathed in deeply, trying to imprint the experience indelibly on the cortex of my brain.

As I stood, transfixed by beauty, tears came to my eyes. It was a bittersweet moment—*what could have been*—for the wedding had been cancelled. Our friend's fiancé had decided he was unsure about proceeding. As we toured the grounds, we saw where the ceremony *would have been* and where the reception *would have been*. Beauty was punctuated by regret, hope replaced by loss, joy usurped by melancholy.

My mind turned to the final, festive feast, the "great banquet" God is preparing for us. We've all been invited to this banquet whose splendor we can only imagine. It will be an eternal banquet in the presence of our Lord and Savior Jesus Christ; the glory of his amazing presence will create the ultimate ambience. One day Jesus will say, "Come, for everything is now ready" (Luke 14:17). This is one banquet we don't want to miss.

WORSHIP WITH ABANDON

David, wearing a linen ephod, danced before the LORD with all his might, while he and the entire house of Israel brought up the ark of the LORD with shouts and the sound of trumpets. (II Samuel 6:14-15)

God calls us to love and worship him with our whole being. In Mark 12:30, we are told to love the Lord with our hearts (emotions), minds (thoughts), souls (spirits) and our strength (bodies). Our Western culture, however, tends to glorify the mind, and this emphasis is reflected in our worship style. While we feel comfortable worshiping God with our thoughts, we're a bit too sophisticated to unleash our emotions and bodies in worship.

In II Samuel we find this story of David praising God with his whole being. It says he danced before the Lord "with all his might." Our reflex "Yeah, but ..." response is that such emotional and physical worship was probably acceptable in his culture but not ours. Yet in verse 20, we find that David was criticized for his "vulgar" behavior, which was said to be particularly inappropriate for his royal position. David responded by saying his praises were unto the Lord and not for anyone else. Furthermore, he said he would be willing to be even more "undignified" or "humiliated" in human eyes, to praise his God.

The question is not, "In my culture and with my personality, what kind of worship is comfortable?" The real question is, "What kind of worship does God desire?" Clearly, God desires sincere, unashamed, wholehearted worship. Are we willing to embarrass ourselves in front of others as David did? Are we willing to swallow our pride and wholeheartedly worship God with abandon? Why not?

PRAYER - GOD'S DESIGN OR OUR DESIRE?

... There was given me a thorn in my flesh, ... Three times I pleaded with the Lord to take it away from me. But he said to me, "My grace is sufficient for you ..." (II Corinthians 12:7-9a)

I believe that God hears our prayers and sometimes answers them in very amazing and miraculous ways. However, I must also acknowledge that at times God inexplicably fails to intervene in situations that cause severe pain and suffering. Where is God at those times?

The Koch family had devoted many years to mission service in Zambia, and they had become our friends. They had foregone comfort, income and security to further God's kingdom in rural Africa. As I stood and watched their newborn baby being lowered into a Zambian grave, my emotions were overwhelmed by grief while my mind was busy searching for answers. Why had God let this happen? We had prayed so hard. What possible purpose could this tragedy serve? Our hearts cried out in anguish, and our minds cried out for answers.

Theologian Eugene Peterson said, "Praying most often doesn't get us what we want but what God wants, something quite at variance with what we conceive to be in our best interests." Country singer Garth Brooks sang that some of God's best gifts to us are when he doesn't answer our prayers.

Our logical minds tell us it is better for an omniscient, omnipotent, loving God to be in control of our world than for us to have the reins. Yet in any given situation when our reasoning is at odds with God's reasoning, we tend to think *he's* the one who is wrong. As we buried the Kochs' baby, no logical argument could quell the questions or heal the hurts. While our God is too great for us always to understand his ways, we can understand his heart. We worship a God who is always faithful, always loving and always just. At times when situations seem to tell us otherwise, we need to remember the heart of God. As we trust the heart of God, our minds begin to find peace, and our hearts begin to find comfort—trust is more often a choice than a feeling.

WELL-EQUIPPED

May the God of peace, who ... brought back from the dead our Lord Jesus, that great Shepherd of the sheep, equip you with everything good for doing his will ... (Hebrews 13:20-21)

I heard Henry Blackaby speak at a fund-raising banquet last night. In his address he reiterated some of the salient points from his book *Experiencing God*. He told us the tasks that God gives us are "God-sized." That means we won't be able to do them ourselves; we will need his help.

I remember in grade school how my parents encouraged me to try a variety of different activities. I played basketball in fifth and sixth grades, took piano lessons for several years and screeched on a clarinet for two years. In high school, however, my parents realized I was a hopeless nerd and let me spend my leisure time in Science Club, Spanish Club, Student Council and reading books. I don't blame my parents, however, for not knowing what I could do well. How could they know I wouldn't be another Michael Jordan or a concert pianist? Of course, the fact that I had to wear shoe inserts to hit five foot eight and my fingers were so short they barely reached the piano keyboard seemed like good clues to me.

Unfortunately, we look at tasks God calls us to do in the same way we look at tasks in the secular world—are we able to do them? In the spiritual realm, however, there is a different set of rules. God often calls people for tasks we are unable to do (e.g., every biblical character who ever did anything significant). Our inadequacy requires reliance on God. As we rely on him, he *then* equips us for the job. This simple truth that God doesn't call the able, but he enables the called, challenges me. Our essential equipment is not gifts and abilities but God himself. I often see needs and assess myself as unable or ill equipped to meet them. I then assume God is calling someone else for the task ... maybe not.

AN EVANGELISTIC CATALYST

This salvation, which was first announced by the Lord, ... God also testified to it by signs, wonders and various miracles, and gifts of the Holy Spirit distributed according to his will. (Hebrews 2:3b-4)

Pastor and teacher John Wimber noted that in the New Testament, Jesus combined the proclamation of the gospel with its demonstration in power. The manifestation of the spiritual gifts authenticated the gospel message and overcame people's resistance to the good news. They saw the gospel message was real, with power to address the problems in their lives. Wimber said this form of evangelism is both powerful and effective, and he called it "power evangelism." The disciples followed Jesus' example and used power evangelism themselves. Luke says, "The apostles performed many miraculous signs and wonders ... [and] more and more men and women believed in the Lord" (Acts 5:12, 14).

While we don't want to promote a theatrical picture of the gospel, effective evangelism involves more than the presentation of an orthodox theology. Correct doctrine alone will not win the world to Christ. Jim Cymbala says, "The gospel must be preached with the involvement of the Holy Spirit." There are too many churches with meager expressions of the miraculous, life-transforming power of the gospel message. Cymbala points out that our faith is based not only on the cross but also on the empty tomb, which clearly demonstrates the supernatural nature of our faith. Non-Christians need to see lives transformed, illnesses and hurts healed, and prayers answered. When these things happen, people see a faith that is alive and attractive, and they are drawn to Christ in a very natural way—by seeing the activity of God's Holy Spirit in the lives of everyday Christians.

A RAINBOW REMINDER

"I have set my rainbow in the clouds, and it will be the sign of the covenant between me and the earth. ... Never again will the waters become a flood to destroy all life." (Genesis 9:13, 15b)

Modern society seldom entertains the idea of covenant. Yet covenant is one of the primary means by which God has chosen to deal with people. In its most basic form, a covenant is a pledge or promise. The promise may be provisional or unconditional. The Mosaic Covenant, given to Moses at Mount Sinai, was a provisional covenant. God would protect and bless the people of Israel as long as they served him and were obedient to his commands. On the other hand, the Noahic Covenant, made with Noah after the flood, was unconditional. God promised never again to destroy the earth with a flood, regardless of the behavior of people.

Covenants often had accompanying signs. The sign of male circumcision accompanied the covenant with Abraham that promised to make him a great nation. The sign of the covenant with Noah was perhaps less personal than circumcision, yet few things are more spectacular to view than the arc of a rainbow with its spectrum of colors painted across the sky.

This past summer I took my daughter Amaris out to eat at a local restaurant. As we arrived, it was starting to rain, and we were fortunate enough to witness a beautiful, bright rainbow that left us awe-struck. We stood underneath the restaurant awning for ten minutes, savoring this unique experience. It was as though our covenant-making God was reaching out and touching us today just as he must have touched a weary Noah and his family so many years ago. That restaurant-rainbow experience was a visitation from God—he gave us a vivid reminder of his faithfulness to us.

UTTER THE UNSPEAKABLE

... At the name of Jesus every knee should bow / ... and every tongue confess that Jesus Christ is Lord, / to the glory of God the Father.
(Philippians 2:10-11)

There is an unwritten yet universally known rule in the book of political correctness: don't mention the name of Jesus. It's okay to talk about Islam, Buddhism, or Judaism, and even talking about Christianity is tolerated if the name of Jesus isn't used. If you mention *his* name, however, you've crossed the Rubicon, you've stepped over the line in the sand, and you've committed a faux pas of significant proportions. You are now also a *persona non grata*.

The problem is that no one can become a Christian by learning about good morals, religious truths and a Greater Power; it's not even enough to believe in God. Scripture teaches that salvation comes by believing and declaring that *Jesus* is Lord (Romans 10:9)! The inconvenient truth is that the same word that gets you in trouble is the same word that saves the lost—Jesus.

Why do we have trouble voicing the name "Jesus" around non-Christians? Jesus tells us "out of the overflow of the heart the mouth speaks" (Matthew 12:34). Defying anatomic explanation, our vocal paralysis (about Jesus) comes from a problem in the heart. Paul tells us we are to have our hearts circumcised (Romans 2:29). This spiritual circumcision removes our fleshly nature as our hearts are covenanted with God. We are then spiritually empowered to speak the name we find so hard to utter—Jesus—and to proclaim the simple message of Jesus crucified, foolishness to the world but power and wisdom to those who receive him (I Corinthians 1:17-25).

PRECAUTION OR PRESUMPTION

Jesus, once more deeply moved, came to the tomb. It was a cave with a stone laid across the entrance. "Take away the stone," he said ... So they took away the stone ... Jesus called in a loud voice, "Lazarus, come out!" The dead man came out, his hands and feet wrapped with strips of linen, and a cloth around his face. Jesus said to them, "Take off the grave clothes and let him go."
(John 11:38-44)

Some Christians believe having health insurance or life insurance shows a lack of faith in God. Others would go further by saying we should not even take medicine or receive immunizations but trust God alone with our health. It may be true that we too frequently rely on our own resources, taking excessive precautions to assuage each anxious thought. On the other hand, is it right to throw caution to the wind by taking on no personal responsibility and presuming God will take care of us?

When Jesus reached Lazarus' tomb, why did he have others remove the stone? He could have miraculously done that himself. I think he had them do it because they *could*. Jesus then raised Lazarus from the dead because they *couldn't*. Lazarus emerged all cocooned with cloth wrappings. Jesus could have "transported" him right through the clothes, but he didn't. Instead, he asked the people to take off Lazarus' grave clothes. Why? Again, because this was something they were *able* to do.

It seems God often expects us to do that which we can while he takes care of that over which we are powerless. Having insurance, taking medication and doing what we are able to do don't necessarily mean we are lacking faith. Indeed, these actions may be the very means God planned on to provide for us. Having faith in God does not preclude us from using our bodies, our minds and the tools he has given us. Let's take away the stone and then trust God to do the rest.

SPIRITUAL FOOD

... [You were] mere infants in Christ. I gave you milk, not solid food, for you were not yet ready for it. Indeed, you are still not ready. (I Corinthians 3:1-2)

Most books have target audiences. They are written to be pertinent to a specific age group or knowledge level. Scripture, however, is amazingly able to provide spiritual nutrition for everyone from the new, clueless convert to the old, scholarly saint. How can the Bible be as appropriate for me today as it was forty years ago when I first became a Christian?

Part of the reason lies in the fact that I need to be instructed repeatedly about the same things; I'm a slow learner. However, much of the reason is that the Holy Spirit just impresses different things on me at different times due to my situation, need or readiness. There may be a particular passage I've read many times without apparent effect, but then for some reason (Holy Spirit prompting) with this reading, it hits me squarely in the solar plexus, leaving me breathless.

There may also be parts of Scripture I don't understand due to the meager nature of my present knowledge and/or experience. I remember two things I didn't understand about my third grade teacher, Mrs. Williams. She had a funny odor, and her teeth were perfectly straight. Both things impressed me as unique and somehow significant. However, it wasn't until many years later that one day it dawned on me—my third grade teacher smoked cigarettes and wore dentures.

Some of what Scripture teaches us will only dawn on us as we gain more knowledge and experience in our Christian walk. Scripture provides all the spiritual food we are in need of—meat, milk and trail mix. Milk is for when we are spiritual babes, meat is for when we are mature in Christ, and trail mix is for the long hike in between.

CONTEMPLATIONS ON PARENTING

These commandments that I give you today are to be upon your hearts. Impress them on your children. Talk about them when you sit at home and when you walk along the road, when you lie down and when you get up. (Deuteronomy 6:6-7)

Doreen and I have been blessed with four wonderful daughters. Dara, our youngest, recently left for college, and for the first time in twenty-four years, we are without children in our home. Several days ago, upon entering the bathroom, I was accosted by a neat and tidy room. The vanity was no longer covered with hairbrushes, curling irons, make-up and hair driers. We no longer have to stay up late at night wondering if our daughters are safe on the roads (or crashed in the ditch somewhere, unresponsive and unable to use their cell phones). The days of running to music lessons, sporting events and concerts are now behind us.

How have I done as a father? Was I able to shield them from injury without being overprotective? Did I help them develop a good self-image without fostering pride? Was I able to minimize their exposure to the world's evil without causing naïveté? And on a more practical level, did I teach them how to change a flat tire, draw up a budget and unclog the sink drain? Did we model how to argue fairly, and do they know the importance of having smoke detectors?

While contemplating all this can foment anxiety and a sense of certain failure, their *spiritual* readiness for life is far more important. As parents, we are to "impress" on our children God's precepts. We are to integrate our faith with the daily activities of life. As we sat around the dinner table, as we drove in the car and when we went to the movies, did we integrate our faith with fun, family, and food? Did we not only "walk the talk," but did we also *talk* about the walk? Will they turn to God in their successes as well as their failures? When circumstances seem dismal, doubts arise and God seems distant, will their faith stand firm? "These commandments ... are to be upon your hearts. Impress them on your children."

ALIENS WITH A MISSION

Dear friends, I urge you, as aliens and strangers in the world, to abstain from sinful desires ... Live such good lives among the pagans that ... they may see your good deeds and glorify God on the day he visits us. (I Peter 2:11-12)

Being a *Star Trek* fan since childhood, when I hear about aliens, I immediately think of images of creatures from another galaxy trying to conquer our world, only to be thwarted by Captain James Kirk and the starship *Enterprise*. Peter tells us, however, that as Christians *we* are "aliens and strangers in the world." We are aliens because this is not our true home—our citizenship is in heaven.

Using a different metaphor, theologian Stanley Hauerwas points out, "We are a *colony* of heaven" (Philippians 3:20, italics mine, Moffatt's translation). In one sense, therefore, as Christians we are "alien colonizers." Like the colonizers who first settled our country, we need to support one another for survival. Yet our mission is not just to survive, nor is it to conquer or destroy. Our mission is to call and encourage others to join our colony (the community of believers).

The Christian colony is crucial for the survival and growth of the colonists, but it is also the *means* for outreach to the surrounding world. Although it may come as a surprise to us, airtight doctrinal orthodoxy is not the most effective way to draw the world to Christ. Hauerwas says the most credible form of witness the church has is the demonstration of love by the "living, breathing, visible community of faith." In John 17:23, Jesus prayed that his body the church would be brought to "complete unity to let the world know that you sent me (Jesus) and have loved them even as you have loved me." The most persuasive evidence of the good news of the gospel of Jesus Christ is the visible, tangible unity and love of his followers—and we wonder why our churches aren't growing!

A LOVING JUDGE

Woe to you who are complacent in Zion, / ... Therefore you will be among the first to go into exile; / your feasting and lounging will end. (Amos 6:1, 7)

We've all heard the skeptical agnostic say, "If there were a God, he would be a God of love, forgiveness and acceptance, not a God of anger, wrath and judgment like most Christians envision." It should be no surprise to us that when persons *create* a God, it ends up being one with whom they feel comfortable. When we try to understand the nature of God, our quest should be driven by a desire for truth, not by a desire to remain comfortable. Even as Christians, however, we tend to squirm a bit when confronted with the Old Testament picture of an angry God of justice. Nonetheless, Christianity presents God as both loving and just, characteristics that are not mutually exclusive.

I've recently been reading the biblical books of prophecy and have been impressed by the fact that God's anger and punishment are not contradictory to his love but a direct outgrowth from his love. God becomes angry when he sees the people he loves involved in self-destructive behavior (i.e., sin). More to the point, how could a God who loves us be apathetic when we engage in behavior that harms us? Christian author Becky Pippert points out that anger is not the opposite of love; hate is. She states God's wrath is simply "his settled opposition to the cancer that is eating out the inside of the human race he loves with his whole being."

As we read the prophets, we find a just God who is angry at sin, but we also see a God who is pleading with his children to repent and avoid judgment. We see a God who is patient almost to a fault, sending one warning prophet after another, ever hopeful his children will change their minds and escape punishment. We see a God who weeps for the people he loves. Perhaps a shallow love is what the agnostic skeptic desires, but God's love is not shallow; his love is too deep and wide not to be angry and disapproving when those he loves engage in behavior harmful to themselves and others.

EMPOWERED WEAKNESS

But [the Lord] said to me, "My grace is sufficient for you, for my power is made perfect in weakness." (II Corinthians 12:9a)

"God helps those who help themselves." We've all heard this verse quoted, yet the reference is never given. This verse, along with "Cleanliness is next to godliness," can be found in the "Collection of Verses Our Parents Wanted to Add to the Bible." Interestingly, the true scriptural perspective on who God helps seems to be just the opposite; God helps those who *don't* and *can't* help themselves.

When we feel strong and able to handle things on our own, we proceed without asking for God's help. When we acknowledge our weakness, however, God comes to our aid to empower us. There seems to be a magnetic spiritual principle in effect, in which "opposites attract" and "likes repel." In other words, God (with his power) is attracted to our weakness. But when we act in our own self-sufficient strength, we repel God, and he steps back, his power not being called on. Paul says, "The Spirit helps us *in our weakness*" (Romans 8:26, italics mine).

When God called Gideon and his clan to deliver Israel from the Midianites, Gideon questioned God's wisdom since his clan was the "weakest" of all the clans of Israel. When Gideon finally assembled thirty-two thousand men to fight the Midianites, God told him, "You have too many men for me to deliver Midian" into your hands (Judges 7:2). Only after paring them down to three hundred men were they "weak enough" to attract God, who intervened with power.

When God calls us to a task, what do we use as a measure of readiness? If we feel confident in our ability to succeed, do we proceed? If we feel inadequate for the job, do we wait? How do God's power and our weakness factor into our overall assessment? Maybe we need to rethink how we think.

LIFE: A BRIEF PROLOGUE

"You have made my days a mere handbreadth; / the span of my years is as nothing before you. / Each man's life is but a breath." (Psalm 39:5)

I can still remember the wise counsel my junior high school English teacher gave me on studying for tests. Mr. Mattingly said the guiding principle should be to "major on the majors and minor on the minors." In other words, I should spend the bulk of my time learning and reviewing the *important* concepts and spend only a small amount of time trying to memorize trivia. It was good advice for school, but it also applies to our Christian lives.

We are here for perhaps eighty or ninety years, depending on the benevolence of our genes and the quality of our health habits. But our stint on earth, measured by a tool called time, is just a prelude to eternity. In spite of this, we often set up camp here as if this were the final destination. It's like an author who gets so caught up in his or her prologue that the book itself is forgotten. Imagine if our country's forefathers had become so enamored with the preamble that they never wrote the Constitution.

Our life on earth *is* a prologue to the real story, a preamble to the major event. We should not become too caught up in earthly things, for we don't ultimately belong here. As citizens of heaven, we are aliens on earth (I Peter 2:11). Our human tendency is to major on the minors (earthly endeavors) and minor on the majors (divine pursuits). However, just like in junior high school, this is likely to result in a poor showing on our "finals."

REST FOR THE WEARY

[Jesus said,] "Come to me, all you who are weary and burdened, and I will give you rest. ... For my yoke is easy and my burden is light."
(Matthew 11:28, 30)

It seems many Christians feel overwhelmed, overworked, weary and wondering. We are *overwhelmed* with busy schedules, appointments, and to-do lists that never get done. We are *overworked* but seem unable to cut back on our workload. We are *weary* from burning the candle at both ends with our activities, and we *wonder* if there isn't some better way.

Jesus' comments in Matthew 11 remind us of two things we should do when we suffer from Christian fatigue syndrome. The first thing we should do is to go to Jesus. He is calling the weary to himself. Entering God's presence through prayer, worship and reading his Word provides refreshment and rejuvenation. God promised Moses: "My Presence will go with you, and I will give you rest" (Exodus 33:14).

Secondly, Jesus says that his "yoke is easy and [his] burden is light." If we seem to have a difficult yoke and we seem to be bearing a heavy burden, perhaps we are not bearing *his* yoke and carrying *his* burden for us. Perhaps we've taken something on ourselves or had something pushed on us by others. If we are involved in truly meaningful ministry that God has called us to, we will more commonly be energized, not made weary by it.

So when weary, we should check our yoke and burden. Are they God's yoke and burden for us? Then we need to go to Jesus, for it is in his presence that we find strength and rest.

THE WISDOM OF FOLLY

But God chose the foolish things of the world to shame the wise; ... so that no one may boast before him. (I Corinthians 1:27a, 29)

If Christianity were complicated and hard to understand, only the smartest could fathom its message. If Christianity required great strength and effort to be a member, only the powerful elite who exhibited immense fortitude and expended vast energy could hope to "arrive." But counter to what we might expect for so great a prize, Christianity is understandable and attainable by the weak and the simple.

Ironically, when we approach God and Scripture with our *own* wisdom, it can be an actual impediment. Columnist Andrée Seu in *World* magazine talks, tongue-in-cheek, about this difficulty: "I have seminary training. Unlike simple people who obey the Bible because they don't realize how complicated it is, I find ambiguity in every verse. I don't obey Scripture, I discuss it."

Before we take too much pride in our own conservative hermeneutics, declaring obedience to Scripture without need for interpretation, we should consider several verses: "Do not be anxious about anything" (Philippians 4:6). "Ask and it will be given to you" (Matthew 7:7). "Consider it pure joy, my brothers, whenever you face trials of many kinds" (James 1:2). Do we take these words at face value or do we feel obliged to spiritualize them or explain what they *really* mean so we don't have to admit our failure to believe/obey these commands?

God has chosen "foolish things" (like the death of a lowly carpenter on a cross) to shame the wise. Let's call our best worldly wisdom by its true name (folly) and lay it at the foot of the cross, for it is only as we embrace the simple truths of God's Word that we truly become wise.

A CONVINCED SKEPTIC

But [Thomas] said to them, "Unless I see the nail marks in his hands and put my fingers where the nails were, and put my hand into his side, I will not believe it." ... Then [Jesus] said to Thomas, "Put your finger here; see my hands. Reach out your hand and put it into my side. ..." Thomas said to him, "My Lord and my God!" (John 20:25b, 27-28)

Although the derogatory adjective "doubting" seems as tenaciously attached to the name Thomas as lint is to your black slacks, Thomas is a more complex character than this one-word descriptor would indicate. When Jesus said he wanted to return to Judea to visit his ailing friend Lazarus, the nervous disciples reminded Jesus that the people in Judea had recently tried to stone him. The disciples were probably worried for their own well-being. Thomas, however, bravely encouraged the disciples to return even though it was dangerous (John 11:4-16).

While Thomas was skeptical of the other disciples' claim that Jesus was raised from the dead, can we blame him? When Thomas did come face to face with the risen Jesus, Thomas' confession of faith went beyond, "Yes, I believe you were raised from the dead," to "Yes, I believe you are the Messiah; you are God himself!" Thomas had a questioning nature, but he also exhibited courage and a perceptive faith.

According to tradition, Thomas was sent to take the gospel message to the skeptical people of India. Arriving in AD 52, Thomas' evangelistic work was accompanied by signs and wonders as he established the first Christian church in India. Today, more than 2.4 million Indian Christians attribute their origins to the Apostle Thomas. In AD 72, Thomas was stoned and then stabbed to death with a spear. When Thomas touched Jesus' side, I wonder about Jesus' unspoken thoughts: "My dear Thomas, one day I will send you to a skeptical people with questions like your own. You will give your life for me, the one you doubted. The pierced side you touch today, you will share with me on your final day."

THE PATHWAY TO SIN

One evening David got up from his bed and walked around on the roof of the palace. From the roof he saw a woman bathing. The woman was very beautiful ... David sent messengers to get her. She came to him, and he slept with her ... (II Samuel 11:2, 4)

Much of the "success" of sin can be attributed to its insidious nature. We are seldom ensnared when candidly presented with black and white options. Usually, however, the path to sin is paved with off-white or shades of gray. The path we follow so imperceptibly morphs into wickedness that we find ourselves justifying each step that somehow unfairly got us into this mess.

Certainly it wasn't David's fault that he couldn't sleep that night and ended up walking around on the roof. It was just by the vagaries of chance that Bathsheba was bathing at that very time. Noticing her beauty was merely an objective evaluation. And there's nothing wrong with a king wanting to meet with one of his subjects; no evil was planned here. Why didn't *she* come up with an excuse to refuse his invitation? She should have known better. And what do you expect to happen when a beautiful woman is alone with the king in his chambers? After all, the king is still a normal man with natural needs. If it's anyone's fault, it's hers—she should have been the one to resist. Do our own rationalizations seem any less contrived than David's probably were?

James says we are tempted or enticed by our own evil desires. The desire then conceives, giving birth to sin. And "sin, when it is full-grown, gives birth to death" (James 1:14-15). Falling into sin often begins as a subtle process that coaxes us insidiously along the path to a disastrous end. We need to realize that if we don't want to end up in "Oz," we need to stay off the "yellow brick road."

A FRIEND IN NEED

Do not forsake your friend ... / better a neighbor nearby than a brother far away. (Proverbs 27:10)

Tom was my friend. To say he had a checkered past would be an understatement. It was while he was in prison that he gave his heart to Christ. God gave him a heart of love and service for others. I first met him when my car was stuck in the mud, and he pushed me out. I can still see him smiling, all covered with mud spots; he looked like a giant Jackson Pollock painting. In the winter he would come unsolicited to plow away the snow in our driveway and refuse payment. Tom employed numerous ex-prisoners in his business. He wanted to give them a second chance like he'd been given, even though they often took advantage of his generosity.

Although God gave Tom a new heart, for some reason he didn't take away his dark desire for drugs and alcohol. His addictions, like a bloodhound on the scent, continued to plague him throughout his life. He repented in tears over and over again. We went to several Christian men's retreats together. He freely shared his failures. No one knew God's grace and forgiveness like Tom.

Tom died of a drug overdose. I hadn't seen him for several months before his death. I think I was frustrated at his relapses and felt ill equipped to deal with his problems. But perhaps all he needed was a friend.

Tonight as I look outside, snow is falling with big, wet flakes, and the driveway is hidden beneath a white blanket. No one will be coming, however, to plow us out. I'll have to get out the snow blower and do it myself. Tom was there for me. Was I there for him?

IN VIEW OF DEATH

... Death is the destiny of every [person]; / the living should take this to heart.
(Ecclesiastes 7:2)

The middle-aged couple always showed up for their doctors' appointments together. My presence seemed to have no effect on their constant bickering. They seemed as oblivious to my presence as they might have been to that of a potted plant. They appeared to share no joy together, each serving as a burr in the saddle of the other person's life. Then she developed terminal breast cancer, and their relationship did an "about face." He became a supportive caregiver, and she became an affectionate, doting wife. The transformation was startling and almost uncanny. I was a bit skeptical, but they maintained their warm relationship until her death a year later.

I was delighted they had one good year together but wondered about the many wasted years. What was it about the reality and imminence of death that changed their relationship so dramatically? How did disease, suffering and dying serve as a mentor for their marriage when family, friends and counselors had failed?

It's been said that you watch someone die to learn how to live. This couple seemed to have learned how to live well together only when they realized her death was imminent. Impending death gave them both an incentive and a perspective without rival. It is unfortunate that although we all know we will one day die, we tend to live in denial, thereby losing any potential benefit that awareness might bring. "Death is the destiny of every [person]." What comes after depends on whether we have a relationship with Jesus before—"the living should take this to heart."

May 24

THE OBJECT OF OUR DESIRE

So I hated life, because the work that is done under the sun was grievous to me. All of it is meaningless, a chasing after the wind. (Ecclesiastes 2:17)

The French philosopher Sartre, in his novel *Nausea*, described the gut-wrenching horror people have when they realize the unexplainable fact of their existence. "I had appeared by chance. I existed like a stone, a plant, a microbe … here we are eating and drinking, to preserve our precious existence, and there's nothing, nothing, absolutely no reason for existence." Why do we, unlike any other created entity (e.g., stones, trees and chimpanzees), despair at the thought of a meaningless existence?

We have a deep desire to know not only our present purpose but also our past origin and our future destiny. Many books have explored these questions. Cows, on the other hand, seem to have very little interest in any of this. This may partially explain why they have written so few books, although their lack of opposable thumbs may be a contributing factor.

Timothy Keller, in *The Reason for God*, states that our innate desires must point toward a reality that can fulfill them. Hunger is satisfied by food, sexual desire by sexual intimacy, tiredness by sleep, and relational desire by friendship. However, our desire for meaning cannot be fulfilled if we don't believe in God, since our existence, without a Creator, would be accidental.

But, what if our deep desire for meaning is a *clue* programmed into our inner being to make us search for God? Solomon said, "[God] has also set eternity in the hearts of men" (Ecclesiastes 3:11). We sense that our existence is not all there is, there must be some purpose in life, and death is not the end. Perhaps, like a compass needle points toward the North Pole, our yearnings point us toward God.

THE HOVERING HOLY SPIRIT

As soon as Jesus was baptized, he went up out of the water. At that moment heaven was opened, and he [John] saw the Spirit of God descending like a dove and lighting on [Jesus]. (Matthew 3:16)

John the Baptist saw something descend and light "like a dove" on Jesus. John somehow perceived it to be the Spirit of God. John's Jewish upbringing would have given him a visual image from the Torah that may have helped him interpret what he saw that day. Genesis draws this picture at the dawn of Creation: "The Spirit of God was hovering over the waters" (1:2). At Jesus' baptism the Spirit of God again hovered over the waters. This time it had the appearance of a dove, hovering over the waters of the Jordan River.

Genesis says at Creation "the earth was formless and empty, darkness was over the surface of the deep" (1:2). Into that "formless" world of chaos, God brought order as he separated the land from the sea, the day from the night, and the sky from the earth. Into that "empty," lifeless world, God brought life beyond imagination—lush vegetation teeming with animals. And finally, into that "dark" world, God brought the light of the Sun, moon and stars.

Jesus' formal ministry, which started at his baptism when the Spirit of God hovered over the waters, echoed what happened at Creation. A "formless" spiritual chaos was crying out for a new order that was realized in Christ (Hebrews 9:10). "Empty" spirituality was replaced by a new spirituality that was abundant and full of life (John 10:10). And finally, a spiritually "dark" world would meet the illuminating light of Jesus (John 8:12).

God's Spirit also hovers over us today. He wants nothing more than to land on us to bring order to the chaos in our lives. He wants to replace our empty, meaningless lives with abundant lives of purpose. He wants to shine the light of truth into our darkness. If we listen closely, we may hear the beating of wings—a dove searching for a place to land.

ACCIDENTALLY ON PURPOSE

To keep me from becoming conceited … there was given me a thorn in my flesh … That is why, for Christ's sake, I delight in weaknesses … For when I am weak, then I am strong. (II Corinthians 12:7, 10)

My family and I were on our way to Africa, where my wife and I would be working at a mission hospital in the hinterlands of Zambia. I was excited to be fulfilling a dream I'd had since high school. I had worked hard and done well through college, four years of medical school and three years of residency training. Although I knew there would be more to learn, I was confident in my ability to acquire information and adapt. God was pretty lucky to have me on the job. Such was my pompous state of mind twenty-four hours before I was hit by a car, breaking both bones in my left leg and setting forth a cascade of events that would dramatically change me and our first year of mission life.

At the time, the accident seemed unfortunate, unfair and untimely. Where was God when I needed him anyway? However, with a tincture (defined here as a rather long period) of time, I came to realize I'd been too proud and too confident for God to use me effectively. God allowed a "divine wrench" to be thrown into the works, helping to bring some needed changes in my life. My confident independence crumbled as I was forced to depend for assistance on my wife, my children and even the Zambians whom I had come to serve. After six months and a dozen different plaster casts for a bone that refused to heal, I was reminded that I needed to put my trust in God alone. Then, two surgeries and a stint with depression later, God finally had me where he wanted me (at least for the time being), dependent on him.

God used that accident to make me not only a better missionary but also a better husband and father. I grew in empathy and became softer. Before the accident I hardly ever cried. After the accident, I would get misty-eyed just singing "Puff the Magic Dragon" to one of my daughters at bedtime. The truth of Paul's words found a home in my heart. Only when I am weak in my own strength can I be strong with God's strength.

GOOD GUILT

Therefore, brothers, since we have confidence to enter the Most Holy Place by the blood of Jesus, ... let us draw near to God ... having our hearts sprinkled to cleanse us from a guilty conscience and having our bodies washed with pure water. (Hebrews 10:19, 22)

I was discussing Christianity with an unbeliever who suddenly looked at me and said, "The trouble with Christianity is that it lays a big guilt trip on people." I began to ponder: "How is it that we even know right from wrong, which lays the groundwork for guilt?" Author Donald Miller, in *Blue Like Jazz*, says, "It's as if aliens were sending transmissions from another planet, telling me there is a right and wrong in the universe." Instead of aliens, however, it is our Creator who is sending us those communications.

The fact that we all have sinned and are moral failures is a given. In response to this fact, there are several possible responses. We could develop a *jaded* conscience, numbed by ever escalating wrongdoing. Alternatively, we could have an *ignored* conscience as we brazenly practice denial. Or, we could have a *guilty* conscience, one painfully aware of our shortcomings. A guilty conscience is actually the healthiest condition, as long as it is not an endpoint. Paul talks about a guilty conscience, a sprinkled heart, and a washed body. The purpose of guilt is to draw us to God. Christ's blood is then applied ("sprinkled") to our inner beings ("hearts"), a process that cleanses our guilty consciences. Not only are our consciences being cleansed, but also our external practices and actions ("bodies") are being made holy as though "washed" with "pure water."

So, yes, as Christians we do experience guilt. However, the only thing worse than a sinner experiencing guilt is one who doesn't. The good news is that through the blood of Christ we can be forgiven and set free from guilt. We can enter into the Most Holy Place with confidence and a clear conscience, not because of our own merit, but because we've been forgiven by accepting the finished work of Jesus Christ on the cross.

COMPLACENCY

At that time I will search Jerusalem with lamps / and punish those who are complacent, / who are like wine left on its dregs … (Zephaniah 1:12)

Isn't God overreacting about complacency? It doesn't seem like feeling secure and comfortable with one's present state of affairs should be such a negative thing. God ought to search out and punish those who are overtly evil, rather than those of us who just lack a bit of fervor for doing good. Nonetheless, there is the warning from Revelation 3:16, "Because you are lukewarm—neither hot nor cold—I am about to spit you out of my mouth." Perhaps I shouldn't be so complacent about my complacency.

God compares the complacent to "wine left on its dregs." As wine ages, sediment (dregs) precipitates out and settles on the bottom. The wine's color and body are "fixed" by the dregs. If left too long, however, the wine thickens and becomes syrupy and moldy. What was good has been ruined. When we are complacent, we suffer a similar fate. What was good has gone bad, and this ruination is the reason for God's anger.

Opposing complacency would be enthusiasm, zeal, and passion. God has often expressed approval for persons with these characteristics (Romans 12:11). King David loved to worship God passionately in song and dance. God called David a "man after his own heart," in spite of David's glaring shortcomings (adultery and murder–2 Samuel 11)—perhaps David's zeal for the things of God was his redeeming feature.

If we are feeling smug, secure and comfortable with our present spiritual life, perhaps we've been on the "dregs" too long and what was previously good is beginning to spoil. Let's ask God to replace our complacency with an ardent passion for him.

MERCY

[God] saved us, not because of righteous things we had done, but because of his mercy. (Titus 3:5a)

Growing up, I remember hearing that grace and mercy were two sides of the same coin. Grace is getting what we don't deserve (blessings), and mercy is *not* getting what we do deserve (judgment). Implicit in the definition of mercy is the fact that we are in a situation of need but have no right to expect help; we have erred and rightly deserve punishment. Although acknowledging our fallen nature is an unpopular thing to concede, it is still the reality of our experience.

My wife, Doreen, vividly remembers when she banged up the family car at the age of sixteen. Although her father had every right to criticize her carelessness, he gave no words of criticism. He extended mercy, and she never forgot it.

We Christians are often experts at being judgmental toward those we consider to be in error—to abortion rights activists, to the homosexual community, to divorced persons, etc. We seem to have reflex judgment as though our collective knees had been tapped with a giant hammer. This judgmental reaction, however, contrasts sharply with Jesus' response to the woman caught in adultery (John 8:1-11) and the father's response to the prodigal son (Luke 15:11-32). We so quickly forget our own sins— gossiping, pride, impatience, envy, overeating and judgmentalism.

God's mercy is a natural outgrowth of his love and compassion for us. We are called to be merciful just like our heavenly father is merciful (Luke 6:36). As Christians, we have received God's greatest mercy. If we pause to let our hearts feel and our minds grasp the deep significance of God's loving mercy to us, it will be easier for us to extend loving mercy to others.

A SIMPLE CREED

Therefore God exalted him to the highest place / and gave him the name that is above every name, / that at the name of Jesus every knee should bow, / in heaven and on earth and under the earth, / and every tongue confess that Jesus Christ is Lord. (Philippians 2:9-11a)

My denomination recently went through a merger. Although better than going through a split, it was not without elements of stress. In the process, we reviewed and defined our core beliefs. What is the creed by which we live? What is our confession of faith? In one sense, the whole Bible is our creed, but that's a bit unwieldy and perhaps a cop-out. The Apostles' Creed is one commonly accepted synopsis of basic Christian belief. In his words to the church at Philippi, the apostle Paul gives us the simplest and most basic of all Christian creeds: "Jesus Christ is Lord."

When we truly declare that Jesus is Lord, we are acknowledging his oneness with God, for no one is above him. The exalted position of "Lord" puts all things under him. It means he is Lord of the universe and Lord of time (past, present and future). On a personal level, he is Lord of our lives and therefore in a position to be worshiped and obeyed.

In 1742, Handel's *Messiah* was performed in the presence of King George II. When the "Hallelujah Chorus" was sung, King George stood to his feet in awe to honor a king greater than himself, the "King of kings and Lord of lords" (Revelation 17:14). When King George stood, everyone else stood, and a tradition was born. Yet it was more than a tradition. Standing for the "Hallelujah Chorus" was, and still is, an affirmation of the most basic Christian creed and the most fundamental truth of all time: "Jesus Christ is Lord!"

A STUMBLING BLOCK

Now about food sacrificed to idols: ... But food does not bring us near to God; we are no worse if we do not eat, and no better if we do. Be careful, however, that the exercise of your freedom does not become a stumbling block to the weak. (I Corinthians 8:1, 8-9)

The church service was about to begin. As a college student home for the summer, I naively sat in the pew, wearing blue jeans and a T-shirt. I was surprised when a man sitting nearby leaned over to talk to me. He told me the clothes I wore were inappropriate for the house of God, where we should bring only our best. He said the way I dressed was a stumbling block for him, and therefore I should change the way I dressed.

While eating food sacrificed to idols is no longer a raging issue in most of our churches, it was when Paul wrote to the church at Corinth. Perhaps drinking alcohol, watching R-rated movies or wearing certain types of clothing might be similar issues for us today. Clearly, there will always be issues that, although not basic to Christianity or salvation, will be debated by sincere Christians. Some Christians believe the church needs clear behavioral guidelines to promote holiness and to have a clear witness to the secular world. Other Christians emphasize the freedom from legalism that we have in Christ and the importance of a pure heart over external appearances.

Paul cautions us to be careful that our freedom does not become a "stumbling block" to others. A stumbling block is anything that causes one to trip or fall into sin. By definition, a stumbling block should be something we don't see or can't avoid. If we see a potential stumbling block, at that point it becomes our responsibility to try to avoid it. Also, things that offend one's personal taste do not qualify as stumbling blocks because personal taste does not define sin. While we want to be sensitive to other people's feelings, that doesn't necessarily mean being controlled by them. While I rarely wear T-shirts to church anymore, I still often wear blue jeans—watch your step please, lest you "stumble."

June

TRUSTING GOD WITH OUR OWN

Not one [sparrow] will fall to the ground apart from the will of your Father
... So don't be afraid; you are worth more than many sparrows.
(Matthew 10:29b, 31)

My daughter Amaris is a fourth-year medical student presently doing a rotation at a rural mission hospital in Zambia. She emailed several days ago to tell us she had drawn blood from a patient who was HIV-positive and had accidentally stuck herself with the needle. She has started on medication to decrease her chance of becoming infected.

Since I've heard about the needle-stick, anytime I'm not actively engaged with some activity or thought, my mind goes to the default position of ruminating: "My daughter might get AIDS." I'm her father. I'm supposed to protect her from harm, fix her problems, hold her in my arms and reassure her that everything is going to be okay. But she's half a world away and has already been exposed to harm. I'm impotent to fix her problem, and I'm hugging empty air. Even as I write these words, however, I realize her heavenly Father is there with her. He is omnipotent, and he who loves her more than I could ever imagine is holding her in his arms.

I am reminded that "in all things God works for the good of those who love him" (Romans 8:28). I also know that God's goal is not to prevent difficulties or tragedies but to reveal himself to us. It is often in difficult or even disastrous circumstances that God's purposes are realized, and he nourishes our faith or makes us more Christ-like. Frequently, it is only in retrospect that we can see God's hand. As Søren Kierkegaard said, "Life is lived forward but understood backward."

Right now, however, there is a disconnect between what my head knows and what my heart feels, and I find myself in tears. Nonetheless, I know that while God's ways may be perplexing, they are purposeful. As I pray for my Amaris, I cling to this truth, and I cling to The Truth, Jesus.*

*Thankfully, Amaris ended up not contracting HIV from her dangerous needle-stick.

June 2

POINTING TO CHRIST

The bride belongs to the bridegroom. The friend who attends the bridegroom waits and listens for him, and is full of joy when he hears the bridegroom's voice. That joy is mine, and it is now complete. He must become greater; I must become less. (John 3:29-30)

The imagery of the Church as the bride of Christ seems both brazen and humbling. How could we as the Church, with our unkempt hair, poorly proportioned body, deaf ears, hard hearts, feeble minds and stumbling gait, be a desirable bride for Christ? Certainly he deserves better. Nonetheless, he has chosen us to be the object of his affection. His love is unconditional, which is fortunate since we are seldom capable of fulfilling any conditions.

John the Baptist, who is speaking in the above passage, is portrayed as the bridegroom's friend. John worked hard on the preparations for the wedding celebration. Although he achieved some degree of notoriety, he did not dream of usurping the position of the bridegroom. John said his joy was "complete" as Jesus (the bridegroom) took center stage.

I've always admired the way John the Baptist stepped aside to let Jesus take his rightful position. He directed the bride–the people of Israel–to the bridegroom and then appropriately faded into the background. "He must become greater; I must become less." We are also to direct those around us to Jesus. If persons around us are impressed with how good we are, how great a teacher, pastor or parent we are, but they are not drawn closer to Jesus, then we have failed. We are coming *between* the bride and her bridegroom. Imagine if the best man stood between the bride and the groom as the bride approached the front of the church and refused to get out of the way to let the groom take the bride's hand. This is what it is like when we let people be drawn to *us* without getting out of the way to point them to *Jesus*, the groom. Our joy will not be complete until we are less and he is more.

PAIN, EVIL AND SUFFERING

Where were you when I laid the earth's foundation? / Tell me, if you understand. / Who marked off its dimensions? Surely you know! (Job 38:4-5a)

The problem of pain, evil and suffering is a difficult one. It's been said that perhaps the only more difficult one would be to define God and give two examples. The classic statement of the problem of pain, evil and suffering is that either God is all-powerful but not all-good and therefore doesn't stop evil because he doesn't care about it, or he is all-good but not all-powerful and therefore is *unable* to stop evil.

God could have made us never to sin and to love him unquestioningly, but obedience and love lose their meaning when they are involuntary. Evil (choosing to disobey God) is therefore an inherent possibility with the gift of free will. Christian apologist C.S. Lewis explains, "God cannot both give us free will (which allows us to truly love him) and at the same time withhold it from us (to keep us from sinning); not because His power meets an obstacle, but because nonsense remains nonsense even when we are talking about God."

The biblical character Job asked God why he was suffering when he had lived a righteous life. Like Job, we too often arrogantly assume we have the right to understand everything. A God who denies us any information on matters that we feel entitled to comprehend frustrates us. God answered Job with a question: "Where were you when I laid the earth's foundation?" God wanted Job to realize the appropriateness of human limitation. We delude ourselves by thinking our finite minds not only *can* know but also *should* know everything about everything. To understand God and his ways completely, we would have to *be God.* Since we are not God, some limitation on our understanding should not only be allowable but should also be the normal expectation.

GOD HUMBLED HIMSELF

Who, being in very nature God, / ... made himself nothing, / taking the very nature of a servant, / being made in human likeness. / ... he humbled himself and became obedient to death— / even death on a cross! (Philippians 2:6-8)

Can God make a stone so heavy he can't lift it? Islam and Christianity would answer this question differently. Allah, the god of Islam, has a "greatness" that causes a separation from humanity and the created world. The transcendent Allah does not condescend to have feelings toward humanity. He does not lower himself to be a personal god in fellowship with us. Showing mercy is a sign of weakness, and Allah is anything but weak. To think of Allah stooping to incarnation, suffering and death is blasphemous. Allah can lift any stone.

Christianity, on the other hand, shows us a view of God who is paradoxically both transcendent (above us) and immanent (with us). God is full of mercy and compassion (James 5:11). He grieves for his children (Jeremiah 14:17) and even sees each sparrow fall to the ground (Matthew 10:29). Motivated by his great love, God humbled himself to dwell among us, to suffer, and ultimately to die on the cross. Christianity's view of an almighty God who nonetheless is loving and personal is so unexpected that it lends credence to its truth—who could make up such things?

Our God's love is so great that he humbled himself by giving up power when he became a man. By relinquishing his power, God demonstrated that he *could* make a stone so heavy that he would be unable to lift it. Our God, the one and only true God, is willing to limit his power because of his great love for us. The only reasonable response is thanksgiving, praise, worship, and a life devoted to the One who loves us so well.

A HOLY TIME

Then God blessed the seventh day and made it holy, because on it he rested from all the work of creating that he had done. (Genesis 2:3)

The first thing in Scripture that God made holy was not a person or a place but time itself. "God blessed the seventh [Sabbath] day and made it holy." His reason for making the Sabbath holy is even more surprising. For six days God had been the epitome of productivity as he spoke the very world into existence, yet none of these days was sanctified and set aside as holy. God chose to make the day when he rested and was "unproductive" a holy day.

We tend to think of holiness as being based on what we *do*. This reflects our culture, in which value is placed on persons in relationship to their productivity. As a result of this cultural value, we've become a very *busy* people. Pastor and best-selling author Max Lucado says only Americans would name a mountain "Rushmore." We need to reverse the way we think. "Don't just do something, stand there," may be a call to holiness as well as sanity. Our *being* (resting in Christ) is the real basis for our holiness, and the Sabbath is a reminder of that truth.

Holiness involves being set apart from the world and being consecrated to God. It is often easier to give God our money and our labor than to give him our *unbusy* time. Perhaps that's one reason he requests it of us.

BIGGER BARNS

'I will tear down my barns and build bigger ones, and there I will store all my grain and my goods. And I'll say to myself, "... Take life easy; eat, drink and be merry."' But God said to him, '... This very night your life will be demanded from you. Then who will get what you have prepared for yourself?'
(Luke 12:18b-20)

Although our culture specializes in unfettered striving for the "good life," we may be confused about what that good life is. We devote much of our energy to acquiring and maintaining a certain standard of living. The assumption is that happiness and contentment will follow—a precarious assumption.

A young capitalist once visited a wise hermit who lived on a mountaintop. Incredulous that he would waste his life like this, the young man challenged the recluse, "Don't you realize that if you worked hard for the next thirty years you could retire and live a life of leisure?" The hermit replied, "But that's what I'm doing *now.*"

It's very easy to get seduced into the mindset that "building bigger barns" is the way to happiness. Millionaire Lee Iacocca once said, "Here I am in the twilight years of my life, still wondering what it's all about ... I can tell you this, fame and fortune is for the birds." Nonetheless, we continue to idealize the poor who become rich (Horatio Alger theme), while forgetting the rich who voluntarily become poor (e.g., St. Francis of Assisi). Which one, though, is truly happier and more content? The obvious answer is counter-intuitive, and we continue to build bigger barns.

FOLLOWING THE SHEPHERD

"... He goes on ahead of them, and his sheep follow him because they know his voice." (John 10:4)

David said, "The LORD is my shepherd ... he leads me ..." (Psalm 23:1-2). In both the Old and New Testaments, we are compared to sheep following God. Jesus said the sheep know their shepherd by his voice. If they hear a voice, they know if that voice belongs to their shepherd and whether or not they can trust him. Although identifying the shepherd is based on hearing, following the shepherd is based on seeing. They *see* where the shepherd is going and follow him. If we were sheep, what would we actually see? Since sheep are short of stature, we would mainly see feet and legs. Sheep follow the shepherd by watching to see where his feet and legs go.

During the Exodus, the children of Israel were led through the wilderness by a pillar of fire by night and a pillar of cloud by day (Exodus 13:21). Pastor and teacher Ray Vander Laan notes that these two pillars are described as "standing" (Exodus 14:19). It's as though these two huge pillars were the legs of Yahweh himself, guiding the Israelites like the legs of a shepherd guide the sheep.

Jesus is "the good shepherd" (John 10:14), and he calls us with two simple words, "Follow me" (Matthew 9:9). If we are to follow as sheep, we must watch Jesus' feet and legs. We must see where they have gone and then follow in his steps.

TRUE APPEARANCES

" ... The LORD does not look at the things man looks at. Man looks at the outward appearance, but the LORD looks at the heart." (I Samuel 16:7b)

Psychologist Samuel Gosling did a personality study among college students. First, a personality assessment was done on each student by one of their close friends, and then a complete stranger who was allowed to visit their dorm room for fifteen minutes also did an assessment. Surprisingly, the complete strangers had more accurate assessments than the friends. The books we read, the pictures on our walls and the logs of our Internet surfing may paint more accurate portraits of us than the groomed images we project to our friends.

I will soon be going to my fortieth high school reunion. In preparation for this event, I lost a few pounds, got a fresh haircut and fretted about what clothes to wear. There were 206 students in our graduating class. So, by my calculations, there are probably about 205 other middle-aged, overweight, graying alumni who are presently involved in similar endeavors. We are fixated on outward appearances, and we give little thought to our true selves lying largely hidden under the surface.

A friend once told me that when large symphony orchestras have auditions, the candidates perform behind a screen to prevent appearance bias. It doesn't matter if the violinist is male, female, black, white, fat, skinny, ugly or pretty; what matters is the sound they produce on the violin. Similarly, God is uninterested in our external appearance that we have so carefully groomed. He is interested in matters of the heart. We need to learn to value what God values. Let's echo the psalmist David, whose heart pleased God: "Search me, O God, and know my heart; / test me and know my anxious thoughts. / See if there is any offensive way in me, / and lead me in the way everlasting" (Psalm 139:23-24).

THOUGHTS ON CREATION

In the beginning God created the heavens and the earth. (Genesis 1:1)

Science proposes the Big Bang as the first event in the creation of our universe. However, if nothing existed before the creation of the universe, then nothing was there to cause the Big Bang. But no event or thing has *ever* been observed to originate from *nothing*. Philosopher John Locke said, "Man knows by intuitive certainty that bare nothing can no more produce any(thing) than it can be equal to two right angles." If that is the case, then the beginning of the world requires a non-physical reality (since nothing physical yet existed) to be the first cause. Otherwise our universe is an uncaused reality, a conclusion scientists and philosophers find uncomfortable and untenable, if not impossible. This line of reasoning provides for the possibility of God.

No one would look at a modern jet plane with all its aerodynamic engineering, electrical systems, jet propulsion technology and computer systems and say, "There was no intelligent design behind this plane. It just came into existence by some random cosmic accident." Albeit such a claim seems preposterous, our bodies are many times more complex than a jet plane, yet people are content to believe we just evolved by chance.

One of the reasons we intuitively don't believe that a jet plane just "happened" is the second law of thermodynamics (the law of entropy). It states that all changes in the universe are moving in the direction of greater entropy (i.e., greater disorder or randomness). Things left alone over time deteriorate. Evolution (unless God-driven) flies in the face of the law of entropy by creating *more* order and complexity over time.

In addition to contradicting evolution, the second law of thermodynamics also points back to a time when things began (creation). If, as most persons agree, the world is becoming more disordered with time (winding down), it must have had a time when it was very ordered (wound up). Perhaps it's not as illogical as some would say to believe that in the beginning *God* "created the heavens and the earth."

PRAYER: PRELUDE TO GROWTH

They devoted themselves to the apostles' teaching and to fellowship, to the breaking of bread and to prayer. (Acts 2:42)

The early church realized the importance of prayer in their lives. Prayer is our umbilical cord to God, supplying us with the mystical nutritional elements necessary for spiritual life. There is no formula, set of instructions or recipe that will rejuvenate our spirituality—it has to come from God. Life-giving prayer is a spiritual conduit through which God infuses more of himself and his life-giving power to us. Prayer is one of the primary ways spiritual refreshment occurs. A vital prayer life readies our hearts, minds and spirits to receive the taught Word as well as the "still small voice" words spoken by God's Spirit.

We've all heard stories from non-Christians who had read the Bible and gotten little from it. When they became Christians, suddenly the same Scripture became alive, speaking wisdom and truth directly into their lives. The difference was the presence of God's Holy Spirit in them.

A vital prayer life also primes our spiritual ears to be in tune with God's Spirit throughout the day. There is a phenomenon called sympathetic resonance where if two violins are both finely tuned, and the A string of the one violin is plucked, the A string of the other violin across the room will vibrate in resonance with it. Prayer can help us to be spiritually in tune such that our spirit resonates with the Holy Spirit. This resonance can be either a warm communion or instructive communication between God and us.

As we pray, spending time alone in God's presence, his Holy Spirit ministers *life* to our spirits, hearts and minds. This spiritual invigoration prepares the way for spiritual growth to occur. Like the first Christians in the book of Acts, we are still called to devote ourselves to teaching and to fellowship, to the breaking of the bread and to prayer.

GOOD FOR EVIL

... "If your enemy is hungry, feed him; / if he is thirsty, give him something to drink. / ..." Do not be overcome by evil, but overcome evil with good.
(Romans 12:20-21)

If actions and responses are characterized as good or evil, and one looks at the possible ways to combine these, three general categories emerge: 1) Evil for good, 2) Evil for evil and good for good, and 3) Good for evil. In the first case, an evil response to a good action might be described as unjust, immoral or even brazenly evil. Such a person would be thinking only of himself.

The second category, returning good for good or evil for evil, describes conventional morality. If someone returns your lost purse, you might give her a reward (good for good). If someone punches you, you are justified in punching him back. Or, in a more sophisticated society, he might be punished with a fine and/or jail time (evil for evil). These responses provide appeasement and promote order and justice in society by protecting each person's rights.

The final response is perhaps the most difficult to understand and certainly the hardest to do—returning good for evil. As is often the case, the response most foreign to our nature is the one God calls us to adopt. This response requires us to surrender our "rights" and relinquish feelings of anger and revenge to practice a selfless (*agape*) love. In a unique way, practicing *agape* love takes the situation and its outcome out of our own hands and places them in God's hands. When we return good for evil, our response causes the offender to pause in their tracks and ask, "Hey, what's going on here?" That moment of wonder produces fertile ground for God's Holy Spirit to sow seeds.

"If your enemy is hungry, feed him"—this is not doormat theology practiced by the impotent. Rather, it is the courageous imitation of Christ that unleashes the power of God's Holy Spirit for the good of our enemy and his potential salvation.

WHEN GOD SAYS "NO"

Then Jesus went with his disciples to a place called Gethsemane, … and he began to be sorrowful and troubled. … He fell with his face to the ground and prayed, "My Father, if it is possible, may this cup be taken from me. Yet not as I will, but as you will." (Matthew 26:36, 37, 39)

Why are so many of our prayers "unanswered" (i.e., not answered the way we wanted)? From our perspective, our prayers seem simple enough for an almighty God to answer. They are prayers for good things, not greedy or evil things. So why do we still experience problems, pain, sickness and suffering, all of which we had clearly asked to be spared?

While there is no one answer to why God says "no" to some of our prayers, there may be both some consolation and revelation in seeing that God's own son Jesus also experienced unanswered prayer. God allowed Jesus to suffer and die even though he had prayed, "If it is possible, may this cup be taken from me."

Jesus' unanswered Gethsemane prayer illustrates an important spiritual truth. To us, it seems like a no-brainer that good would always be better than evil. However, God often chooses a third option—evil redeemed, which is the best of all. God delights in taking that which was meant for sorrow, destruction and defeat and redeeming it to bring joy, growth and victory. The cross, the grave and the empty tomb are an excellent example of why God sometimes says, "No."

ALIENS AMONG US

Do not oppress an alien; you yourselves know how it feels to be aliens, because you were aliens in Egypt. (Exodus 23:9)

We are presently embroiled in a rather nasty national debate about what to do with the huge influx of immigrants (a.k.a. illegal/unregistered aliens) from our southern border. It is estimated there are eleven to twelve million illegal Latino immigrants residing in the United States, and the number continues to grow. The arguments regarding the immigrant dilemma are multifaceted and focus on social, economic, political, ethical, legal, humanitarian, patriotic and pragmatic considerations.

As I found myself arguing both sides of the issue, changing colors like an epileptic traffic signal, it became apparent that the crux of the issue for me was how I define myself: "Am I first an American or first a Christian?" If I am first an American, then my patriotic mindset must be based on what is best for America. However, if I am first a Christian, then what Jesus would think and do should mold my attitudes and determine my actions. Unfortunately, the Golden Rule and patriotism seldom share the same elevator.

A biblical perspective, based on looking up the words *alien, traveler* and *stranger* in Scripture, yields very one-sided results; God's love and mercy rule the day. "Do not mistreat an alien" (Exodus 22:21). "The LORD watches over the alien" (Psalm 146:9). "My door was always open to the traveler" (Job 31:32). And lastly, at the final judgment Jesus' words resound, "I was a stranger and you invited me in" (Matthew 25:35).

Paul reminds us that we Christians are also aliens, for "our citizenship is in heaven" (Philippians 3:20). Our spiritual citizenship trumps our earthly one, and we should therefore care more about others' well-being and less about preserving our own comfortable American lifestyle. These ideas may seem naïve and impractical. It is difficult, however, to rationalize away Jesus' lingering words: "Whatever you did for one of the least of these … you did for me" (Matthew 25:40).

KNOWING GOD THROUGH WORSHIP

Come, let us bow down in worship, / let us kneel before the LORD our Maker. (Psalm 95:6)

Scripture says our love for God should include our minds, bodies (strength), spirits (heart) and emotions (soul) (Deuteronomy 6:5, Matthew 22:37). Loving God with our whole being enables us to understand and experience God more fully. It's similar to how we learn about the world around us by using all five senses. The fewer senses we use, the more incomplete and inaccurate our understanding of the world. Worshiping God is one way we show our love for him, but worship is also one way we learn to know God.

For many of us, most of what we understand about God has come through our minds. I fear this may give us a distorted and dwarfed picture of God. If we can summon our courage and obedience to love God with our whole being, we may be surprised to experience and know God in some dramatic new ways.

When we worship God without reservation, he responds in kind. Body postures (bowing down before him, raising hands up to him and lying prostrate in his presence) help put our spirits, bodies and emotions in positions of openness and vulnerability before him. Many who have engaged in such unrestrained worship report their bodies have tingled, felt warm or even experienced physical healing. Emotions have bubbled over with tears or with joy. An overwhelming sense of unworthiness or unconditional love may be felt. Some have also spoken utterances they do not understand. During such worship experiences, God's Holy Spirit may minister to the worshipers' inner spirits, causing emotional healing and wholeness.

Some of us think we know God very well but have never ventured beyond knowing him with our minds. Only knowing God with our minds is like getting to know an elephant using only our sense of smell—we're missing a lot! We need to learn to worship with abandon and let our bodies, emotions and spirits complement our minds in order to experience and know God more fully.

FEAR--THE ANTIDOTE FOR FEAR

A furious squall came up, and the waves broke over the boat, … Jesus was in the stern, sleeping on a cushion … He got up, rebuked the wind and said to the waves, "Quiet! Be still!" Then the wind died down and it was completely calm. He said to his disciples, "Why are you so afraid? Do you still have no faith?" They were terrified and asked each other, "Who is this? Even the wind and the waves obey him!" (Mark 4:37-41)

When Jesus rebuked his disciples, he contrasted their fear with faith. A complete trust in God would have left no room for worries and anxieties. However, since we (like the disciples) fall short of perfection, we also routinely contend with fears in our lives. What do we do when the storms rage, our ship is about to capsize and our Lord seems inaccessible? It may be helpful to reframe our perspective by realizing that fear is an opportunity. How can one learn the virtue of trust if we are never fearful? David learned this truth, stating, "When I am afraid, / I will trust in you / … what can mortal man do to me?" (Psalm 56:3-4)

It is interesting to note it was *after* Jesus calmed the sea and the storm that the disciples were described as "terrified," asking, "Who is this?" They appear to have exchanged one fear for another. No longer frightened of possible shipwreck and drowning, they turned their anxieties toward the one who commanded the very forces of nature. Their reaction of fear after seeing a glimpse of Jesus' divine power was a very appropriate response. When we view Jesus as only "our buddy along life's journey," we do a grave injustice to the Creator of the world. We need to recapture some of the terrifying awe that belongs to our God. This tends to happen as we spend time with him and witness him calming the wind and the waves in our lives. As we develop an "awe-full" fear of God, it replaces the "awful" fears in our lives.

QUESTIONS

... I will meditate on your wonders. (Psalm 119:27)

To wonder and to question come as naturally to humanity as running downhill comes to mountain streams. Our nature is to ponder. Who? What? Where? When? Why? and How? Over the centuries, this questioning perspective has led to many discoveries and inventions. More importantly, however, looking at our world and ourselves causes us to ponder our origin, our purpose, and our destiny. These questions have led many to consider the possibility of God.

When one realizes that meaningful questions may lead persons to God, it's ironic that much of evangelical Christianity seems uncomfortable with meaningful questions in the arena of faith. One of our close friends, who became a Christian as an adult, said one of the things that made her keep Christianity at arm's length was her perception that she had to believe with an *unquestioning* faith. If one thinks about it, however, unquestioning faith is an oxymoron. Faith by its very nature must have space for questions—if one has no questions, no faith is required.

Scripture is jam-packed with people who had questions for God. Moses questioned God's ability to pick the right leader (Exodus 3:10-4:17). Job challenged God as to why he allowed calamity to strike him (Job 31:35). David wondered how long God would forget him (Psalm 13:1-4). Rather than belittle the questioners, God seemed very engaged with each of them, even though he didn't always answer their questions. Honest faith questions reveal two things God likes to see. First, they reveal the questioner is humble enough to admit ignorance. Secondly, an honest questioner is seeking an answer (i.e., truth). The writer of Hebrews said, "[God] rewards those who earnestly seek him" (Hebrews 11:6). Just as the plumb bob will consistently point us toward earth's center, honest faith questions will consistently point us toward God.

June 17

AWE IS LOST

Having believed, you were marked in him with a seal, the promised Holy Spirit, who is a deposit guaranteeing our inheritance. (Ephesians 1:13b-14a)

Our sun is 93 million miles from Earth. Light, traveling at 186,000 miles per second, takes over eight minutes to travel from the sun to us. The volume of our sun is 1,300,000 times that of Earth. Only about one two-billionth of the sun's heat and light reaches the earth; the rest is lost in space. Earth lies at exactly the right distance from the sun to allow animal, plant and human life to exist (otherwise we'd be a hot glowing orb or a frozen ice ball). As amazing as all this is, when was the last time we considered the huge importance of the sun to our very existence? We are jaded by the busyness of our lives.

In our spiritual lives, we also are often under-amazed. In Ephesians, Paul tells us that as Christians, we have the Holy Spirit within us. We tend to read this "la-la-la," taking this amazing fact for granted. At the beginning of Scripture, we read about the dawn of Creation. "Now the earth was formless and empty, ... and the Spirit of God was hovering over the waters" (Genesis 1:2). That would be the same Holy Spirit that hovers over our activities today! At the end of the Bible, we read about the return of Christ, when time will be no more. The end will be ushered in when "the Spirit and the bride say, 'Come!'" (Revelation 22:17). That is also the same Holy Spirit that speaks into our minds and thoughts each day. After Jesus' ascension, the Holy Spirit came at Pentecost: "Suddenly a sound like the blowing of a violent wind ... filled the whole house ... tongues of fire ... came to rest on each of them" (Acts 2:2-3). That Holy Spirit, as mighty as the wind and intense as blazing fire, enables and empowers our daily Christian lives today!

We take too much for granted. We need to rekindle our sense of awe and amazement. Each day as we see our remarkable, incredible sun rise in the morning and set in the evening, let us be reminded of the amazing, awesome Holy Spirit, who resides in us as a "deposit guaranteeing our inheritance."

FIRSTFRUITS GIVING

David longed for water and said, "Oh, that someone would get me a drink of water from the well near the gate of Bethlehem!" So the Three broke through the Philistine lines, drew water from the well near the gate of Bethlehem and carried it back to David. But he refused to drink it; instead, he poured it out before the LORD. (I Chronicles 11:17-18)

I recently heard some rather startling statistics about the financial giving of Christians in the USA. One might assume that the richest Christians in the world would be quite generous. However, instead of exceeding the expected ten percent tithe, we are giving a meager 2.7 percent! It seems that instead of adhering to the principle of *first*fruits giving, we've resorted to *last* fruits giving; after all our other spending is done, we become charitable with whatever remains.

I fear we've lost much of the biblical perspective on giving offerings and sacrifices. Scripture teaches us that our offerings and praises are sacrificial acts of worship (Hebrews 13:15-16). As such, our giving has always been a part of sinful humans' drawing near to a holy God.

Giving up that which is most dear to us demonstrates the depth of our gratitude or devotion. David demonstrated his love for God by giving that which he profoundly treasured to his LORD—the sweet water from the well at Bethlehem, his hometown, obtained by three of his men, who risked their lives to get it. God demonstrated the supreme example of love when he sacrificed on our behalf that which was most dear to him, his only son, Jesus Christ.

When we practice firstfruits giving, we not only demonstrate a correct priority in our lives, but we also demonstrate trust. When we give our offerings *first* (before we pay all our bills), we are trusting that God will provide for our needs. Giving our firstfruit offerings is an act of worship, and worship brings us into God's presence. It is in his presence that we experience transformation and blessing—this could be material and/or spiritual blessing. The spiritual reality is that in firstfruits *giving*, we end up *receiving*.

FIX IT OR FEEL IT?

Do nothing out of selfish ambition or vain conceit, but in humility consider others better than yourselves. Each of you should look not only to your own interests, but also to the interests of others. (Philippians 2:3-4)

My wife had just shared from her heart a difficulty she was going through. Fortunately, she had me for her husband. I knew I possessed a unique set of skills (kind of like Liam Neeson did in the movie *Taken*) that made me particularly good at problem solving. I had several good ideas already formulating that could certainly put her well on her way to fixing this problem. She wouldn't have told me about her problem if she didn't want a solution, right? So why was this neon sign flashing in my brain that said: "No. Don't go there. Wrong way. Danger"? I had been there before, and déjà vu was doing its best to warn me of looming disaster. With an intuitive speed rivaling a 200-pound Galapagos tortoise, I realized that what she needed was not my solution but my empathy. It is uncomfortable for me to describe just how much I resisted and resented her not needing my unique problem-solving skills.

God dawned a truth on my mind and heart. I was really putting my wants before her needs. I wanted to be the hero who saved the day while my wife needed someone to share the pain of her struggle. The Apostle Paul reminds us to be unselfish and to consider the interests of others before our own. Having the right answer isn't all that helpful when no one is asking a question.

THE BEST LAID PLANS

Many are the plans in a man's heart, / but it is the LORD's purpose that prevails. (Proverbs 19:21)

There is nothing wrong with planning ahead. However, it behooves us as Christians not to become too attached to our own plans. Several years ago I was discussing a birthing plan with one of my patients and her husband. "I don't want any pain medicine during labor," she declared. "That's fine with me," I told her. "I never push for pain medicine during labor, and if you don't want it, we certainly won't give it." But she persisted, stating that during the stress and pain of labor she might say things she really wouldn't mean. She wanted me to agree that *even if she were to ask* for pain medicine, I would refuse her request based on her present clearly stated desires. I looked to her husband, hoping for an easy way out of this awkward arrangement, but he was adamantly nodding his head in agreement. I naively consented.

As fate would have it, two weeks later we found ourselves in the throes of a very difficult labor. The inevitable question came, "Dr. Miller, can I have a pain shot now?" Remembering our recent, lengthy discussion, I calmly reminded her of her desire to do this without pain medication. "D-O-C-T-O-R M-I-L-L-E-R!" she screamed at the top of her lungs. "GIVE ME A SHOT!" I turned to her husband, who reluctantly shrugged his shoulders. I acquiesced.

Like this woman, we are often quite certain about what is best for our future, in spite of our ignorance about what actually lies ahead. As we enter into the "labor" God has for us, the best plan is to hold loosely to our plans, to cry out to him in our travail, and to let his plans prevail.

June 21

WHY NOT SHARE?

But Peter and John replied, "... For we cannot help speaking about what we have seen and heard." (Acts 4:19-20)

Incessant evangelistic fervor is not one of the problems that plague the contemporary American church. We seem quite capable of restraining our zeal for faith-sharing. We need to be careful, however, for the church will cease to exist without evangelism.

Why do we avoid sharing our faith? We may fear we won't know all the answers to questions nonbelievers have. However, if we wait until we know all the answers, we'll *never* share our faith. Besides, we can only witness to that which we know, not that which we don't know. Even brand new Christians, who think the "Romans Road" is a street in Italy, can share their own story about what God has done in their lives.

"Yes, but evangelism is not my spiritual gift." That does not get us off the hook, since we are all called to share our faith whether it's our spiritual gift or not. In fact, only ten to fifteen percent of new Christians responded to an altar call by a pastor or evangelist. The great majority of conversions occur in the context of relationships between non-Christians and lay believers.

"But they'll think I'm a religious nut." If we share in the context of an ongoing relationship, non-Christians are not likely to fear they'll get a Kool-Aid party invitation. Yet even if they do think we are peculiar, is our pride so great we won't risk appearing foolish for the cause of Christ?

"But who am I to tell them they're wrong and I'm right?" First of all, we're all "wrong"; we were born that way. However, our attitude in faith-sharing should not be judgmental but humble. We should remember the vivid imagery that defines what a Christian is: "I am only one beggar telling another beggar where I found bread."

I think we often dwell on our fears and forget that what we are sharing is *good* news, not *bad* news. It's news of acceptance and love, not rejection and hatred. Christ offers forgiveness and serenity in a culture of guilt and worry. The Good News is that we can have an abundant and meaningful life, not just a superficial existence. How can we help but speak about what we have seen and heard?

CREATED BY DESIGN

The LORD will fulfill his purpose for me; your love, O LORD, endures forever. (Psalm 138:8)

Secular scientists tell us we are the result of an improbable cosmic accident. If one begins with the assumption that there is no God, this conclusion would be a logical explanation for our presence. It might be better, however, to start with the idea that "nothing is assumed." One would then want to include the possibility of God and look for evidence to support or refute his existence. Wouldn't it be better not to discard any potential possibilities without first objectively examining them? Science usually prides itself on being free of prejudicial bias.

Christian apologist Ravi Zacharias points out three implicit ramifications of denying God's existence: 1) There would be no meaning to life since we are here by chance; 2) There could be no moral absolutes, suggesting ethics are arbitrarily set; and 3) There would be no hope for the future since this life is all there is. The Bible, however, presents a scenario in opposition to the cosmic accident assumption.

Scripture tells us that God created each of us while we were still in our mothers' wombs (Isaiah 44:2). We were made for a purpose (Psalm 138:8), and God planned even the details of our lives (Acts 17:26). According to Scripture, we are not the unintended result of the forces of evolution. Our lives are not the arbitrary product of time and circumstances. Albert Einstein noted, "God does not play dice." Every aspect of who we are—our minds, bodies, personalities, talents and experiences—serves a specific function. The Christian perspective suggests that our lives are full, with meaning and purpose given by our Creator and growing out of his love for us. We are the objects of God's love and attention, and it is because of that love that we have great value and eternal significance.

These are two separate worldviews. Sometimes we adopt a particular perspective without even realizing there are other ways to look at things. If you have never truly examined the Christian worldview, an exciting adventure awaits you. Enter with an open mind.

GROWING AND BEARING FRUIT

But the fruit of the Spirit is love, joy, peace, patience, kindness, goodness, faithfulness, gentleness and self-control. (Galatians 5:22-23a)

It's a little discouraging to scroll down through the fruit of the Spirit and find that I'm lacking in every single one. Yet it's encouraging to see that I've grown in some areas. Each of us probably has one or two "fruit" that we find lacking more than the rest. For me, patience seems to have gone missing.

Several years ago my wife had an idea to help me with my impatience. She suggested I memorize and meditate on Scripture verses about patience. A week later I was reciting one of these new verses while driving home. Unfortunately, an extremely slow driver had thoughtlessly gotten in front of me and interrupted my recitation. Needless to say, I was forced to give her several friendly beeps on my horn, encouraging her at least to try to approach the speed limit. As I was beeping my horn and reciting my verse on patience, the irony of the situation dawned on me, and I broke out in laughter.

As I pondered my situation, two truths were apparent. First, I cannot bear the fruit I want by force of will, any more than an apple tree can grit its teeth to bear a plum. *God* has to change my heart. Memorizing verses may be the means he uses for transformation, but the mechanics of the process alone are fruitless. The second revelation was that the only way to develop patience is by being in situations where I am tempted to be *im*patient. I think this is a general truth for any of the fruit of the Spirit.

If we want to grow in an area of righteousness, we can expect to be tempted by the sin that opposes that virtue. For example, how can one be characterized as honest without being tempted to lie? Growth often occurs as we make right choices when tempted. Sage Moses Maimonides argued that repentance is only complete when the sinner has the chance to sin again and does not. Consequently, when we pray for growth, we need also to pray for strength to resist the temptation that will surely come. As God enables us to obey, growth occurs. During this mystical process of growth, blossoms suddenly appear, and the fruit is born.

CALLED TO SUFFER

But if you suffer for doing good and you endure it, this is commendable before God. To this you were called, because Christ suffered for you, leaving you an example, that you should follow in his steps. (I Peter 2:20b-21)

We should know that as Christians living in a fallen, sinful world, we will experience suffering. If this were not apparent based on reasoning alone, we should see it through the example of Jesus and his disciples and from the clear teaching of Scripture. Yet in spite of all this evidence, when we personally experience suffering, it's very hard not to cry out, "Unfair!" or, "Why me?"

I have a friend who was recently convicted of a crime she did not commit. There was a long and complicated trial involving her service to an alcoholic and his drug-addicted son. I believe the jurors' final decision was based on their belief that it was inconceivable she could have given so much of her time and subjected herself to fleas, the constant foul odor of urine, and physical danger, without the expectation of financial reward. It just wouldn't make sense any other way; thus she must have taken the money from the alcoholic. She ended up losing her job and a substantial sum of money. In addition, the press subjected her to public humiliation throughout the trial. No good deed goes unpunished.

The New Testament perspective on suffering for following Christ, however, is different than the world's perspective and involves more than passive acquiescence. We are called to rejoice in suffering (I Peter 4:13). Peter goes on to say that when we suffer for Christ's sake, we somehow engage in a mystical participation or fellowship (*koinonia*) with Christ's suffering. Furthermore, because of the suffering, we are in some unexplainable way blessed, and God's "Spirit of glory" rests on us (4:14).

I don't pretend to know what it means to be blessed by God's "Spirit of glory," and I literally tremble to think of suffering as my friend has. Yet this promise of blessing can still give us a measure of comfort in times of anguish.

AN INCURABLE CONDITION?

What a wretched man I am! Who will rescue me from this body of death?
Thanks be to God—through Jesus Christ our Lord. (Romans 7:24-25a)

I can still envision the old man as he crawled on all fours into our mission clinic in rural Honduras. His feet were carefully wrapped with banana leaves since no shoes were large enough to cover them. I could see the humiliation in his eyes as he crawled past a downpour of stares. Unwrapping the bright green leaves revealed the source of his embarrassment. Both feet had been completely overgrown with huge, fungating, cauliflower-like growths. He had been living in pain, shame and fear for years. I have seldom been so happy to see such a terrible problem as I was that day. His disease, which seemed so incurable, was "yaws." This malady can be treated and cured with high doses of the common antibiotic penicillin. He had been living in fear and suffering when there was a remedy at hand.

Sometimes we are like that poor old man. When we take an honest, objective look at ourselves, it's not a pretty sight. Even on a good day, our irritability, insensitivity, impatience and self-centeredness keep the indicator needles on our depravity gauges in the zone somewhere between bad and terrible. If we can hardly stand ourselves, how can a holy God stomach our presence? Our condition seems hopeless ... even terminal. Yet like the old man who had been crawling around without hope, there is a remedy for our condition; his name is Jesus. Let's unwrap the banana leaves and receive his healing, forgiveness and unconditional love.

JOINING GOD'S WORK

We are therefore Christ's ambassadors, as though God were making his appeal through us. (II Corinthians 5:20a)

An ambassador is an authorized representative or messenger from one country to another. He is to represent his country's interests, not his own. As Christians, we are Christ's ambassadors, but we often forget that our desires should be focused on his interests, not ours. It's hard to put our ideas, plans and goals in the back seat when they are such good ones.

The truth of the matter is we tend to be so self-centered that we don't even consider the possibility that God had a plan of action and was actively orchestrating people, time and events before we ever came onstage (how could there have even been a stage without us?). Pastor and author Henry Blackaby, in *Experiencing God*, points out that God is always at work around us and that he invites us to become involved with him in his work. Not surprisingly, we often have it backward. We tackle what seems to be a good project and ask God to join us and bless our work. We need to adjust to what *he's* doing, not vice versa.

Ice hockey legend Wayne Gretzky was once asked the key to his great success. After a moment's reflection, he replied, "I skate to where the puck is going to be." Our spiritual eyes need to home in on God's activity as though it were the puck. We need to ask, "Where is God moving, and in which direction is he going?"—and then move in that direction to join him. For as we pursue God's activities, he grants us the amazing privilege of joining him with his plans and purposes for our world.

THE WRITTEN WORD VS. THE LIVING WORD

You diligently study the Scriptures because you think that by them you possess eternal life. These are the Scriptures that testify about me, yet you refuse to come to me to have life. (John 5:39-40, emphasis mine)

It's good to read about the importance of eating the proper foods and getting the right vitamins and nutrients for optimal health. Some cookbooks even have tantalizing pictures of dishes that can make one's mouth water. However, reading books about good nutrition or looking at pictures of tasty foods is of no benefit for someone suffering from malnutrition. The person in need has to *partake* of that which is described; otherwise, it's all a cruel charade.

Scripture teaches us many things about God, and that's a good, helpful thing. However, learning more *about* God is useless unless it's actually a prelude to knowing God better. Christianity is not about some special knowledge; it's about a special relationship. Scripture is "God-breathed" and useful for teaching and training (II Timothy 3:16). However, Bible study cannot be seen as an end in itself lest it become a subtle form of idolatry. The holy *Word* of God is just a sign pointing us to the Holy *One* of God—Jesus. The Bible in itself does not have life-changing power, but a relationship with God through Jesus Christ does.

A GOD'S-EYE VIEW

A champion named Goliath came out of the Philistine camp. ... David said to the Philistine, "You come against me with sword and spear and javelin, but I come against you in the name of the LORD Almighty ..." As the Philistine moved closer to attack him, David ran quickly toward the battle line to meet him. Reaching into his bag and taking out a stone, he slung it and struck the Philistine on the forehead. ... and he fell facedown on the ground.
(I Samuel 17:4, 45, 48-49)

When I was in junior high school, my fellow students and I used to draw schematic pictures and then ask each other, "What's this?" The key to figuring out the drawings was being able to look at it from a different perspective (e.g., that's a "bird's-eye view" of a man on a bicycle, or an "ant's-eye view" of an elephant stampede). It's surprising (and often humorous) how much a different perspective can change one's overall view.

Pastor and teacher Joseph Garlington points out a similar difference between the Israelites' view of Goliath and David's view of Goliath. The Israelite soldiers said, "Such a huge giant, how could we ever defeat him?" On the other hand, David said, "Such a huge head, how could I ever miss it?" The difference in perspective came from David looking not at his own abilities but at his God.

Hudson Taylor, the famous missionary doctor who pioneered Christian mission work in China, said, "Many Christians estimate difficulties in light of their own resources and thus attempt little and often fail. All of God's giants have been weak men who did great things for God because they reckoned on his power and his presence being with them." We can also reckon on that same power and presence being with us.

SPIRITUAL PREY

Your enemy the devil prowls around like a roaring lion looking for someone to devour. Resist him, standing firm in the faith. (I Peter 5:8b-9a)

Peter paints the picture of the devil pursuing us like a lion after its prey. Our pastor, Dave Musser, suggested there are spiritual lessons we can learn from the tactics lions use to hunt.

Separate them from the herd. When lions want to bring down a powerful animal like an elephant, they try to separate one from the herd. Isolated, the elephant becomes more vulnerable. In our churches, members who are marginalized become spiritually vulnerable.

Frighten them into flight. The wildebeest has powerful horns that make it difficult to bring down. However, if the lion can frighten a wildebeest into running, its backside is unprotected, and it can be brought to the ground for the kill. Like the wildebeest's horns, our spiritual armor is on the front of our bodies (Ephesians 6:11-17). We have no protection on our backside because we are to resist the devil actively, not retreat (James 4:7).

Make them fall. A giraffe's height makes him a difficult prey. Lions may try to chase one to slippery or irregular terrain to make him fall. If the giraffe falls, the lion attacks his exposed neck (going for the jugular), and the struggle is soon over. When Christians fall into sin, we too become vulnerable. Having sinned, we feel ourselves a failure, making us prone to further sin. Eventually we feel beyond hope of redemption and give up even struggling.

Watch for movement. Some animals' camouflage offers excellent protection. Movement, however, will draw the lion's attention. When we begin to move forward spiritually, we also draw the devil's attention. This knowledge, however, need not paralyze us with fear. We should not be surprised when satanic attacks occur. Peter tells us to stand firm in our faith and *resist* him.

GOD'S PROVISION

"The fire and the wood are here," Isaac said, "but where is the lamb for the burnt offering?" Abraham answered, "God himself will provide the lamb for the burnt offering, my son." (Genesis 22:7b-8a)

This is an amazing story of obedient faith. Isaac, the result of a miraculous geriatric conception between Abraham and Sarah, was the only hope of fulfilling God's promises to Abraham. Yet God told Abraham to offer as a burnt sacrificial offering his beloved Isaac, his only son, the heir of promise.

As Abraham drew his knife to slay Isaac, God intervened. He revoked his own previous order, allowing Isaac to live. Abraham looked up and saw a ram in the thicket. The ram was offered in Isaac's place as a sacrificial offering. Abraham called the place "The LORD Will Provide" (*Jehovah-jireh*).

God, however, had provided for his people in many different times and places before this event and would provide for his people in many instances after this event. God provided for the needs of Adam and Eve in the Garden of Eden. He also provided for the needs of Noah and his family during and after the flood. Later, he provided water, manna and quail for the children of Israel in the wilderness during their exodus. Yet in none of these cases of provision is God named the "provider-God," *Jehovah-jireh*. In *this* story in which God is called *Jehovah-jireh*, it is worth noting what God provided. God provided the sacrifice.

This Old Testament story of provision is a foreshadowing of the most important provision of all time. Just as the ram took the place of Isaac on the sacrificial altar, so Jesus' sacrificial death was in our stead. As the Lamb of God (John 1:29), Jesus was God's sacrificial provision for us. Abraham spoke in faith, "God himself will provide the lamb." We must accept in faith that God has provided the Lamb for the sacrifice. Jesus is our provision from the God who is our provider, *Jehovah-jireh*.

July

A SANCTIFYING TOUCH

May God himself, the God of peace, sanctify you through and through. May your whole spirit, soul and body be kept blameless ... (I Thessalonians 5:23)

God's dealing with humanity is not compartmentalized. He cares about all areas of our lives. His holistic approach is seen in the *mitzvot*, the 613 commands from the Torah. The *mitzvot* go beyond the prayer and worship practices of the Jews to include their health practices, business dealings, sex life and even cooking and eating practices. Similarly, at the onset of Jesus' ministry, he declared he had come to touch *all* areas of human need—the poor (economic), prisoners (legal), blind (physical) and the oppressed (political) (Luke 4:18-21). Jesus also reiterated the *Shema* (the Jewish confession of faith) when he stated we are to love God with our whole being: heart, mind and soul (Matthew 22:37).

The truth of God's holistic concern for us is also embodied by the Jewish ritual cleansing bath called the *mikvah*. When participating in this cleansing, one must be totally immersed in the water of the *mikvah* so that it touches all parts of the body. All clothes, jewelry, bandages and fingernail polish must be removed before entering the water. The hair cannot be braided or knotted so that each strand can be soaked by the water. The fingers and toes should be splayed apart so the web spaces are not missed, and some even suggest flossing the teeth so food particles between the teeth don't leave an area untouched by the purifying water. While the *mikvah* practices may seem extreme if not compulsive, they do demonstrate a truth about our God–he wants to touch *all* aspects of our lives.

Most of us have areas in our lives we are covering, preventing exposure to God's purifying waters. Those areas may include our leisure time, social interactions, business practices, thoughts, emotional wounds or eating habits. Let's get out our spiritual floss to uncover those areas and let God's purifying waters sanctify us "through and through."

HOLY, HOLY, HOLY

[The angels] were calling to one another: / "Holy, holy, holy is the LORD Almighty; / the whole earth is full of his glory." (Isaiah 6:3)

In my marriage I'm learning the importance of knowing my wife Doreen well. As I learn to know her well, I can better understand the things she does and the desires of her heart. It's the same in our relationships with God—as we know him better, we can better understand what he is doing and his desires for us and the world.

To know God well, we must understand his basic nature and attributes. While God is faithful, loving, just and merciful, one of God's paramount characteristics is his *holiness*. It may be significant to note that the Bible never says God is "loving, loving, loving" or "faithful, faithful, faithful," but it does say he is "holy, holy, holy" (Isaiah 6:3 and Revelation 4:8). The three-fold repetition in Hebrew writings indicates a word's importance and therefore should encourage us to ponder the word's significance.

One definition of holiness is to be "separate or set apart" from evil. Interestingly, God's holiness can be conferred on places, things and persons. When God spoke to Moses at the burning bush, he said, "Take off your sandals, for the place where you are standing is holy ground" (Exodus 3:5). Things set apart for sacred use, like animal sacrifices (Numbers 18:17) or a tithe (Leviticus 27:30), were also called holy. Perhaps most amazing, however, is the fact that we Christians are also made holy (I Peter 2:9). We share in the glory of God by the holiness he confers on us. Our response to this awesome, undeserved gift can only be one of worship, in which we join the angels in declaring, "Holy, holy, holy is the LORD Almighty; / the whole earth is full of his glory."

OUR FATHER'S LOVE

"O my son Absalom! My son, my son Absalom! If only I had died instead of you—O Absalom, my son, my son!" (II Samuel 18:33b)

Absalom killed his brother Amnon and staged a coup to overthrow his father, the king. When King David fled the city to avoid turning Jerusalem into a bloody battlefield, Absalom pursued his father to finish him off. Yet David's unconditional love for his son never wavered, and he later grieved sorely at Absalom's death. David was described as being a man after God's own heart (I Samuel 13:14), and David's fatherly love certainly demonstrated one facet of God's heart.

As I read David's lament, I can feel David's deep anguish as a parent. My wife sometimes quotes author Elizabeth Stone, who said that having children is "to have your heart go walking around outside your body." Loving makes us vulnerable to injury and pain. Although our children are now adults, I still remember some of those pains—when one was made fun of at school, when false rumors were told about another, and when difficult circumstances were endured by a third. When an arrow pierced one of our children, my wife and I would bleed.

As imperfect as our parental love may be, it is still a reflection of our heavenly Father's love for us. God suffers, grieves and endures with us. And somehow in that knowledge, I find reassurance and comfort.

A NEW CREATION

Jesus looked at him and said, "You are Simon son of John. You will be called ... Peter." (John 1:42b)

Jesus had a unique way of seeing beyond what was painfully apparent to others. Looking at Simon, he saw more than a coarse, unschooled fisherman. Beyond the dirt under his nails and the unmistakable odor of fish, Jesus saw a diamond in the rough. He saw a potential friend, a disciple and a leader of the church.

In Matthew 16:18, Jesus said, "You are Peter, and on this rock I will build my church." The Greek demonstrates a play on words here. You are *petros* and on this *petra* I will build my church. *Petra* is a rock that symbolizes stability. Peter, however, was a poor metaphor for a stable rock. Indeed, he was impulsive and *un*stable. But Jesus saw beyond what he was to what he could become.

Jesus seemed able to find something redeemable among even the most undesirable people—the woman at the well, the tax collector, the woman caught in adultery and the man with a legion of demons. He touched their lives, and they were forever changed.

"You are Simon ... you *will* be called Peter" is actually the story of the whole New Testament–individuals who are transformed by meeting Jesus. Paul says in II Corinthians 5:17, "If anyone is in Christ, he is a new creation; the old has gone, the new has come!" It is both exciting and humbling to know that Jesus looks at each of us and sees great spiritual potential. He speaks to us as he did to Simon, "You are Myron, son of Mahlon. You *will* be called ..."

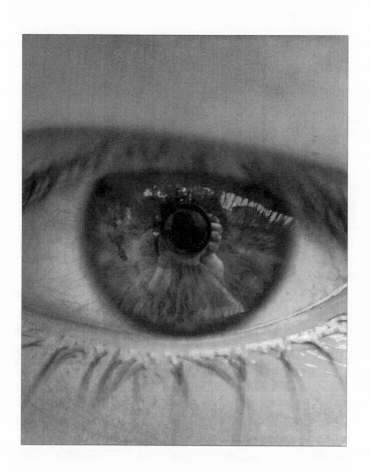

THE LAMP OF ILLUMINATION

"The eye is the lamp of the body. If your eyes are good, your whole body will be full of light." (Matthew 6:22)

The eye is an amazingly complex and helpful organ. Sight allows us to take in more information than any of our other senses. Our eyes enable us to gaze at the heavens and see galaxies that are light years away or lie on our bellies in the backyard and examine the smallest details of a delicate flower. We can see colors, shapes and sizes as well as perceiving depth and movement. It's easy to understand why many persons fear blindness more than any other sensory loss.

Jesus says, "The eye is the lamp of the body." A lamp's function is to illuminate or reveal things. While certainly our eyes reveal the world to us, it is also true that our eyes reveal us to the world. We've all noticed how someone wanting to conceal his or her thoughts or feelings will try to avoid eye contact. Yet even the process of averting one's gaze sends a message.

The information we glean from watching someone's eyes is so important that most of us find it disconcerting to carry on a conversation with someone wearing sunglasses (especially the mirror type). I find myself thinking that although their head may be pointing in my direction, they could be watching someone else.

How does our eye, the lamp of the body, spiritually reveal both the world to us and Jesus-in-us to the world? Jesus said, "I am the light of the world" (John 8:12). If he is the light of our lamp, he will help us view the world as *he* sees it. On the other hand, when the world looks at us they will see a reflection (poor though it may be) of the light that is in us and transforming us; that light is Jesus.

TOLERATING INTOLERANCE

Instead, speaking the truth in love, we will in all things grow up into him who is the Head, that is, Christ. (Ephesians 4:15)

What is the most important virtue in America today? In the Sixties, we heard a lot about love, peace, equality and justice. Today, however, Christian writer and apologist Josh McDowell suggests that these virtues have been supplanted by the virtue of tolerance. Moreover, tolerance has been redefined. He says tolerance no longer means just allowing others to have different opinions and beliefs, and treating those opinions and beliefs in a fair, objective way. The new definition of tolerance says that we also need to accept other persons' beliefs, lifestyles and truth claims as being as valid as our own. There can be no hierarchy among belief systems, or we have become intolerant, if not bigoted.

McDowell says there are significant ramifications resulting from this shifting definition of tolerance. Since truth is now considered to be relative and not absolute, one can no longer evaluate the truth claims of various religions. All religions have their own truth and are on an equal footing. Justice can no longer coexist with tolerance, for justice assumes an absolute right and wrong. Tolerance says no one is wrong—we are just different. Firmly held beliefs are now labeled intolerant. Although we may like being described as tolerant, Christian author G.K. Chesterton astutely noted a hundred years ago, "Tolerance is a virtue of a man without conviction."

Furthermore, Christians are called to something higher than tolerance; we are called to love. Christian love cannot be passively inactive when others need the Good News of the Gospel of Jesus Christ. We cannot be indifferent while persons engage in harmful, destructive behavior; God has so much more available for us. Truth by its very definition must be intolerant of that which is false, and we are called to speak the truth in love. Indeed, the consequences of not doing so would be intolerable.

ANCESTRAL BLESSINGS

"... I, the LORD your God, am a jealous God, punishing the children for the sin of the fathers to the third and fourth generation of those who hate me, but showing love to a thousand generations of those who love me and keep my commandments." (Exodus 20:5b-6)

In the 1800's, in the rural mountain regions of Appalachia, feuding between families was quite common. The legendary Hatfield-McCoy feud was only one of many. In the late 1990's, two psychologists, Cohen and Nisbett, conducted a provocative experiment on descendants from the area where these feuding clans lived to see if any remnants of the inclination for hostility had been passed down through the generations. Surprisingly, these modern-day college students from Michigan, five or six generations and 700 miles removed from the legendary feuds, still held hostile tendencies similar to their nineteenth-century Appalachian relatives! One can certainly speculate about possible explanations for this observation. What I found interesting, however, was that this modern-day study confirmed to me what God had spoken to Moses almost 3,500 years ago.

Our personal decisions and actions may have consequences that extend beyond us. These consequences may be passed on to our descendants for generations to come, which is a sobering if not frightening thought. We've all caught ourselves having the same quirks we smugly disapproved of in our parents. Realizing that we may one day see these same foibles pop up in our own children is a bit daunting. Fortunately, this bucket brigade of familial flaws is not a *fait accompli*; there is no genetically irresistible mandate at work here.

As Christians we have been "born again" (John 3:3). We have new parentage. God is now our father, and we are thus heirs to new things (Romans 8:15-17). Part of what we receive upon adoption into this new family is the transforming inner power of the Holy Spirit (Acts 2:38-39). We can break free of our familial weaknesses and inclinations, but the good news doesn't stop there. Not only can we *stop* passing on that which is harmful, but we can *start* passing on that which is good, holy and righteous. We can begin a godly legacy. And while the effects of sin can last a long time—"to the third and fourth generation," the effects of loving God and righteousness endure much longer—"to a thousand generations." Which spiritual inheritance are we leaving for our descendants?

ANXIOUS WITH WORRY

Do not be anxious about anything, but in everything, by prayer and petition, with thanksgiving, present your requests to God. (Philippians 4:6)

We are a culture of the anxious. We worry about big things like terrorism, global warming and nuclear war. And we worry about small things like how often we should pump out our septic tank, that funny clicking sound in the car engine, and whether or not we should eat tofu. Most of our worries fall into two categories: 1) trivial things that make us disproportionately distraught and 2) significant things that are God's responsibility, not our own.

The stellar, Olympic-class worriers tend to suffer from the proverbial inability to distinguish a mountain from a molehill. Sometimes we take our lives too seriously, and everything seems of monumental importance. We need to remind ourselves of "Lazlo's Chinese Relativity Axiom." This axiom states that no matter how great our accomplishments or how terrible our defeats, there are about one billion Chinese who couldn't care less.

On the other hand, some of our concerns are not petty, and our natural inclination is to ruminate on them. Paul, however, says we are not to worry about anything but to present our concerns to God in prayer; they are *his* responsibility. Rick Warren says thinking about a problem over and over again is worry, while thinking about God and his Word over and over again is meditation. So if we know how to worry, we also know how to meditate. We just need to change the focus for our ruminating thoughts. Reflect on that for a time.

TOUCHING HIM TOUCHING ME

That which was from the beginning, which ... our hands have touched—this
we proclaim concerning the Word of life. (I John 1:1)

We cannot touch what is intangible. When we touch something or someone, a part of us comes into contact with that person or object. Old Testament Mosaic Law had a long list of things forbidden to touch (Leviticus 11-15), to avoid defilement.

Jesus, however, had no fear that contact with evil, sickness or death would defile him. He allowed a sinful woman to wash (touch) his feet; she experienced love and forgiveness (Luke 7:37-48). Jesus touched an unclean leper, healing him (Mark 1:41), and a dead girl, raising her to life (Mark 5:41). Instead of someone's defilement (sin, illness or death) flowing into Jesus through physical contact, Jesus' power and love flowed into *them*.

Most scriptural admonitions regarding touch are negative: "You must not touch" (Genesis 3:3) and "do not touch" (Colossians 2:21). But on two separate occasions, Jesus asked *to be* touched, once by Thomas (John 20:27) and once by the disciples (Luke 24:39). Jesus asked them to touch him so they would know he was real.

Seminary professor H. Douglas Buckwalter points out that touch was also part of what characterized God in the Old Testament. God touched the ground to form man from the dust of the earth (Genesis 2:7). God also touched Jeremiah's mouth as he began his prophetic ministry (Jeremiah 1:9). This is in stark contrast to the wood and metal idols of the day, which were impotent and unable to touch: "they have hands, but cannot feel" (Psalm 115:7). Our God is real, and he wants to touch us and asks us to touch him. When we "touch" God, he is not tainted by our contact, but rather, we are healed by his touch—we experience his love, his forgiveness, his power, and his life.

DEFENDING OUR FAITH
WITH GENTLENESS AND RESPECT

Always be prepared to give an answer to everyone who asks you to give the
reason for the hope that you have. But do this with gentleness and respect.
(I Peter 3:15b)

Dan Brown's *The Da Vinci Code* (DVC) was a bestseller when it was published in 2003. More than one hundred million people have read the book, and millions more saw the movie released several years later, directed by Ron Howard and starring Tom Hanks. While the book is appropriately labeled fiction, it weaves fact, legend and conjecture via a vivid imagination into an intriguing story, which convinced many that its underlying claims must be true. One study indicated that fifty-two percent of Christian readers said it caused them to question some aspect of their faith!

The two most basic tenets of the Christian faith, the written Word (the Bible) and the living Word (Jesus Christ), are undermined in the DVC. As evangelical Christians, we are accustomed to defending our beliefs by using Scripture. However, the DVC challenges biblical authority by suggesting the New Testament gospels were just the arbitrary result of manmade political decisions. As Christians, we should be prepared to make a cogent defense for the reliability of Scripture.

We need not fear the DVC. When one looks carefully, truth has a way of standing firm. As John Adams succinctly stated, "Facts are stubborn things." We have, however, a responsibility for due diligence to know church history and Scripture so that we are prepared to give an answer for our hope.

Anger directed at Dan Brown, Tom Hanks, Ron Howard, or Hollywood in general is not helpful. Standing in picket lines and ranting about how Hollywood is going to hell in a handbasket will only serve to marginalize Christians as right-wing religious fanatics and diminish the chance for meaningful dialogue. We are encouraged to defend our faith but "with gentleness and respect." We need to remember that the sacrificial love that Jesus demonstrated on the cross is not only for us but also for those who made this movie, those who wrote the book, and those who may be deceived by it. We want to reflect that same love as we point them toward the true Jesus. He alone can meet our needs, and he alone is the reason for the hope we have.

SPIRITUAL DISCERNMENT

"Sir," the woman said, ... "Our fathers worshiped on this mountain, but you Jews claim that the place where we must worship is in Jerusalem." Jesus declared, "... God is spirit, and his worshipers must worship in spirit and in truth." (John 4:19-20, 24)

It's easy to be distracted from underlying issues and problems by trivialities. When the woman at the well felt uncomfortable with Jesus' probing questions, she tried to distract him with one of the frequently argued issues of the day regarding where they should worship. Jesus was not to be sidetracked by trifles. He brought her back to the proper focus by pointing out that it doesn't matter *where* we worship; what's important is *how* we worship—"in spirit and truth."

I have a non-Christian friend who has problems with smoking, drinking, and infidelity in his marriage. While these problems are significant, *focusing* on them would be a mistake. Even if he could change his bad behavior patterns, he would be no more "Christian" than before. It's easy for his unsavory habits to distract me, but they are just symptoms of the larger fundamental problem—he needs Christ in his life.

During the winter months it's common for patients with pneumonia to show up at my office. Typically they complain about a fever and cough. I could give them acetaminophen for the fever and guaifenesin for the cough, but such treatment would be grossly inadequate. Someone with pneumonia needs an antibiotic for their underlying infection. Treating the symptoms alone could be dangerous by masking the primary disease, which needs a more definitive therapy.

With spiritual matters, however, it may seem difficult to discern the fundamental issues. Yet Paul reminds us that through God's Holy Spirit we have *spiritual* discernment because we have the "mind of Christ" (I Corinthians 2:14-16). We need to humble ourselves and subjugate our human wisdom to God's wisdom. As we allow this to happen, we can do what Jesus did and avoid unfruitful diversions. In submission to God, a spiritual focusing occurs that allows us to see beyond what is visible and hear beyond what is audible, and by the enlightening power of his Holy Spirit, discern what is truly important.

CHANGING EXPECTATIONS

"You have heard that it was said, … But I tell you that …" (Matthew 5:27-28)

While all Scripture is inspired and profitable for us (II Timothy 3:16), most Christians do not have a "flat Bible" hermeneutic that puts Old and New Testament teachings on the same plane. The Old Testament provides general moral teachings (often in story form) and gives us insights into the nature of God and his ways. The New Testament gives us the story of salvation through Christ, the coming of the Holy Spirit and the birth of the church. Our present-day theology and spirituality derives primarily from the New Testament because it is the fuller revelation of God's written message to us. Yet few evangelicals clearly articulate this approach without some element of uneasiness.

How does one explain a view of the Bible that seems to show, at first blush, a God whose actions and expectations change from the Old to New Testaments? Yet Malachi declares, "I the LORD do not change" (3:6), and the writer of Hebrews tells us, "Jesus Christ is the same yesterday and today and forever" (13:8). The dilemma, however, can be understood if we recognize there is a "moral progression" from the Old to New Testaments. God progressively revealed himself and his will to people over time, with the full and complete revelation in the New Testament through the life and teachings of Christ (Hebrew 1:1-2).

Although we value the Old Testament and the Law, they are viewed through the perspective of the New Testament and the New Covenant in Christ, the fullest revelation. Our God has not changed. However, God's dealings with us and even his expectations of us have differed at various points in time.

As parents, we have different expectations for our one-year-olds than we have for our five-year-olds. When our infants learn to pick up food with their hands and manage to get more in their mouths than their noses, we are delighted and clap our hands to show pride and affirmation. However, if our kindergartners exhibit the same behavior, we are no longer proud parents. We now expect spoon and fork aptitude and will be happy with nothing less. As parents we have not changed, but as our children's dexterity and understanding have grown, our expectations for them have also changed.

The Bible is the story of God's working with his people from the time of Creation to the establishment of the Church. Like a parent, God works with his children where we are, while always striving to bring us to where he wants us to be.

WE HAVE JESUS

The point of what we are saying is this: We do have such a high priest [i.e., we have Jesus] ... (Hebrews 8:1)

Contemporary Western culture tends to place a book's climax or most important point at or near the end of the story. Ancient Hebrew culture, however, placed the dominant theme in the middle of the story, and the book of Hebrews follows this pattern. In the middle of the book, the author tells the readers the main point of the story—we have Jesus.

Let's first look at the story as a whole. The book of Hebrews has been said to demonstrate the all-sufficiency of Jesus as the revelation of God and as the mediator between God and man. Hebrews has also been called "the book of superiors" because the words "better" or "superior" occur fifteen times, describing Jesus or his works. Jesus is said to be the *superior* revelation of God (1:1-3). Jesus is *superior* to the angels (1:6), *superior* to Moses (3:3), and *superior* to the high priests (7:26-28). The main point of the book is stated at this point—we have Jesus—this is then followed by showing how Jesus' work as our high priest produced a *superior* covenant (8:6), a *superior* tabernacle (9:11) and a *superior* sacrifice (10:8-12).

The main point is sandwiched in between the theological teachings on Jesus' superiority, and that main point is that we have Jesus! The theological truths are important, but even if we can't understand all the theological implications and intricacies, we can know that we have Jesus—and that is enough because Jesus is enough.

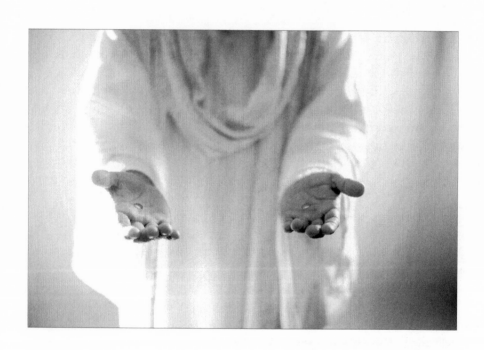

SCARS OF PERFECTION

[Thomas] said to them, "Unless I see the nail marks in his hands and put my finger where the nails were, and put my hand into his side, I will not believe it." ... Then [Jesus] said to Thomas, "Put your finger here; see my hands. Reach out your hand and put it into my side. ..." Thomas said to him, "My Lord and my God!" (John 20:25b, 27-28)

In our Bible study group last week, we were talking about Jesus' resurrection. One of the group members asked why Jesus' resurrected body wasn't perfect; why did he still have the scars? Certainly, if God could raise Jesus from the dead, he could have also erased the scars.

We discussed several possible reasons for Jesus' retaining the scars from his suffering and death. **1) Proof.** When persons saw Jesus in his resurrected body, the scars drained all of the skepticism out of the room. The scars left no doubt that this was the same Jesus who had been crucified. **2) Essence.** When John the Baptist, Christ's forerunner, first saw Jesus, he said, "Look, the Lamb of God, who takes away the sin of the world!" (John 1:29). Jesus' atoning work as the sacrifice for humanity's sin was the *sine qua non* of his life on earth, the essence of who he was. Because of Jesus' redemptive work, the scars are an essential part of his incarnate being. Jesus' scars make him *more* perfect, not less so. **3) Memorial symbol.** The final possible reason for Christ's persistent scars is perhaps the most intriguing of all. In Isaiah, God promises that he will never forget his children. Though a "mother [might] forget the baby at her breast," God will not forget his children (49:15). God must have anticipated their doubtful thoughts, so he offered a confirmation that he would remember them: "See, I have engraved you on the palms of my hands" (49:16). By Jesus keeping his scars, we are also engraved on his hands—a promise we will never be forgotten.

July 15

HUMANITY'S PLANS & GOD'S SOVEREIGNTY

But Joseph said to them, "Don't be afraid ... You intended to harm me, but God intended it for good to accomplish what is now being done, the saving of many lives." (Genesis 50:19-20)

Who would have thought the jealous actions of Joseph's brothers, who sold him off into slavery in Egypt, would somehow become part of God's master plan? Humans' evil schemes and activities are not beyond being used by God to bring about *his* results.

I was about eight years old when Dad told me an amazing yet awful story. Five young men had gone to share the good news of Jesus Christ with a dangerous group of Indians in the hinterlands of Ecuador. All five men were killed, leaving behind stunned, grieving wives and children. I don't remember many of the details of Dad's recounting of this now famous story of the Auca Indians (today called the Waodani). However, I do still remember how moved my father was that these brave young men had given the ultimate sacrifice of their lives in an effort to share the good news of Jesus.

Many mission agencies expected this tragedy would be a setback to the foreign missionary effort. However, just the opposite was the case. In the year following this deadly incident, mission agencies were astounded by thousands of persons who volunteered for missionary service. A wife and a sister of two of the men killed were subsequently able to bring the message of Christ to the very Indians who had killed their loved ones. The gospel pathway had been paved by the lives of those martyred.

God is not surprised or defeated by evil or the disobedience of humans. Nor is he overwhelmed by natural disasters, atom bombs or acts of genocide. When situations seem dismal, and evil and suffering seem to be winning, remember that God is ultimately sovereign. God can take what humans meant for bad and use it for good to accomplish *his* purposes for *his* glory.

SET UP TO FALL

Pride goes before destruction, / a haughty spirit before a fall. / Better to be lowly in spirit and among the oppressed. (Proverbs 16:18-19a)

Logic tells us that placing ourselves on a lofty pedestal will increase our chance of a painful fall. On the other hand, presenting ourselves in a lowly position is more likely to result in being raised up a notch. Although this is common sense, we seldom follow this path of logic.

No individual or group (not even doctors) has a corner on pride. I'm not proud of it, but I can't help pointing out that self-importance is certainly one of the things we doctors excel at. Almost all doctors, for instance, defy statistics by believing we provide better quality care than the "average" physician does—apparently, there are no average doctors.

As a resident physician in training, I remember trying to impress my mentoring physician with my skills at delivering babies. One notable delivery was going quite well until we got to the cutting of the umbilical cord. The umbilical cord is somewhat like a slippery garden hose, with a great deal of pressure inside looking for a way to express itself. As I cut the cord, it slipped from my novice fingers and flailed around like a snake with epilepsy, spraying blood all over my esteemed mentor. The blood even hit a spot on the ceiling, which the nurses later told me was the most impressive thing they remembered. "A haughty spirit [goes] before a fall," and the landing from that fall was quite painful.

True humility is not self-deprecation, however, but an objective understanding of who we are before God. This understanding includes both our strengths and weaknesses. When we see ourselves as God sees us, with all our weaknesses and failures, it's hard to remain pompous. When we realize that anything good we have is a gift from God and not something we've created or earned, it's easier to be humble.

EXPERIENCING GOD'S TRUTH

And my God will meet all your needs according to his glorious riches in Christ Jesus. (Philippians 4:19)

I may give mental agreement to words on a page, but they don't have full meaning until I've experienced them in my life. We were doing mission work in rural Zambia when I had such an experience, and "God as my provider" were words that took on life. My wife, Doreen, was pregnant with our fourth daughter and developed a blood clot in her thigh. Clots can be very dangerous since they can break off, travel to the lungs and cause a life-threatening situation for both the mother and the baby. The treatment needed was IV heparin, a blood thinner. Unfortunately, this was not a medicine stocked in Zambian hospitals.

Phil, one of our fellow missionaries, remembered that he'd brought over heparin some years back when his wife had surgery and thought he still had a few vials "squirreled away" somewhere. To deliver IV heparin, however, we needed an infusion pump, which we didn't have. But then Les, another missionary friend, remembered that some visitors from the U.S. had just brought over some used medical equipment, and he thought he had seen an infusion pump among the items. We immediately started treatment and scrambled to get additional heparin from the neighboring country of Zimbabwe that arrived just hours before our first few vials ran out. My wife went on to recover and eventually delivered our fourth daughter safely, without any lasting effects from her blood clot.

"God will meet all [our] needs." We had now experienced the truth of these words in our lives. Christian author Henry Blackaby distinguishes between knowing *about* God and knowing *God* when the knowledge becomes personal and intimate. It is one thing to have head knowledge that God is our provider, but it is something very different, deeply significant, and life-changing to experience it.

UNIQUE OPPORTUNITIES

[Jesus] said to Simon, "Put out into deep water, and let down the nets for a catch." Simon answered, "Master, we've worked hard all night and haven't caught anything. But because you say so, I will let down the nets." When they had done so, they caught such a large number of fish that their nets began to break. (Luke 5:4-6)

Doesn't it seem that God often asks us to do something when we're all tired out? When our muscles are fatigued and our backpacks of stress are full is precisely when God asks us to hike up the mountain. Couldn't he have a better sense of timing?

I slowly handed my daughter the key. "Whatever you do," I warned her, "don't lose that key!" The next day my wife told me Charis had lost the key. "Don't be too hard on her," my wife cautioned. "She feels bad enough already." Her words came just in time to prevent my "I-told-you-so" response from pummeling my poor daughter like a toy boat caught under the Niagara Falls. My wife reminded me that our heavenly Father had extended mercy to us and we (meaning I) needed to model that same merciful attitude. With a changed perspective, I talked with my daughter, and we shed a few tears together—it was a precious moment I had almost missed.

When we're dead tired, angry as a cat thrown in the water, or stressed to the point of breaking down, how do we respond to a situation that tests us? In those moments when it is most difficult to respond appropriately, there is ironically the greatest potential for benefits if we do. Peter was tired, discouraged and probably defensive about a carpenter telling him how to fish. But although he whined a bit, he ultimately listened to Jesus. I was angry with my daughter and "justifiably" upset. However, through a few wise, Spirit-inspired words from my wife, God changed my attitude. In both cases, a "miracle" happened. We need to remember that when we feel most justified in having a disobedient, angry or ungodly response, we may have a unique opportunity for something really great to happen with an *unexpected,* Christ-like response.

July 19

TRANSITION FROM OLD TO NEW

Remember the law of my servant Moses, the decrees and laws I gave him at Horeb for all Israel. See, I will send you the prophet Elijah before that great and dreadful day of the LORD comes. (Malachi 4:4-5)

Malachi is the last book of the Old Testament (OT). The author, bearing the same name as his book, is believed to be the last OT prophet. When his words ended, the 400 "silent" years of the intertestamental period began. The silent era ended with the "sound" of Christ's birth in the New Testament (NT) gospels.

The transitional position of Malachi, as well as the content of the book, spurs us to look both backward and forward. This is a healthy practice, for as we look in both directions, we gain a perspective to see more clearly where we are presently. First, Malachi looks backward and summarizes the OT by reminding us of the Law (Moses) and the Prophets (Elijah). He also looks forward, however, for the coming of the messenger of God, a *new* Elijah, whom Jesus reveals to be John the Baptist (Matthew 11:12-14). With these prophetic words, Malachi provides an anticipation of the Messiah, who is the fulfillment of so many OT promises and the subject matter of so much of the NT, thus linking the Old and New Testaments.

Reflecting on Malachi's transitional function for the testaments, German scholar Nagelsbach in Herzog's *Cyclopedia* says, "Malachi is like a late evening, which brings a long day to a close; but he is also the morning dawn, which bears a glorious day in its womb."

"UNANSWERED" PRAYER

These were all commended for their faith, yet none of them received what had been promised. God had planned something better ... (Hebrews 11:39-40)

Twenty-six years ago today I stood gazing at my newborn daughter—all one pound and fourteen ounces of her. She and her identical twin sister had been born prematurely. She had a tube in her trachea to help her breathe, one in her stomach to drip in feedings and an intravenous line in a scalp vein through which she was receiving antibiotics.

As I watched my tiny daughters struggle for life, I couldn't help but wonder why God had not answered our prayers. Why were my wife and newborn daughters having all these problems? When Doreen had starting having troubles with her pregnancy, we even had a special prayer and anointing service for her—and now this.

Luke 1 tells an interesting story of another "unanswered" prayer. Zechariah was an old man when an angel of the Lord came to him telling him his prayer had been heard, and his wife would bear him a son. Zechariah must have been initially puzzled. It had been so long since he'd prayed for a child that he must have long since considered that prayer "unanswered." Yet God had not forgotten his request and decided to answer it in an unanticipated way and time. God's answer went beyond the faith and even imagination of Zechariah. Bible teacher Ed Miller says God has a habit of doing this and calls it "God's over-answering our prayers."

Those twin daughters I was so worried about—one is now a high school teacher taking seminary courses part-time, and the other one is finishing medical school. The next time it seems that God has not answered your prayers, or that he's given the wrong answers, keep in mind he may be over-answering your prayers because he has "planned something better."

SPIRITUAL BATTLES

For our struggle is not against flesh and blood, but against the rulers, against the authorities, against the powers of this dark world and against the spiritual forces of evil in the heavenly realms. (Ephesians 6:12)

I remember when my family and friends were going through a flurry of difficulties. There were issues at work and at church, financial problems, interpersonal difficulties and health maladies. These troubles curtailed our feeding the poor and sharing the gospel message because we were busy trying just to keep our heads above water. Anne Lamott described a difficult situation as being like "trying to put an octopus to bed." That's what we were doing too—we pushed one tentacle under the covers, and another one invariably popped out.

At some point we became aware of the same reality that the apostle Paul pointed out to the church at Ephesus: "our struggle is not against flesh and blood, but ... against the spiritual forces of evil." Instead of focusing on this or that tentacle, we needed to focus on the creature beneath the sheets that controlled the tentacles.

It is very important to know with whom we are struggling. Paul says we cannot wage spiritual battles with worldly weapons (II Corinthians 10:4). In spiritual battles, pistols and spears are worthless while prayer and Scripture are essential. The devil is unfazed by guns and grenades, but speaking the name of Jesus and claiming the cross of Christ can take out entire demonic brigades.

Many in our Western culture (including Christians) are hesitant to believe in invisible spiritual forces of evil. Perhaps that is why we continue to struggle, trying to push one tentacle after another back in under the sheets.

FALLING ASLEEP

Brothers, we do not want you to be ignorant about those who fall asleep, or to grieve like the rest of men, who have no hope. (I Thessalonians 4:13)

It was a plastic bag filled with ashes, similar in size to a bag of flour. It contained the mortal remains of my brother-in-law Dan. How could the life of this gentle Irishman, who could weld, plumb, do electrical work and spin a yarn with the best of them, be reduced to this gray, powdery residue? Paul addressed the issue of death in his letter to the Thessalonians.

First, Paul said we should not be ignorant. Those who have "fallen asleep in him [Christ]" (4:14) will be raised to eternal life. In this passage, "fallen asleep" needs to be understood as more than a euphemism for death. It is a descriptive metaphor that conveys truth—our lives don't end at death.

Secondly, we are not to grieve like others. This doesn't mean we should keep a stiff upper lip or that we shouldn't cry or even wail. There is a sadness and grief that is appropriate with the loss of one we love, but it is a sadness tempered by hope.

Finally, we have a hope that lies in Jesus himself. Jesus died; he's been there and done that. More importantly, however, Jesus rose again. He conquered death. It is precisely because of his victory over death that we have hope. Our separation from our loved ones is only temporary, and we look forward to an eternal reunion with them in heaven.

Yes, Dan's mortal remains are ashes, but a plastic bag cannot contain his immortal essence. Dan's real life was not reduced to ashes but released to God.

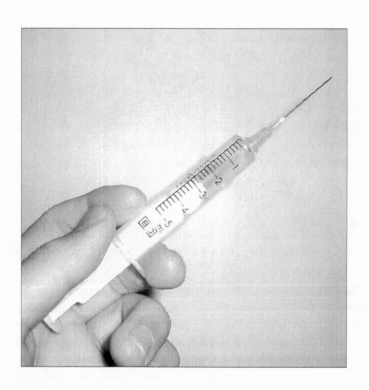

THEN FOLLOW ME

Now a man came up to Jesus and asked, "Teacher, what good thing must I do to get eternal life?" … Jesus answered, "… go, sell your possessions and give to the poor, and you will have treasure in heaven. Then come, follow me." When the young man heard this, he went away sad, because he had great wealth. (Matthew 19:16, 21-22)

It's been said that although salvation is a free gift, that doesn't mean there is no cost. Indeed, "counting the cost" is part of making an informed decision to become a Christian. Yet I can't help but believe that often the cost-to-benefit analysis, when applied to making a decision for Christ, is poorly understood.

One day while I was working at a medical mission hospital in rural Honduras, a man who had passed out came in complaining of chest pain. Our ultrasound machine revealed his problem. He had a huge pericardial effusion. The sack around his heart was filled with fluid and was literally crushing his heart. He needed an emergency procedure called a pericardiocentesis, in which a large bore needle is inserted through the chest wall, directly into the sack around the heart to draw off the offending fluid. I explained the risks and benefits of the procedure to the patient and his family. To my dismay, they refused the procedure; the patient died six hours later. I was very frustrated with their decision, but they couldn't seem to get past the idea of sticking a very large needle into his chest despite the fact that the seemingly dangerous procedure could have saved his life.

In the same way, the rich young man couldn't get beyond the idea of giving up his great wealth. He thought there had to be another way, yet Jesus made it a prerequisite for following him. Most of us have something we find difficult to give up so that we can walk with Christ. It's for that very reason he asks us to relinquish it; there can be nothing between God and us. The rich young man "went away sad." May the same not be said of us.

GOD IS A PACKAGE DEAL

Where can I go from your Spirit? / Where can I flee from your presence? / If I go up to the heavens, you are there; / if I make my bed in the depths, you are there. / If I rise on the wings of the dawn, / if I settle on the far side of the sea, / even there your right hand will guide me, / your right hand will hold me fast. (Psalm 139:7-10)

This is a beautiful psalm of David reassuring us of God's presence wherever we go. God's "hand" of protective guidance is always present. However, there is a passage in Amos that creates an ominous echo to this soothing psalm. Amos also says no one can escape God, though they dig to the depths of the grave or climb to the heavens. They may try to hide at the bottom of the sea or on the highest mountaintop, but God's eyes will see them, and in this case, his hand of judgment will find them (9:2-4). So which is it, God's loving hand of protection or his righteous hand of judgment? Although we may prefer one hand over the other, the unavoidable truth is that both hands belong to God. He is a package deal.

As I was once discussing the nature of God with a nonbeliever, he said, "If that's the kind of God you believe in, I don't want any part of him"—as if we could choose what God is like. God is who he is completely apart from what we might imagine or hope him to be, and he has revealed himself to be both righteous and loving.

There is more to the story, however. God sent Jesus, who took our judgment on himself. The two attributes of God that seemed irreconcilable (his absolute justice and his infinite love) are reconciled by the sacrifice of Christ on the cross. Though we may fear God's righteous hand, because of the cross, it is his hand of love that finds us in our hiding place and gently holds us to his chest.

THE WIPER OF TEARS

"And God will wipe away every tear from their eyes." (Revelation 7:17b)

This has been a difficult year for my mother's side of our family. A teenager was killed in a car accident, a middle-aged wife and mother took her own life and an elderly patriarch died after struggling with Alzheimer's disease. We've seen intense grief grip hearts, numb minds and gel bodies. The age-old questions of suffering and death, thought to have been previously dealt with, have inevitably returned—like a baseball thrown with all one's might toward the heavens. The questions often originate more from our hearts than our minds. Does God really care? Doesn't he notice my world collapsing around me like a sand castle in the waves?

While God only sometimes delivers us *from* hard times, often he delivers us *through* them. In other words, we may not be spared the troubles, suffering and pain, but God is there with us through it all. In Acts 7, we read the story of the stoning of Stephen, the first Christian martyr. God did not spare Stephen a painful execution, but neither did God abandon him. As Stephen looked toward heaven, he saw "the glory of God, and Jesus standing at the right hand of God" (7:55). Eleven of the twelve disciples, even though they were Jesus' closest friends, met a violent end. They were not spared suffering and death, yet we are comforted in the knowledge that Jesus was with them in their last hours, just as he was with Stephen.

During times of pain and suffering, God has not abandoned us. When a child falls and skins her knee, she runs crying to her mother for help. The child is comforted with a hug and a bandage. Similarly, when we are hurting, we can run to God; he is our loving Father. In this world we will experience pain and suffering, but God wants to hold us in his arms and care for our wounds, and one day he will "wipe away every tear."

MISSION FULFILLED

And Moses the servant of the LORD died there in Moab ...
(Deuteronomy 34:5)

The life of Moses is an amazing story. Moses bravely confronted Pharaoh, king of Egypt, demanding the release of the enslaved Israelites. After their release, Moses led the children of Israel on a forty-year journey through the wilderness. Moses put up with the Israelites' continual grumblings, and he provided for their welfare for forty long years. Yet when they finally arrived at the threshold to the Promised Land, "the land flowing with milk and honey" (Exodus 33:3), the object of their desire for all those years, God told Moses he could not enter the land because of his itsy-bitsy disobedience in the Desert of Zin (Numbers 20:8-12).

God seemed unfair in his judgment with Moses. My wiser and more equitable plan would have allowed Moses to lead the Israelites into the Promised Land. What harm could have come from that? But God's ultimate purpose was to call a people to himself. If Moses had continued to lead, perhaps the people would have begun to see *him* as their deliverer and not God (*Yahweh*). By using different leaders, it was clear they were just instruments, and God himself was the true deliverer. In addition, by showing the consequences of Moses' disobedience, God sent a clear message on his opinion regarding sin.

Although God did not allow Moses to enter the Promised Land, he did let him view it with his own eyes (Deuteronomy 34:4). While Moses must have been disappointed at not being able to enter the Promised Land, he must also have felt a deep sense of accomplishment and privilege. God had spoken with Moses "face to face" (34:10) and entrusted him with the Ten Commandments. God's special love for Moses was demonstrated as God buried him with his own hands (34:5-6). The last moments of Moses' life were in intimate communion with his God. ... The children of Israel, stunned at the loss of Moses, were reminded that God was their true deliverer. Okay, so maybe God's plan was a little better than mine.

SELF-CENTERED EXEGESIS

All Scripture is God-breathed and is useful for teaching, rebuking, correcting and training in righteousness ... (II Timothy 3:16)

A woman was defending her doctoral thesis, and she had just finished her presentation based on the Reader Response Theory. Her basic tenet was that the truth of Scripture is not dependent on the purpose of the writers but is only dependent on whatever it means to the reader. One of those critiquing her presentation tried to synopsize what she had been saying. "No, no," she said. "That's not what I meant," and she again explained her thesis. The critic again wrongly interpreted her intent, causing her no small degree of exasperation. Finally, the critic explained, "Well, that may not have been what you meant when you wrote it, but that's what it means to me, the reader."

A big problem with the Reader Response Theory of biblical interpretation is that authority for truth has been usurped from the text and author and given to the reader. When we interpret Scripture subjectively, we get it to say what we want it to say. Not surprisingly, we then have a docile God created in our own image, with scriptural instructions that fail to challenge the way we live. When the readers' ideas have authority over the text and the purpose of the writers, the Bible can then have different meanings for each person, with a God who looks very different to each of them, and there is no basis for discernment among them.

Instead, however, if we can agree that the original meaning of the text, in the language, culture and time from which it came, is the focus for the meaning of the passage today, we can have an objective basis for interpretation (exegesis). As biblical scholars Gordon Fee and Douglas Stuart stated in *How to Read the Bible for All Its Worth*, "A text cannot mean [today] what it never meant [when it was first written]." The text itself, the author's intent, and God all exist and are what they are, completely independent from the reader's understanding of them. It is important to remember that we, the readers, are not the center of the exegetical universe.

NATURAL GLORY

And [the angels] were calling to one another: "Holy, holy, holy is the LORD Almighty; / the whole earth is full of his glory." (Isaiah 6:3)

When I first saw Victoria Falls, one of the seven natural wonders of the world, I was in awe. The falls stretch a mile wide along the border between Zambia and Zimbabwe. A sheer 355-foot drop-off creates a drenching mist with a multitude of intensely colored rainbows. As I gazed, dumbstruck by the beauty and grandeur, I realized this was more than a physical reality—it was a spiritual experience.

Nature is sacred, created by God and used by him as one means to reveal his glory. When we gaze into a starry night sky, admire a beautiful sunset, startle at a crash of thunder or sniff a blooming rose, we are encountering the Creator and his majesty as he reveals a portion of himself to us.

When God became flesh in Jesus, the ultimate revelation, the apostle John said, "We have seen his glory" (John 1:14). Some people, however, did not see God's glory in Jesus; they saw only a carpenter. Similarly, some people today see only a flower, a star in the sky or a waterfall. For them, God remains veiled and silent. They have eyes but do not see and ears but do not hear (Mark 8:18). All of nature, however, continues to proclaim the glory of God. The skies proclaim the work of his hands (Psalm 19:1); the mountains and hills burst into song (Isaiah 55:12). Look, and listen ...

SPIRITUAL RISK TAKING

"For if you remain silent at this time, relief and deliverance for the Jews will arise from another place, but you ... will perish. And who knows but that you have come to royal position for such a time as this?" Then Esther sent this reply to Mordecai: "... I will go to the king, even though it is against the law. And if I perish, I perish." (Esther 4:14-16)

Whether in the stock market, table games, or our jobs, we all engage in a certain amount of risk taking. If a situation becomes too risky, however, we become uncomfortable. Nonetheless, God seems to have a habit of calling persons out of their comfort zones. Noah was called to build an ark, Abraham was called to leave his homeland and Esther was called to put her life in jeopardy (not the game show).

Esther had beauty, prestige and wealth—why risk all that? Mordecai's response demonstrated great wisdom. First of all, he acknowledged Esther's free choice in tandem with God's sovereignty. "If you remain silent ... deliverance for the Jews will arise from another place." In other words, Mordecai told Esther she didn't *have* to do this thing; but if she passed up the chance, God would probably get someone else to do it. He also pointed out that her current position might not be by chance or personal effort but by divine design.

Esther saw the godly wisdom in Mordecai's words and boldly stepped out of her comfort zone. She seized the opportunity God presented her, although uncertain of the outcome: "If I perish, I perish."

Pastor and author David Mains says that to become part of the plans God has for us, we need to become "spiritual risk takers. We have to break out of our comfort zones. We need to dare to dream." In big and small things, we need to be ready to step out in courageous faith. For who knows but that we have come to our position for such a time as this?

THE SALT OF THE EARTH

... Zacchaeus; he was a chief tax collector and was wealthy. ... [Jesus] said to him, "Zacchaeus, come down immediately. I must stay at your house today." So [Zacchaeus] came down at once and welcomed him gladly. All the people saw this and began to mutter, "He has gone to be the guest of a 'sinner.'" (Luke 19:2, 5-7)

Have you ever been accused of spending too much time with nonbelievers? If not, why not? While it's true that Christian fellowship is important, it's also obvious that the Great Commission cannot be fulfilled in a Christian environment.

If we have no non-Christian friends or contacts, our opportunities to share the good news about Jesus vacillate somewhere between zero and none. On the other end of the spectrum are those of us who have a lot of non-Christian friends, yet we blend in so well with them that they aren't even aware we have any faith beliefs.

For those of us living in Christian ghettoes, we need to start interacting with and befriending non-Christians. As Rebecca Pippert says, we need to get "out of the saltshaker and into the world." On the other hand, those of us who blend in too well with the secular world need to get out of our "chameleon mode" and let our true colors show.

Several years ago a young woman came into my office with an unplanned pregnancy. She proudly wore several tattoos and a black leather jacket. She glibly spoke about her planned abortion. She didn't go to any church and said she was an agnostic. Somewhat tentatively I asked if I could pray with her. Before the short prayer was half over, she was sobbing in tears.

Sharing God's love with those around us can serve as an entryway for God's Spirit to touch their hearts and lives. Christ's example calls us to love and befriend the Zacchaeuses around us.

A HOLISTIC APPEAL

Praise the LORD, O my soul; / all my inmost being, praise his holy name.
(Psalm 103:1)

Like commercial breaks during the Super Bowl games that allow time for bathroom duties and preparing snacks, I once viewed the psalms as an interesting poetic interlude to the truly important substance of the rest of Scripture. I have learned, however, that my comparison of the psalms to TV commercials was in error.

Learning theology with our minds alone gives us knowledge in a vacuum, knowledge awaiting meaning in the framework of the rest of our lives. The poetic imagery of the psalms, however, gives us theology in the context of life and emotions, saturated with significance. The psalms express emotions that are real and often raw—anger, fear, shame, anxiety, joy and celebration. In the psalms, we are presented with not just words but also pictures (verbal vignettes) that resonate with our souls. The Hebrew word for soul, *nephesh*, refers to our entire being. Old Testament scholar Tremper Longman III asserts that the psalms "inform our theology, stimulate our imagination, arouse our emotions and appeal to our wills." The psalms, written in widely variable circumstances and moods, provide revelations not only about God but also about us. Poetic ruminations rooted in the context of life can help us see what is often hidden, hear what is frequently muffled, and voice what is typically muted.

The historical narratives, the practical proverbs and the theological epistles remain important. However, the poetic psalms, with their potential for holistic appeal, call for a total response, which I believe resonates with the very heart of God.

August

HIS WAYS

"For my thoughts are not your thoughts, / neither are your ways my ways," de-clares the LORD. / "As the heavens are higher than the earth, / so are my ways higher than your ways and my thoughts than your thoughts." (Isaiah 55:8-9)

In the abstract it's very easy to acknowledge that God's "thoughts and ways" are superior to mine. In practical everyday life, however, I usually find myself trusting my own ways above all others.

When we first went to do mission work on the Mosquito Coast of Honduras, Dr. Rudy tried to warn us about some of the unique problems encountered when practicing medicine among this indigenous Indian group. One of the commonly held local beliefs he described was the "tube in any orifice causes death" theory. Sick patients sometimes needed a tube in an orifice—a stomach tube, a rectal tube, a bladder tube, a breathing tube, a tube in the chest wall to drain pus from the lung cavity, etc. It's understandable that people came to fear these tubes, since patients sick enough to need one would sometimes end up dying—though the tube was not the cause of the serious illness but its result.

My first experience with this problem was when a four-month-old baby was brought in with a severe case of bronchiolitis. His oxygen level was dangerously low, so I carefully taped an oxygen tube into his nose. When I returned to check on him a short time later, the oxygen tube and the tape were completely off the baby and now aerating the room with our precious and limited supply of oxygen. When questioned, the mother was completely oblivious as to how this could have happened, even though she had been holding him the entire time. The "tube in any orifice causes death" theory had struck again! In spite of my explanations, the mother had reverted to her own fears and understandings and had pulled the tube out as soon as I left the room.

We are often like this mother. Our knowledge seems superior to God's, so we let it direct our actions. We wisely loosen the tape and pull away the offending tube, unaware that our spiritual lungs are gasping for oxygen. It's difficult for us to really believe that his thoughts and ways are higher than ours.

FIGHT THE GOOD FIGHT

I have fought the good fight, I have finished the race, I have kept the faith. Now there is in store for me the crown of righteousness, which the Lord, the righteous Judge, will award to me on that day. (II Timothy 4:7-8a)

Our local church body recently lost one of our eldest members. Charles Neff was eighty-nine years old when he was called to his final home after a five-month struggle with leukemia. Charles was one of those rare individuals who related well to persons of all ages. His wisdom, humor and ardent love for his Lord were an engaging combination. His life, like the wake of a great ship, touched the lives of hundreds of people in a positive way. The ripples his life set in motion will continue to touch many more persons long after he is gone.

However, I don't want to eulogize his life apart from his faith—nor would he have wanted that. For me, his life was a living witness to the fact that "fighting the good fight" and "finishing the race" are not lofty, unattainable ideals. Christ's enabling power within us makes holy living a potential reality. When we face death (and we all will), we need not say, "I should have done more." Instead, we can join Charles and the apostle Paul and say, "I have fought the good fight, I have finished the race, I have kept the faith."

In the few months before Charles' death, one of the books he read was Randy Alcorn's *Heaven*. In the book, Alcorn talks about the possibility our resurrected bodies will "shine." In Matthew we read: "Then the righteous will shine like the sun in the kingdom of their Father" (13:43). A conversation Charles had several days before his death indicated he must have agreed with this "shining" idea. A visitor at Charles' hospital bed said that he would be looking forward to seeing Charles in heaven. Charles, his wit and humor still intact, replied, "I'll meet you at the Eastern Gate, and be sure to wear your sunglasses."

A LIVING SACRIFICE

Therefore, I urge you, brothers, in view of God's mercy, to offer your bodies as living sacrifices, holy and pleasing to God—this is your spiritual act of worship. (Romans 12:1)

I was always told that whenever you see a "therefore" in Scripture, you should determine what it is *there for*. In this passage, the "therefore" seems to emphasize our offering should be in response to God's mercy already demonstrated to us. That mercy is clearly detailed in the first eleven chapters of Romans prior to the above verse. In these chapters we see how Christians, through no merit of their own, are made righteous, made holy and made heirs to their heavenly Father—amazing! Yet we do not serve God to earn his blessings. Rather, because he has already blessed us, we respond by offering him all that we are on the sacrificial altar.

The Jews were well acquainted with the practice of animal sacrifice. The killing of an animal and shedding of its blood was an essential part of Old Testament worship. Now that Jesus' atoning blood has fulfilled the Old Testament model, however, Christians can be offered as "living sacrifices"; we don't have to die physically. It's been pointed out, however, that the problem with putting living sacrifices on the altar is that we keep trying to crawl off again. One day we tell God, "Yes, Lord, I'm all yours." But the next day we say, "I didn't mean *that* part, God. Come on, give me a break."

When we think of giving God offerings, I suspect we tend to think of our money, our talents, our good deeds, and perhaps our time. While those are all good things, Paul says we are to give *ourselves*. Knowing ourselves as we do, it's hard to understand why God would want us. God, however, looks at us and sees what we will be with Christ in us. As a result, God wants us more than anything else! Because of his great love for us and his desire to be in relationship with us, he delights when we give ourselves to him. Paul describes this offering: "holy and pleasing to God" and our "spiritual act of worship."

TESTS, TRIALS, AND TEMPTATIONS

When Jesus looked up and saw a great crowd coming toward him, he said to Philip, "Where shall we buy bread for these people to eat?" He asked this only to test him, for he already had in mind what he was going to do. (John 6:5-6)

Wouldn't our Christian lives be better off and perhaps even flourish if we didn't have to have tests, trials and temptations? Yet James tells us that we should not just endure trials, but we should, "consider it pure joy" when we meet various trials (1:2). He reminds us that trials produce perseverance. Scottish author and pastor George MacDonald sagely noted, "For man to rise above temptation, it is necessary that he be tempted." While one can hardly argue against the truth of this statement, few would argue for it to be implemented for them.

The example of Scripture is certainly full of stories with stressful trials, seductive temptations and severe tests. Satan tempted Jesus himself, so why should we expect immunity from temptation? Not all the stories, however, show God's people responding to testing and temptation in godly ways. The children of Israel were tested in the wilderness for forty years. Their faithless grumblings might seem humorous if they didn't sound so much like us. While Joseph resisted the propositions of Potiphar's wife, David succumbed to the beauty of Bathsheba.

James tells us that God does not *tempt* us (1:13), but he does *test* us—what's the difference? When a teacher gives us a test, it is with the hope that we will *pass*, whereas when a co-worker tempts us to cheat on our time cards, it is with the hope that we will *fail*. The former is testing us; the latter is tempting us. God tests us for our good, to demonstrate and develop godliness. The devil tempts us to bring us down and to smear our Christian witness.

Bible teacher Ed Miller says that testing in its simplest form is an opportunity to trust Jesus. As we respond with trust, God produces greater holiness in our lives. Our testimony of God's sufficient grace will bring honor to God and encouragement to others who are going through similar circumstances. It is by God's design that our daily tests, trials and temptations are opportunities to trust Jesus and to witness to his all-sufficient grace.

THE BELOVED BRIDE

Husbands, love your wives, just as Christ loved the church and gave himself up for her ... to present her to himself as a radiant church, without stain or wrinkle or any other blemish, but holy and blameless. (Ephesians 5:25, 27)

The Bible has numerous metaphors for the church, such as "the body of Christ" (I Corinthians 12:12-31), the family of God (Galatians 3:26-29) and "a holy temple" (Ephesians 2:21-22). The metaphor I find most intriguing, however, is the image of the church as the bride of Christ (Revelation 21:2). The church depicted as a beautiful, pure bride seems like a can of Spam labeled "filet mignon"; it's false advertising on steroids. The church I know, and am a typical member of, is self-righteous, hypocritical, apathetic and egocentric. We are confused about our purpose and content in our pride. Doesn't God know Christ's bride is an imposter and a harlot? Shouldn't someone tell him there's a vermin under the veil?

Yet God, in his omniscience, says the church is "chosen," "holy" and "royal" (I Peter 2:9). As the bride of Christ, we are "radiant," "blameless" (Ephesians 5:27) and beautiful (Revelation 21:2). In Ephesians 5:1-20, Paul explains the key to understanding this paradox of the holy harlot. God did not love us and choose us because we are holy and blameless; we are holy and blameless because God loved us and chose us. The church, despite its many flaws, has been God's object of affection and blessing for two thousand years. The church has survived persecution, criticism and neglect, and it *will* persevere.

In Genesis 1:2, at the dawn of time, Scripture says, "The Spirit of God was hovering over the waters." If we fast forward to the very end of time in Revelation 22, the Spirit of God is still present but has been joined by the church, the bride of Christ. Together, "The Spirit *and* the bride say, 'Come!'" (22:17, italics mine). Here we see the purpose of all history and the theme of all Scripture; the triune God will secure for himself a people, his bride. This is the mysterious, wonderful and eternal destiny of the church—we are the beloved bride of Christ!

DIVERSIONARY TACTICS

Put on the full armor of God so that you can take your stand against the
devil's schemes. For our struggle is not against flesh and blood ...
(Ephesians 6:11-12)

Some years ago my church seemed engulfed by the tyranny of the trivial.
For several years, it seemed our time and energy were consumed by issues
with pastoral transition, a building program, denominational affiliation,
leadership structure, and defining who we were and where we were going
(nowhere it seemed). While all these things needed to be addressed, they
distracted us from the weightier work of the church—worship, fellowship, missions and discipleship.

Frank Tillapaugh, in *Unleashing the Church*, recounts a former
veteran's story from his time in military service. He noted that the front-
line troops, who were directly engaged in battle with the enemy, seldom
complained about their food or supplies. However, one or two miles back,
the rear guard tended to complain about everything, from the quality of
their food and their commanding officers to the inclement weather.

There is a similarity for us as Christians. When we're on the front
lines, actively involved in outreach, discipleship or worship ministries,
other issues seem insignificant. When we stay in the rear guard too long,
however, we become spiritual nitpickers. We're so consumed with minor
issues that we are distracted from the real battle and unable to engage the
enemy. Being bogged down in the rear guard can be one of the "devil's
schemes," a diversionary tactic to keep us off the front lines. We need to
remember, "Our struggle is not against flesh and blood," and move to the
front lines to take our stand.

THE WHOLE PICTURE

Now Sarai, Abram's wife, had borne him no children. ... so she said to Abram, "... Go, sleep with my maidservant ..." He slept with Hagar, and she conceived. (Genesis 16:1, 2, 4a)

God had promised Abram that his descendants would be counted "like the stars." And while Abram wanted to believe God, there was one annoying detail—the stark and visible reality that his wife was barren. In view of the discrepancy between what Abram saw and what God had promised him, Abram decided to go with plan B. This involved taking action to help God's plan come to fruition; he slept with his wife's maidservant. The problem, of course, was that what Abram thought was a clear picture of his situation was really only one corner of the canvas. And as is so often the case when we take things into our own hands, he caused more harm than good.

Last year an elderly, demented gentleman came in to my office for a yearly check-up. I wanted to listen to his lungs, but his thick undershirt made it difficult. I tried to pull the undershirt out of his pants, but it just kept coming and coming. Suddenly, it seemed stuck, and I could pull it no further. His wife was watching me struggle and got out of her chair to try to help me by pulling on the other side of his undershirt. We made a little more progress, but once again it seemed immovable. Finally, we had him stand up and unbuckled his pants; pulling them down, we discovered the problem. His undershirt was a one-piece bodysuit snapped together between his legs. Our ardent, well-intentioned tugging had done nothing more than to give him what must have been a very uncomfortable "wedgie." Embarrassed, I looked over at his wife. A smile spread across her face like butter over bread, and we both shared the humor of an awkward situation as we corrected our error.

With undershirts, as with Abram and God's promises, we often don't see the whole picture. Rather than presumptuously forging ahead, causing more damage than benefit, we should wait on God to reveal the next step.

IN BUT NOT OF THE WORLD

Do not love the world or anything in the world. If anyone loves the world, the love of the Father is not in him. For everything in the world—the cravings of sinful man, the lust of his eyes and the boasting of what he has and does— comes not from the Father but from the world. (I John 2:15-16)

In the third and fourth centuries AD, a strange thing happened. Hundreds and then thousands of Christians began to leave the comforts and pleasures of life in the cities to devote their lives to God in the harsh conditions of the Egyptian desert. These radical Christian nonconformists became known as the "Desert Fathers." They escaped traditional societal life in their quest for a more holy, undefiled spiritual life. These ascetic hermits had seen how difficult it was to pursue God among the harried demands and temptations of everyday life. Their solution, which is not dissimilar to that of modern-day monks or the Amish, was to create an alternate Christian society separate from the entanglements of the world.

The remedy may seem extreme, but the stakes could not be higher. Our relationship with God should be the most important thing in our lives. Yet how do we expect to develop intimacy in that relationship when we dole out such small investments of time? The busy multitasking lifestyle of the twenty-first century may be seductive and compelling, but it is not conducive to spiritual growth—and we know it!

As Christians in a secular society, we should be swimming against the current of the world around us. We dare not forget that the values, priorities and lifestyles around us are not godly. If we want our relationship with God to grow, we must take time away from the world to focus solely on God. Let's commit to flee the pressures and influences of the world for at least 10-15 minutes each day in a place where we can be in silence, alone with God. If we can't do this, where does our true love really lie?

CALLING EVIL GOOD

Woe to those who call evil good / and good evil, / who put darkness for light / and light for darkness ... (Isaiah 5:20)

On January 22, 1973, the Supreme Court passed the *Roe v. Wade* decision. According to many persons, this went a long way toward liberating women. It gave pregnant women the legal right to choose whether or not to give birth or to have an abortion. This decision has been lauded for preventing millions of unwanted babies from being born into unloving environments. The law also supposedly demonstrates compassion for many women who find themselves in very difficult situations—not being ready emotionally or financially to take care of a new baby.

"Woe to those who call evil good." The debate about abortion has too often been framed in the language used above. The basic question is not one of choice, however, but whether or not an unborn baby is a human life. Consider the fact that virtually no one believes that the mother of a newborn baby has the right to "choose" if she wants to be a mother, and she can take the life of the baby if she decides to do so. If an unborn baby is also a human life, then logic would mandate that "choice" is not an option in this situation either. Therefore, the debate actually hinges on the question of whether an unborn baby (a fetus) is a human life.

Let's look at a one-day-old newborn baby. What is different about the baby now compared to twenty-four hours earlier? In both situations the baby is dependent on someone else for life. Location is really the primary difference (inside or outside the mother). A baby in her mother's uterus has no rights, and her life can be terminated on a whim. But once outside the mother, the baby suddenly becomes a sacred entity with rights and protection by law—the location confers humanity!

Approximately 1.2 million American women have abortions each year. At least nine thousand of these are at or beyond twenty-one weeks gestation (i.e., potentially viable). The overwhelming majority of abortions are chosen for reasons of convenience. The mother lacks financial resources or emotional support, or it's just bad timing. I believe we as Christians can do better to support these women so they won't feel the "choice" of abortion forced on them. Woe to those who call evil good, but also woe to us who do so little to prevent that evil.

A LOSS OF INNOCENCE

From everyone who has been given much, much will be demanded; and from
the one who has been entrusted with much, much more will be asked.
(Luke 12:48b)

Some years ago now, my wife and I went on a trip to the Dominican Republic with our church youth group. As a former missionary, I've always felt it's good for Americans to visit developing nations. Such an experience shows us how most of the rest of the world lives. It gives us a feel for being a minority and struggling with language and cultural differences. We also discover that survival is possible without a TV, microwave or air conditioning. The illusion that financial wealth is necessary to enjoy life is exposed as a bad case of false advertising. We are accustomed to feeling in control of our lives here in the US. When that safe feeling of control is lost, we learn from necessity to rely on God.

While all these lessons are good, with this trip I was impressed with a new thought: being exposed to poverty causes a loss of innocence. Each of us, when first confronted with the obvious disparity between *our* riches and *their* destitution, loses forever our simple, blissful naïveté.

When my daughter Rebekah was in college, she spent a semester abroad in Central America. When she returned, she struggled to sort out her feelings and thoughts about her experience in developing countries. With tears in her eyes, she told me how seeing severe poverty had impacted her. She explained, "What they said is true. I can never again say, 'I didn't know.'" One can't "un-see" the reality of those who suffer in need.

An anonymous quote enunciates the logical conclusion to our loss of innocence. "'It all seemed so wrong,' I said to myself. '*Somebody* ought to do something about this!' Then I realized that *I* am somebody." Maybe our one-week trip abroad gave us more than we bargained for. We have been entrusted with more, which means that more will be expected of us, and we cannot return to the ease of ignorance.

A COMPLETE LOVE

But if anyone obeys his word, God's love is truly made complete in him.
(1 John 2:5a)

I had good intentions of getting the dirty laundry done. My wife Doreen was gone for the evening, and she had asked me to help wash the dirty clothes. How was I to know that the Monday night football game would be so engrossing? The next thing I knew, I heard her driving into the garage, and the clothes were no closer to being clean than when she had left. Somehow my sincere words and good intentions fell short of being enough.

When I'm picking up trash on an inner-city mission trip, I like to quote James: "Faith without *works* is dead" (James 2:26, NASB, italics mine). However, most of the rest of the time, I prefer Paul: "For it is by grace you have been saved, through faith ... *not by works*" (Ephesians 2:8-9, italics mine).

The truth of the matter is that without both sides of the coin, we are dealing with counterfeit money. If I had done the laundry as promised, my words and intentions would have found completeness through my deeds. In the same way, John points out that we should not "love with words or tongue [alone] but with actions and in truth" (1 John 3:18). Otherwise, we're just practicing sloppy *agape*, and our love is incomplete.

For God's love in us to be complete, we need to express it by what we do (obedience) in our daily lives. Nineteenth-century pastor and author Charles Spurgeon said, "An unchanged life is the sign of an uncleansed heart." A cleansed heart produces a changed life and a desire to be obedient. This obedience demonstrates God's love coming to completion in us. Put more simply, I just should have washed the dirty laundry.

August 12

A TINCTURE OF TIME

As the rain and the snow come down from heaven, / and do not return to it without watering the earth / ... so is my word that goes out from my mouth: / It will not return to me empty, / but will accomplish what I desire ...
(Isaiah 55:10-11)

We Americans are very time conscious. We want instant gratification and instant results. Our cupboards reveal our culture: instant rice, instant oatmeal and instant pudding. Anything that takes very long is a waste of time. We stand, impatiently pacing in front of the microwave oven while waiting for the water to boil in our tea mugs. Physician and author Richard Swensen tells a story of a man who bought a microwave fireplace so he could spend a whole evening in front of the fireplace in just eight minutes. We live a fast-paced life.

It's no wonder our impatience spills over into our spiritual lives. If we share a testimony, teach a Sunday school lesson, or share a Bible verse, we expect immediate results. If nothing happens right away, we assume nothing will happen. God, speaking through the prophet Isaiah, gives us a caution and a promise.

The *caution* is that sometimes we won't see immediate results. Although rain immediately waters the earth, snow does not. One must wait for the warmth of spring to melt the snow before the water can moisten the earth. The *promise* is that God's word will not return void; it will ultimately accomplish God's purpose. So, while the waiting in winter may be difficult, the certainty of spring is a comfort.

BRING THEM TO JESUS

Some men came, bringing to [Jesus] a paralytic, carried by four of them. Since they could not get him to Jesus because of the crowd, they made an opening in the roof above Jesus and, after digging through it, lowered the mat the paralyzed man was lying on. (Mark 2:3-4)

Little is said about the paralytic's four friends, yet we can surmise several things. First, they must have cared deeply about their friend's plight to do so much for him. Not only did they feel compassion, but they were also willing to act on it. Obstacles, such as huge crowds and a doorway blocked with people, failed to thwart their mission. Digging through the roof and lowering their friend through the opening revealed their boldness and persistence. Finally, they must have had great faith, believing that Jesus would actually meet their friend's need.

When my mother was eighteen years old, she was drinking, smoking and running around with young people with similar interests. Evangelist George Brunk had revival tent meetings in the area, and my aunt and uncle invited Mom to go to the meetings with them. Mom laughed at them and told them that kind of thing wasn't for her. They came back a second night and asked her again, only to be rudely rebuffed. The third night they stopped by once more to ask if she'd consider going with them. Mom finally said she'd go with them just so they would leave her alone thereafter. To everyone's surprise, that week in July of 1952, my mother gave her life to the Lord.

My aunt and uncle were like the four friends of the paralytic—they brought someone they loved into the presence of Jesus. Do we care enough to act as they did? Are we bold and persistent, even when faced with obstacles? Do we have a faith that is confident Jesus can meet every need of those who come to him? We cannot heal those who are crippled, but we can *bring* them to someone who can.

AN ORIENTED REST

There remains, then, a Sabbath-rest for the people of God; for anyone who enters God's rest also rests from his own work, just as God did from his. (Hebrews 4:9-10)

It's Sunday afternoon, and I'm tired. I worked all day yesterday, and I taught the adult Sunday school class this morning—now I'm ready for some rest and relaxation. An after-dinner nap is always a popular option, or I could read a book, play a card game with my wife, or turn on the TV and let time ebb away unnoticed. Does God really care how I spend my free time? Does how I rest reveal anything about me?

While living in Zambia, we learned the importance of watching a mosquito at rest. If a mosquito's body is parallel to the surface it is resting on, it is a harmless mosquito species, and one can relax. However, if a mosquito's body is at an angle to the surface on which it rests, that angle indicates it is an *Anopheles* mosquito that could be carrying the dangerous malaria parasite. A mosquito's orientation at rest reveals its inner nature.

How are we oriented when we rest? What do our rest-time activities reveal about us? I normally just *take* my rest; I've worked hard, and I deserve it. But Jesus said, "Come to me ... and I will *give* you rest" (Matthew 11:28, italics mine). Jesus calls us to orient ourselves toward him, even during our times of rest. If we offer our rest time to God, he will give it back to us in the form best for us. "God, I have this afternoon free. How do you desire I spend this time?" Even mosquitos can teach us spiritual truths.

THE LAST RESORT

"Ask and it will be given to you ..." (Matthew 7:7)

It was the middle of the night, and I'd just delivered a healthy baby girl. It should have been a time of rejoicing, but the mother was bleeding profusely from a relaxed uterus and a torn cervix. This would have been a significant problem in the best of situations. I, however, was in a tiny mission hospital along the Mosquito Coast of outback Honduras. We had no electricity since our kerosene-run generator was broken and awaiting replacement parts. I had done the delivery by the light of a few candles, which might have provided a romantic ambience for dinner with my wife but was inadequate light for sewing up a cervix. We also lacked sterile surgical instruments since we had no electricity to run the autoclave. The nurse couldn't read the mother's blood pressure by candlelight, but I knew it was low since her pulse was weak and she was passing out. We needed an emergency blood transfusion, sterile instruments, bright lights and a miracle, or this new mother would soon die.

What would MacGyver do if he were here? I couldn't envision how a pocketknife and a piece of string could help our situation. I found myself wishing I were back in Pennsylvania, where the hospitals *always* had bright lights, sterile instruments and a blood bank at your beck and call. But I wasn't there; I was here, sweating bullets, trying to suture a cervix I couldn't see while listening to a baby crying in the background for a mother she might never know. I was the patient's only hope (or so it seemed), and I was failing miserably.

Sometime amid the sweating, pouting and fumbling in the dark, I remembered that God said to ask *him* for help—and so I did. I don't know if God gets tired of being a last resort or not, but that night he didn't seem to mind. He spared the young mother's life. And I am forever grateful.

SILENCE IS NOT SO GOLDEN

Elijah went before the people and said, "How long will you waver between two opinions? If the LORD is God, follow him; but if Baal is God, follow him." But the people said nothing. (I Kings 18:21)

It's not that I had said anything *wrong* since I had not actually uttered a word. And yet somehow I felt that my silence was a loud betrayal. I was with a group of my medical student peers, and the discussion had veered into unfamiliar territory—mysticism, prescient crystals and New Age ideas. To bring up Jesus, the cross, and salvation through Christ seemed old-fashioned, unsophisticated and definitely not cool; so I was silent.

Unfortunately, "Silence is golden" is not a biblical proverb. In fact, Scripture admonishes us, "Do not be ashamed to testify about our Lord" (II Timothy 1:8). If we are ashamed of Jesus in this world, he warns us he will be ashamed of us in the next (Mark 8:38). Paul tells us that belief in our hearts should be associated with speaking with our mouths, and that both are somehow interwoven with salvation itself (Romans 10:9-10).

Although my anatomy textbooks never illustrated this particular anatomic truth, Scripture does: the heart and the tongue are connected. In Matthew, Jesus said, "...out of the overflow of the heart the mouth speaks" (12:34). When we fear even to utter the name of Jesus, the problem is not with our tongues but with our hearts. When opportunities arise, may we not be found silent.

THE WAY OF THANKSGIVING

"For the eyes of the Lord are on the righteous / and his ears are attentive to their prayer ... " (I Peter 3:12)

What is it with prayer, and why are we called to do it? Does it change God, moving him to action he otherwise would not have taken? Since God does not need to hear our words in order to to know our desires, is prayer only for our benefit?

An African custom may offer one helpful insight on the issue of why we pray. During the time we lived in Zambia, I was impressed with how even simple tasks such as borrowing a cup of sugar from a neighbor became a protracted production. After a knock on the door, rather than getting directly to the point, our Zambian neighbors began a long process of pleasantries. General greetings were shared at the door; the visitor then entered the house to sit down and engage in irrelevant discussion. "How is the weather?" and then, "How is your health?" Often a cup of tea somehow worked its way into the ritual. Finally, at some unpredictable point in time, they got around to asking for the cup of sugar for which they had come in the first place. The whole process seemed drawn out, inefficient and puzzling. Why not ask for what you want right away, take it and leave? Our Western way is goal-oriented, while the Zambians prefer to put more emphasis on the relational aspects.

This may illustrate one reason prayer is important to God—he places value on the relationship he has with us. We often come to prayer with a goal in mind: "I need this, that, and the other thing, and now that I've made you aware of it, I need to go." But God is inviting us to come inside, have a seat, share a cup of tea, and tell him all about our needs, our wants, and ourselves.

HOLISTIC REDEMPTION

For God was pleased ... through [Jesus] to reconcile to himself all things ...
(Colossians 1:19-20)

When Adam and Eve sinned, they were cursed and banished from the Garden of Eden (Genesis 3:16-24). Yet even as God described the consequences of their sin, he already hinted at a future redemption (Genesis 3:15), a deliverance from the penalties of their sin. We often view redemption on a personal level; we have been redeemed by Jesus' shed blood (Ephesians 1:7). But God wants to redeem more than our eternal souls. Paul says God wants to reconcile "all things" to himself. When God redeems a person or a situation, there is a deliverance from what was and a transformation into what can be.

As a youth, I remember a woman in our church who was involved in an extramarital affair. When this came to light, it affected the whole church body. If a thumb is smashed by a hammer, the whole body experiences the pain (not just the thumb). This woman's sin caused pain for the whole church body. She asked the church for forgiveness and received it. However, she was too embarrassed to continue to fellowship with our church, and she moved away.

The potential for healing and redemption was not fully appropriated in that situation. I believe God's desire would have been to bring good out of that difficult situation. In Genesis we read how Joseph's brothers sold him off into slavery in Egypt. Yet Joseph said that although his brothers had intended to harm him, "God intended it for good" (50:20). God is never surprised or defeated by our circumstances. In fact, he seems to delight in taking difficult and hopeless situations, delivering us from them, and redemptively transforming them for his glory and for our good.

A MEANINGFUL EXISTENCE

"Meaningless! / Meaningless!" / says the Teacher. / "Utterly meaningless! / Everything is meaningless." (Ecclesiastes 1:2)

I can't read Ecclesiastes without remembering a story about Christian apologist, Ravi Zacharias, who gave a lecture at Harvard. One of the students stood up and said, "Everything in life is meaningless." Ravi responded by saying, "I assume that you assume that your statement is meaningful. If your statement is meaningful, then everything in life is not meaningless. On the other hand, if everything *is* meaningless, then what you have said is also meaningless. So in effect you have said nothing."

The question of whether or not there is a purpose or meaning in our lives is a question frequently pondered. Austrian psychiatrist and Holocaust survivor Victor Frankl defined despair as "suffering without meaning." The recent great success of pastor and teacher Rick Warren's book *The Purpose Driven Life* is related to his theme, which states that we each have a purpose; we all matter. British author and lay theologian G.K. Chesterton said, "You matter. I matter. It's the hardest thing in theology to believe."

Ecclesiastes gives us a look at life "under the sun," a phrase used thirty times in this short book. These three words seem to refer to an earthly existence without God. The Teacher/writer of Ecclesiastes concludes that life without God is senseless and meaningless. Yet he goes on to say that God has "set eternity in the hearts of men" (3:11). This yearning God has put in mankind indicates there is something more than just life "under the sun," life without God. Since the writer has made the case that life without God would be a meaningless existence, he ends by calling us to life *with* God (12:13-14). "You matter. I matter. It's the hardest thing in theology to believe."

INSTRUCTIONS FOR TEACHERS

Not many of you should presume to be teachers, my brothers, because you know that we who teach will be judged more strictly. (James 3:1)

This verse contains a word of counsel and a word of warning. The counsel is that we should not presume to be teachers. The warning is that teachers will be judged more strictly. James expresses concern about too many people wanting to be teachers. Clearly, it's a problem if everyone is a teacher, for there is no one left to be taught. According to Scripture, teachers are not self-appointed based on their desire to teach. Instead, one is called to teach based on gifting from God (Ephesians 4:11). We should not casually or presumptively step into the role of teaching.

James warns us that teachers are judged more strictly. Accountability is a logical consequence that goes along with the power and influence teachers have. A small rudder exerts great power and influence as it directs the path of a large ship (James 3:4). Many of us can remember a schoolteacher from decades ago who had a great influence on our lives (either positive or negative). Their instruction may continue to act as a rudder, giving us direction long after the teachers themselves are gone.

As stewards of God's Word, teachers have even greater responsibility. They are called to teach sound doctrine and to teach with integrity (Titus 2:1, 7). But most importantly, teachers are to point others to the great Teacher, Jesus, who through the work of the Holy Spirit instructs our hearts (Luke 12:12). Scottish pastor and author George MacDonald said, "I believe that no teacher should strive to make men think as he thinks, but to lead them to the living Truth, the Master himself, of whom alone they can learn anything, who will make them in themselves know what is true by the very seeing of it."

NEED-FELT PRAYER

The widow who is really in need and left all alone puts her hope in God and continues night and day to pray and to ask God for help. (I Timothy 5:5)

We've all noticed that when life is easy and circumstances favorable, our prayer life suffers. Our *perceived* need for God is low, and as a result our prayers are feeble. Conversely, when times are tough and our needs are more obvious and urgent, no one needs to remind us of the importance of prayer.

Some years ago our family spent five months in rural Honduras working at a Moravian mission hospital. One afternoon we got caught in a flash thunderstorm while in the small mission schoolhouse. The building was constructed on stilts that raised it six feet above the ground. It stood in the middle of a big clearing as if daring the lightning to strike. Trapped in a dangerous spot, we were tempted to make a run for it. We deemed it foolhardy, however, to run across an open field, with lightning flashing like a strobe light. My wife Doreen and I had seen many previous thunderstorms, but none matched the ferocity of this one. Lightning bolts and thunder crashed all around us, like experiencing the Fourth of July in a shoebox. Our family huddled together in the middle of the room with several of the children in tears. At that moment, not one of us needed a reminder to pray or instructions on how to do it. The obvious danger and urgency of the situation, coupled with our helplessness, were a powerful prescription for prayer.

It's important to remember that when things seem to be going well and we *appear* to be in control, our need is less apparent but no less real than when we're sitting on a lightning rod in the midst of a thunderstorm. There is an unseen spiritual storm crashing around us on a regular basis. We are vulnerable and in dire need of God's daily protection. English clergyman Stephen Marshall said, "A man that is destitute knows how to pray. He needs not an instructor. Let us *know* ourselves destitute that we may know how to pray."

GOD DESIRES INTIMACY

"For this reason a man will leave his father and mother and be united to his wife, and the two will become one flesh." This is a profound mystery—but I am talking about Christ and the church. (Ephesians 5:31-32)

I've recently been impressed by the fact that not only does God desire a relationship with us (think teacher/student), but he also desires an *intimate* relationship with us. One only needs to look at relational metaphors in Scripture to see this cherished desire. God is our "shepherd" (Psalm 23:1), a protector and provider on whom we are totally dependent. God is also our "Father" (Matthew 6:9) who provides for and protects his children, but also a father who encourages and loves his children unconditionally. Apparently, however, these analogies are inadequate since Scripture uses an even more intimate metaphor, saying we are the "bride" of Christ (Revelation 19:7). While we may be mildly uncomfortable with this comparison, the biblical text unapologetically says that we (the church) are in an intimate covenant relationship with Christ that is *like* marriage.

For humans marriage is the most intimate relationship we can imagine. In marriage there is a sharing of dreams, joys, sorrows, love, and the experiences of life. Even to imagine that God loves us so deeply is amazing, humbling and sacredly beautiful. The metaphor of God's people being his bride shows the intensity of his love for us and his desire for closeness with us. God's deep love for us should not be a novel idea. Indeed, deep, intimate love is the essence of the story of God's relationship with us from Genesis through Revelation.

ABSORPTION INTO THE WORLD

The angel of the LORD appeared to her and said, "... you are going to conceive and have a son. ... the boy is to be a Nazirite, set apart to God from birth, and he will begin the deliverance of Israel ... " (Judges 13:3, 5)

While he was still in his mother's womb, Samson was dedicated to God through the Naziritic vow. The vow had three stipulations: 1) he could not drink wine, 2) he could not come in contact with any dead body, and 3) he could not cut his hair. The word Nazirite literally means "a person of the vow." This person was to be separated from the world and consecrated to God.

Samson's story started with great promise. He was the son of godly parents, gifted with great strength, and chosen to help deliver God's people. Unfortunately, Samson's physical strength was not matched by his moral fiber. His downfall began and ended the same way, with his weakness for women. Samson's choice of a Philistine wife was followed by progressively breaking each pillar of his Naziritic vow. First, he touched a dead lion's carcass (Judges 14:6-9), then he drank wine (14:10), and finally he allowed his hair to be cut (16:17-19). His assimilation into the godless world around him was gradual, and even he himself was unaware of what had happened until it happened. In a statement sadder than any country music ballad, we read that Samson awoke, "But he did not know that the LORD had left him" (16:20). Samson's story of imprisonment and untimely death demonstrates the inescapable truth that God's leaving someone has dire consequences.

As Christians today, we are also chosen to be a holy (i.e., a set apart/consecrated) people (I Peter 2:9). The temptation to conform to our culture is just as strong today as it was in Samson's day. We have been forewarned, however, about being absorbed into our godless culture, lest we awaken one day, after a gradual falling away from God, unaware exactly when the LORD has left us.

A MOMENT OF DECISION

"For whoever wants to save his life will lose it, but whoever loses his life for me and for the gospel will save it. What good is it for a man to gain the whole world, yet forfeit his soul?" (Mark 8:35-36)

In 1569, Dirk Willems escaped from a prison in Holland where he had been imprisoned for his Anabaptist beliefs. As he fled across a frozen pond, his pursuing captor broke through the ice into the frigid water. Willems turned around to save his drowning enemy's life. He was promptly re-imprisoned, later tortured and eventually burned at the stake for his beliefs.

Willems must have been tempted to keep on running toward freedom. He had no death wish, or he would not have escaped in the first place. Just like us, he had hopes and dreams for his future. Willems didn't know he would one day be faced with this very difficult moral dilemma. He had had no extensive spiritual training or philosophical instruction on situational ethics. What enabled Willems, in that moment of decision, to turn around to save his pursuer's life despite knowing he would likely forfeit his own?

Psychological and anthropological analyses cannot adequately explain what Dirk Willems did that day. We can, however, understand his actions by seeing the hand of God in his life. Willems' mind, will and emotions had been transformed by the power of God's Holy Spirit. In the instant that defined his life and eternity, Christ's love shone through his actions like a bolt of lightning on a starless night. In showing love for his enemy, Willems lost his life for Christ and thereby saved it.

A CRY FOR HELP

Hear my prayer, O LORD; let my cry for help come to you. Do not hide your face from me when I am in distress. Turn your ear to me; when I call, answer me quickly. (Psalm 102:1-2)

I was going over for bedtime rounds at Macha Mission Hospital in rural Zambia. I still used a cane since I had a broken leg that had not yet fully healed. Stepping out onto our front porch, I was met by a spitting cobra. These snakes are a double threat since not only is their bite poisonous, but they can also spit blinding venom in your eyes. It was one of the few times in my life I wished I wore glasses.

I initially considered trying to finish the cobra off quickly with my cane. Wisdom, however, triumphed over machismo, and I yelled for my wife (who *did* wear glasses) to come and give me a hand. Maybe she could distract the snake long enough for me to deliver the *coup de grâce* with my cane.

Doreen opened the porch door, and I quickly explained the problem. Before I could clarify her role in my master plan, her maternal instincts kicked into high gear: "Protect the kids—Dad's handled snakes before so he can take care of himself." Unable to hear her thought process, I was surprised as she slammed the door shut. Then I heard her push the inside bolt lock into place! Was it the snake or me she didn't want coming in? She then yelled for the girls to climb up on chairs and jammed a blanket into the crack under the doorway. She yelled out to reassure me: "You'll do just fine, dear." I knew my brave wife (who had killed snakes herself in the past) would come to my aid if I really needed her. Her heart, however, was telling her to guard the children, and I actually agreed with her instinctual prioritization. Nonetheless, there I was on the porch with a cobra; my wife was protecting the kids, and everyone else on the mission compound was tucked snugly in their beds. I suddenly felt very alone.

Fortunately, when we call for *God's* help, his door is always open. He is not limited to being in only one place at a time. God doesn't need to ponder what the best course of action might be, nor does he have to wonder about the outcome. God doesn't question if he is up to the task or if his resources are adequate. He is never too busy, and he always wants to help us. Like the psalmist we can cry out to God in our time of need. He will not hide his face from us in our day of distress.

HERMAN U. TIX

All Scripture is God-breathed and is useful for teaching, rebuking, correcting and training in righteousness, so that the man of God may be thoroughly equipped for every good work. (II Timothy 3:16-17)

For some conservative Christians, hermeneutics is the "H-word." We shouldn't *interpret* the Bible, we should just read it, believe it and do what it says—it's just that simple. Of course this overlooks the fact that unless we're reading it in the original Greek, Hebrew and Aramaic, we're already dealing with interpretation through the translation process.

I don't think we need to fear good, sound biblical interpretation, in which the goal is to reveal the true meaning of the text. Gordon Fee and Douglas Stewart, in their book *How to Read the Bible for All Its Worth*, point out two reasons we need to interpret: **1) The nature of the reader.** We bring who we are (our experiences and knowledge) to our interaction with Scripture. Thus, interpretation is inevitable, and it is best that we be deliberate and conscious about it rather than unwitting and oblivious. **2) The nature of the text.** Scripture has both a human and divine side. It is the Word of God, but it is written by human authors with varied personalities, training and perspectives. The Bible was also written to real people at specific times and places in history, yet it has a message that transcends time, nationality and culture. Therefore, for us to understand what the Bible means for us today, we must do some work of interpretation.

St. Augustine noted several key points about interpreting Scripture. He saw the futility of trying to understand Scripture without the help of the Holy Spirit who inspired its writing. "Understanding is the reward of faith. Therefore seek not to understand that you may believe, but believe that you may understand." Spiritual truths cannot be understood with the nonspiritual mind. Believers, however, have God's Holy Spirit, who quickens our minds to understand his ways.

Augustine also realized the danger of subjective interpretation. "If you believe what you like in the gospels, and reject what you don't like, it is not the gospels you believe, but yourself." While humanism says we have the answers to the questions of life, Christianity says God has the answers, and he has revealed them through his "God-breathed" Word, the Bible.

OBEDIENCE

Then Moses climbed Mount Nebo … Then the LORD said to him, "This is the land I promised. … I have let you see it with your eyes, but you will not cross over into it." And Moses the servant of the LORD died there in Moab, as the LORD had said. (Deuteronomy 34:1, 4-5)

Moses was one of the truly great men in the Bible. He stood up to Pharaoh, demanding the release of God's people, threatening imminent plagues. He parted the Red Sea, leading the Israelites out of their Egyptian captivity. He received the Ten Commandments directly from the hand of God. For forty years, Moses listened to the moans, grumblings and complaints of the Children of Israel as he led them through the wilderness to the Promised Land. That would be the modern-day equivalent of taking a trip to the Grand Canyon with a hundred teenagers in the backseat of your Ford Fiesta. In short, Moses was a saint. And yet, for the itsy-bitsy, tiny mistake of *striking* the rock instead of *talking* to it as God had instructed him, Moses was refused entrance into the Promised Land of Canaan, the "land flowing with milk and honey" (Exodus 3:8).

Moses' response was amazing. He didn't complain of unfairness, nor did he mope around in self-pity. Instead, he pronounced a blessing on the tribes as they prepared to enter Canaan without him. One named Joshua would lead them into the Promised Land. The Grecianized form of Joshua's name is "Jesus." Joshua was the prototype, the predecessor of Jesus who would ultimately lead his people into the Promised Land of Heaven.

It's been noted that God didn't allow Moses in his physical body to set foot in Canaan. However, Moses' spiritual presence at the Transfiguration on Mount Hermon put him right in the middle of the Promised Land (Matthew 17:1-3). God is just, and he calls for strict obedience. Fortunately for us, however, God is also merciful, and he delights to give us the desires of our hearts.

THE GLORY OF GOD

And we, who with unveiled faces all reflect the Lord's glory, are being trans-formed into his likeness with ever-increasing glory, which comes from the Lord ... (II Corinthians 3:18)

I was up late last night, helping one of my patients give birth to her first child. As I examined the newborn baby, I noted something in her face that reminded me of her father. Although this baby couldn't walk or talk, and her repertoire of activities was limited to eating, dirtying her diaper, crying and sleeping, her countenance already demonstrated the uncanny imprint of her parents.

Paul says that we "reflect the Lord's glory." And although we all "fall short of the glory of God" (Romans 3:23), we are being "trans-formed into his likeness with ever-increasing glory." My visceral, reflex response is to dismiss any resemblance between God and me. However holy and humble that dismissal may seem, to do so would disregard the clear teaching of God's Word.

New Testament Scripture defines God's glory as his splendor and majesty seen when he reveals himself to humans. The Psalmist said, "The heavens declare the glory of God" (Psalm 19:1). When John spoke of the Incarnation, he said, "The Word became flesh ... We have seen his glory" (John 1:14). But, in addition to nature and Jesus himself revealing God's glory, *we too* were created to reflect God's glory. While we may feel like poor reflectors, we are still reflectors. Paul says our new self is being renewed "in the image of its Creator" (Colossians 3:10), and our Creator's image exudes glory.

Like the newborn baby, we fall short of the appearance of our Father. Yet there is something in our countenance, something in our actions, and something about our lives that mysteriously reflects an im-pression of God. Although difficult to understand and hard to believe, God has chosen us to reflect his glory so that we might point people to him.

THE CRUSADE OF THE CROSS

On the contrary: "If your enemy is hungry, feed him; if he is thirsty, give him something to drink ..." Do not be overcome by evil, but overcome evil with good. (Romans 12:20-21)

British author, columnist and atheist Christopher Hitchens, in his book *God Is Not Great: How Religion Poisons Everything*, asserts that religion inevitably leads to violence. He notes killing in the name of religion in Baghdad, Bombay, Bethlehem and Belgrade. As Christians, we often cringe in embarrassment when the Crusades of the Middle Ages are brought up. We need to acknowledge the inconvenient truth that much violence has been perpetrated in the name of religion (including Christianity). However, societies that have shunned religion have also been guilty of violent atrocities, so one cannot deduce a unique cause and effect relationship with religion and violence.

I think it's significant, however, that persons committing violence in the name of Christianity are actually going against the life and teachings of Christ himself. Jesus never picked up the sword, and he also stopped his disciples from doing so (Matthew 26:52). Persons who carry out violence toward others are not walking in the steps of the carpenter from Galilee. Jesus taught us to love our enemies (5:44) and turn the other cheek (5:39), and he himself suffered and died (without fighting back) for you and me.

Interestingly, the word "crusade" comes from the Latin word for cross, *crux*. When the soldiers of the church were commissioned during the Crusades, they received a cloth cross to be sewn on their clothes. Using the symbol of the cross to rally soldiers in the Crusades seems ironic. A genuine pursuit of the cross of Christ would lead to a life of suffering for the good of others and a willingness to die (not kill) for them.

OUR CHOICE

It is better for you to enter life maimed than with two hands to go into hell,
where the fire never goes out. (Mark 9:43b)

In ancient times, most societies believed in a transcendent moral law. If one violated that law, there would be consequences (i.e., judgment or punishment). People, therefore, tried to conform their behavior to fit the moral law. Contemporary Western thought, however, says that each culture determines right and wrong for itself. In other words, instead of trying to mold our behaviors to a divine moral law, people today believe our societal behaviors can actually *determine* the moral law, and that moral law can be different for each culture. Conveniently, we have become our own gods. Western culture finds the concepts of a transcendent moral law, judgment and hell to be offensive and lacking sophistication. Nonetheless, these ideas are taught in Scripture.

Although some of the descriptions of hell in Scripture may be symbolic, a reality to which the symbols point cannot be denied. Hell is clearly a separation from the presence of God (II Thessalonians 1:9). In order to experience true love, joy and peace, we need to be in communion with God. If we are separated from every aspect of God, we are left with only self and its minions—pride, greed, lust, anger and envy. These traits, when unchecked by any ray of goodness, suck one's soul into a never-ending downward spiral of depravity. I believe this vortex of corruption is at least one facet of hell.

Sometimes God's punishment is giving people what they ask for. In Romans, the apostle Paul says God gave people over to their hearts' desires (1:24). Similarly, eternity without God is the realization of one's desire to live without God. God doesn't *want* anyone to perish (II Peter 3:9). However, for those who persistently reject him, he honors their right to choose. In *The Great Divorce*, C.S. Lewis says in the end there are "two kinds of people—those who say, 'Thy will be done' to God, or those to whom God says 'Thy will be done.'" In essence, those who spend eternity without God will have chosen it.

FORGIVENESS HEALS

Jesus said, "Father, forgive them, for they do not know what they are doing."
(Luke 23:34a)

In October of 2006, a 32-year-old man, apparently nursing a 20-year-old grudge, entered a one-room Amish schoolhouse in Nickel Mines, Pennsylvania, to obtain revenge. He tied up and shot ten young girls and then took his own life. Five of the girls died. Charles Roberts, the killer, was a husband and the father of three children. While this story is sad beyond the potential for mere words to convey, sadness is not what made the greatest impression on me. Although the wanton violence and slaughter of the innocent evoked shock and anger, there was something else that produced an even more vivid impression.

The peaceful Amish community that had been dealt this devastating blow reached out with *forgiveness*. Within a few days of the tragedy, the Amish church sent representatives to Roberts' wife and family. The message given was one of forgiveness for Charles Roberts and a desire to support his wife and children. The Roberts family was invited to the Amish funeral services to share in their grief. The Amish community even helped set up funds for financial aid for Mrs. Roberts and her children and expressed the hope that they would stay in their community.

We are often jaded by violence—genocide in Africa, another bombing in Iraq, and now another school shooting. Nickel Mines was a shock but unfortunately all too believable. Forgiveness like this, however, is *unbelievable*. It is totally incomprehensible and seems outside the realms of potential human response. How can one give up anger, resentment and a desire for punishment, especially when these responses are so justified? True forgiveness, however, is not a feeling but a decision. It's a decision to respond as Jesus did on the cross when he said, "Father, forgive them ..."

Forgiveness is a healing balm that sets people free. Because forgiveness was extended to Charles Roberts, his wife and children will have a much better chance of emotional, physical and spiritual well-being. And because the Amish community was willing to forgo hate, anger and revenge, they are more likely to experience freedom from the aching heartburn that plagues all of us when we harbor a grudge.

September

September 1

A WRETCH LIKE ME

For what I do is not the good I want to do; no, the evil I do not want to do—this I keep on doing ... What a wretched man I am! (Romans 7:19, 24a)

"Christians are a bunch of hypocrites; they're no better than anyone else." Although this is a common indictment of Christians, it's still hard not to become defensive when I hear it. I think it's important to see the truth in the critique and yet to realize that that truth need not hurt the case for Christ.

There is a common, erroneous line of logic about Christianity that needs to be brought into the light of day. When non-Christians attack the idea that Christians are better people (in character, good deeds and morality) than non-Christians, they are tearing down a straw man of their own making. No one should ever have claimed that Christians were better people than non-Christians; this notion is the straw man. We Christians often take the bait by trying to rebuild the straw man (usually by trying to defend some celebrity Christian's moral failures). It would be better for us to address the false premise—the idea that Christians are morally superior to non-Christians. This premise is based on the assumption that only those who are good enough will merit salvation and heaven. Since Christians think they are going to heaven, they must think themselves better than those who are not heaven-bound.

The scriptural truth on this matter is that we are all sinners, and *none* of us deserves heaven. We are assured of eternal life not because of our goodness or deeds but because of God's grace (Ephesians 2:8-9). It is true that as Christians we should be becoming more Christ-like. However, where we are on the continuum of goodness depends on many factors, including inborn inclinations and environmental influences. Thankfully, our salvation does not depend on what we've done or *our* goodness. Instead, our salvation depends on accepting what Christ has done and *his* goodness.

SUBMISSION

Submit to one another out of reverence for Christ. (Ephesians 5:21)

In the summer of 1986, two ships collided in the Black Sea between Russia and Turkey. More than three hundred passengers were thrown to their deaths in the icy waters. Initial supposition suggested perhaps bad weather and poor visibility caused the accident, or perhaps the radar malfunctioned, or someone fell asleep on the job. The truth, however, was harder to believe. Both captains were aware of the other ship's approach and their collision course. Nonetheless, each felt the other one should give in and change course. Pride and a stubborn unwillingness to yield the right of way caused an unfortunate shipwreck with tragic pain and suffering.

As Christians, we are called to submit to Christ (Ephesians 5:24), to the authorities (Romans 13:1), and to our elders (I Peter 5:5). While these calls to submission are difficult enough, the call to submit to one another—our equals—is perhaps more difficult. My son-in-law recently told me how he and his wife had an argument last week. During the argument he suddenly realized he was wrong, yet it took another twenty minutes of arguing before he was able to admit that he was at fault. I didn't tell him, but it sometimes takes me several days to admit I'm wrong, so I figure he's doing pretty well.

Although it may be hard for us to believe, our value and self-worth do not depend on being right or being in charge. So instead of fighting to be top dog, Paul says we are to imitate Christ in his humility. Christ "did not consider equality with God something to be grasped" (Philippians 2:6) but willingly laid down that which was rightfully his (e.g., omnipotence, omniscience). Christ gave this up in order to show his love for us and meet us where we were.

As we navigate the metaphoric waters of the Black Sea, pride and an unwillingness to yield will shipwreck our relationships. If we can lay down our pride and "submit to one another out of reverence for Christ," we can grow into what God has purposed for us and stay out of the deadly, icy waters of the Black Sea.

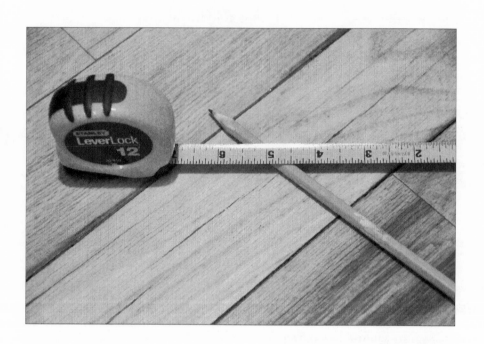

GOD'S TAPE MEASURE

Now we see but a poor reflection as in a mirror; then we shall see face to face. Now I know in part; then I shall know fully ... (I Corinthians 13:12)

Have you ever felt like your life was meaningless? Has it ever seemed as if your circumstances were unfair and senseless? Welcome to the human race! God has given us feelings and thoughts as a reckoning tool to gauge our own significance, to measure justice in the circumstances of life, and to evaluate logic in things that happen. Unfortunately, when we use this divinely bestowed tape measure, things rarely seem to be as long, wide or high as they *ought* to be. Do we blame the measuring tool or the one who gave it to us?

There's an area in Peru where one can find a series of strange lines dug into the ground. For many years these were thought to be the remains of ancient irrigation ditches. However, in 1939 it was discovered that their true meaning could only be discerned from the air. They were actually huge drawings of animals, insects and birds. One just needed the right perspective to see their meaning.

Similarly, Paul reminds us that our perspective is limited. We are able to see "but a poor reflection," and we are only able to "know in part." The problem, therefore, when things do not "measure up," is neither the measuring tool nor the one who gave it to us. *We* are the problem. As American author Anais Nin said, "We don't see things as they are, we see them as *we* are." And we are imperfect viewers.

While our desire to use this tape measure is part of what makes us human, we need to remember that our measurement is unreliable. The difference between the measurements we get and what they *ought* to be is reconciled by faith. From God's omniscient perspective that sees all of time at once, the length, width and height of justice, logic, and meaning measure out exactly right!

GOD USES THE WEAK AND FOOLISH

"But Lord," Gideon asked, "how can I save Israel? My clan is the weakest in Manasseh, and I am the least in my family." (Judges 6:15)

For seven years the Israelites were given over to the oppressive hands of the Midianites. The story of God delivering Israel with Gideon's small army is the story of God using a *wimpy man* from a *weak clan* with a *wild plan* to bring about God's purposes.

When God approached Gideon, he was secretly threshing grain in a wine press to avoid discovery by the Midianites. When God told Gideon he was to deliver the Israelites, Gideon objected, pointing out that he was from the weakest clan in Manasseh and he himself was the "least" in his family. God's reply was, "Go in the strength you have" (6:14), and "I will be with you" (6:16).

The most curious aspect of the story is God's battle plan. Gideon initially had thirty-two thousand soldiers, and although still outnumbered, they might have at least hoped for a victory. God, however, said Gideon had too many soldiers and was only satisfied when the number was whittled down to a meager three hundred men. These few men were then "armed" with an earthen pitcher concealing a lighted torch in one hand and a trumpet in the other. At the appointed time, they were to break the pitchers, blow the trumpets and scream at the top of their lungs. How reassured would you have been with this battle plan?

Gideon and his three hundred screaming, trumpeting pyromaniacs celebrated a great victory that day because they trusted God rather than the strength and wisdom of humans. In I Corinthians, Paul reminds us that God often chooses the foolish and weak things of this world to shame the wise and the strong, so that no one may boast (1:27, 29).

WHY ARE WE?

Jesus replied: "Love the Lord your God with all your heart and with all your soul and with all your mind."' (Matthew 22:37)

Why did God create the cosmos? Before time began, our triune God existed and was complete in himself (i.e., he lacked nothing). Nonetheless, God decided to create the universe. Out of nothing he spoke time, space, matter and energy into existence. The galaxies, solar systems, planets, flora, fauna, atoms, and subatomic particles were God's thoughts transposed into reality. Why? Although we cannot fully understand the mind of God, we have some clues. Just as clues can help us discern if it was Mrs. Peacock in the library with the candlestick, so also clues may help us understand why we *are*, instead of why we are *not*.

In the Gospel of John, we read that love was the motivation for God's becoming flesh to redeem the world: "For God so loved the world that he gave his one and only Son" (3:16). Since love motivated the Incarnation and plan of redemption, it is likely that love also motivated Creation in the first place. God's love, like a culinary masterpiece, is consummated as it is received by others.

One of the innate characteristics of love is that it is in some way incomplete until the one being loved returns that affection. While unrequited love may be a good theme for romantic poetry, it is painful in personal experience. In Victor Hugo's *The Hunchback of Notre Dame*, the love of the grotesque Quasimodo for the beautiful Esmerelda is unfulfilled. However, the very poignancy that makes Hugo's novel interesting is such a love that is *tragically* incomplete (unreturned).

Scripture is chock-full of God's demonstrations of his love for us in myriad and sometimes extravagant ways. By extravagantly demonstrating his love for us, God actually makes himself vulnerable to hurt and rejection since we may choose not to reciprocate his love. God desires for us to love him, but he knows that true love, if it is to have any meaning, cannot be coerced or mandated; it must be voluntary. So he does not impose his will on us but instead simply keeps demonstrating his love for us and inviting us to respond freely in kind. For God so loved that he created the world. For God so loved that he sent Jesus to redeem humanity. It is humbling to realize God has given us the opportunity to complete his amazing love by loving him in return.

TWO GARDEN-VARIETY CHOICES

Then Jesus went with his disciples to a place called Gethsemane, … [Jesus] fell with his face to the ground and prayed, "My Father, if it is possible, may this cup be taken from me. Yet not as I will, but as you will."
(Matthew 26:36, 39)

In some ways, the Garden of Gethsemane is a mirror image of the Garden of Eden. Adam's action in Eden loudly proclaimed, "Not as you will, but as I will." Jesus' prayer in Gethsemane was the very opposite: "Not as I will, but as you will." From Adam's action we see the pain that followed from being self-serving. From Jesus' action we see the power that followed from being submissive to God's will and ultimately to the cross.

The American Dream is to climb the ladder of success and "to do it *my* way." Having more possessions, grasping power, and gaining prestige are assumed to be worthy goals. However, Jack Higgins, author of the book *The Eagle Has Landed*, said there's one thing he knows now at the height of his career that he wished he had known as a child: "When you get to the top, there's nothing there."

Jesus demonstrated this counter-intuitive truth two thousand years ago in the Garden of Gethsemane. True power does not come by climbing over others to get to the top of the heap—there's nothing there. Instead, true power comes when we submit ourselves to the will of the Father—there is something here.

As Christians, we have the influences of Adam and Christ that struggle within us. Do we choose what appears to serve *us* best, or do we submit to God's plan and trust him? These are two "garden-variety" choices with two very different results.

SAFETY IN THE NILE

But when she could hide him no longer, she got a papyrus basket for him and coated it with tar and pitch. Then she placed the child in it and put it among the reeds along the bank of the Nile. (Exodus 2:3)

It started when our children went to school—they were swooped up by that big yellow school bus. We had done our best to prepare them for the harsh influences of the world. We had coated their baskets with tar and pitch, yet the Nile seemed big and foreboding. We were naively unaware at the time, but placing them among the reeds of the Nile would become a repeated pattern, not a one-time event—sleepovers with friends, a week away at camp, getting their driver's license, leaving for college and the coup de grâce, getting married. We would repeatedly have to fight the urge to keep them home under the safety and protection of our care.

Moses' mother must have trembled as she placed her son in the frightening waters of the Nile. Many Jewish babies had drowned in those same cold waters (Exodus 1:22). She undoubtedly overcame fears and tears as she gave up personal control with that moving act of faith. The amazing story of Moses' life, the deliverance of the Hebrews from slavery, the receiving of the Ten Commandments, the journey to The Promised Land and the writing of the Pentateuch—all began with this mother's one heroic act of faith.

We cannot hope for anything better for our family and loved ones than to reside in God's will. We would rob them of God's blessings and purposes by seeking only their safety and comfort. If God calls them to a place of discomfort or danger, that is the best place they could be, even if they die there. It would be far worse to seek a place of safety and comfort that is *outside* God's will. There can be nothing better than placing our loved ones in the almighty, loving hands of God. Coat the basket with tar and pitch, then place it among the reeds along the Nile; God is trustworthy.

A PERMISSIVE ENVIRONMENT

"If your hand causes you to sin, cut it off. It is better for you to enter life maimed than with two hands to go into hell ... " (Mark 9:43)

Hyperbole is a figure of speech in which exaggeration is used to emphasize a point. Jesus' use of hyperbole seems obvious in the text, but what point does he want to emphasize? Jesus' emphasis appears to go beyond merely stating that sin is wrong. He seems to be stressing the seriousness of sin and the importance of taking steps to avoid recurrent sin.

In criminology, the "broken windows theory" looks at the significance of how one responds to criminal activity. If a window in a building is broken but not repaired, it sends a message that no one here cares and wrongdoings are allowed. It gives subtle permission for further criminal activity by being an environment with no apparent rules. On the other hand, if the window is repaired immediately, the chance of further broken windows drops dramatically. With a rapid repair, the message sent is that there are people here who care. Not only a window but also a rule was broken, and things will be corrected.

The broken window is similar to sin in our lives. If sin is not taken seriously, dealt with and eradicated, *tolerated* sin creates an atmosphere of leniency where more sin can flourish. However, if we take all sin seriously and respond to sin in our lives by asking God's forgiveness and calling on his purifying power, we then create a haven of holiness, where evil must struggle to make any inroads.

A PERSISTENT IMAGE OF BLESSING

When he had led them out to the vicinity of Bethany, he lifted up his hands and blessed them. While he was blessing them, he left them and was taken up into heaven. (Luke 24:50-51)

My family moved from western Maryland to northern Indiana when I was ten years old. It was a stressful event in my young life. All our belongings were snugly packed in a cattle truck and two cars. As we pulled out of our driveway for the last time, I can still vividly remember taking one last look out the car's rear window. The visual image of our house with the big tree out front was at that point in time indelibly seared on my brain. The intensity of emotion associated with that last glimpse served to imprint the scene permanently.

I suspect the disciples' last view of Jesus as he ascended into heaven must have also had great emotional intensity and a similar imprinting effect. The disciples' final encounter with their risen Lord would have had special significance even had he not so blatantly defied the law of gravity. As Jesus raised his hands to bless the disciples, he ascended into heaven. Jesus' last action revealed the passion of his heart to bless those he loved. As the disciples saw his arms outstretched in blessing, they would have seen his nail-scarred hands. It was a reminder that his blessing was not a cheap gift but a costly sacrifice.

Jesus' posture and passion toward us today are unchanged from when he left the disciples two thousand years ago—his arms are still outstretched with a desire to bless us. Jesus impressed that imagery on the disciples' minds not only so they would remember and benefit from it themselves but also so they would remember to write it down to share with Christians through the centuries. As we read this Scripture, we can envision Jesus today like they saw him then, with nail-scarred hands outstretched over us in blessing.

CULTURALLY CORRECT

"It is by the name of Jesus Christ of Nazareth, … Salvation is found in no one else, for there is no other name under heaven given to men by which we must be saved." (Acts 4:10b, 12)

We've all heard the mantra in one form or another. "Religious beliefs are culturally conditioned and therefore cannot hold any universal truths for all people. To assume your culturally biased beliefs are the right ones for others is arrogant ethnocentrism."

It is true that our cultural context affects our belief system. However, to use this as an argument that no faith beliefs can be absolutely true, since all are relative to one's social milieu, relies on logic that self-destructs. Sociologist Peter Berger notes that stating that all beliefs are relative is itself a belief and therefore must be relative. As he puts it, "Relativity relativizes itself." He says one can't assert, "All claims about religion are [culturally] conditioned except the one I am making right now."

In his book *The Reason for God*, Timothy Keller points out that Christians are often criticized as narrow and arrogant for believing their religion is superior to others. Yet the idea that we shouldn't claim our religion better than others is in itself a very Western idea. Keller concludes, "It is no more narrow to claim that one religion is right than to claim that one way to think about all religions (namely that all are equal) is right." Each thought pattern is exclusive in a different way.

The claim that salvation is found in no one but Jesus Christ is exclusive. As such, it is either true or false but cannot be both. Regardless of cultural background, such an absolute claim must be evaluated. It is either folly to be discarded or truth to be embraced.

DELIVERANCE: A PROCESS WITH A PURPOSE

... 'I am the LORD, and I will bring you out from under the yoke of the Egyptians. I will free you from being slaves to them ...' (Exodus 6:6)

God could have delivered the Israelites out of their slavery in Egypt in many different ways. However, he chose to deliver them by using ten plagues that probably occurred over a period of a year or more. The manner of deliverance was not just a means to an end but also a process with a purpose.

The ten plagues described in Exodus are often considered God's judgment against Pharaoh and Egypt. That assessment is true, but they also demonstrated God's mercy. The plagues were progressively more severe, interspersed with pleas to release the slaves, which gave the Egyptians opportunities to avoid further suffering.

The plagues were also faith invitations to the Egyptians. Because of them, God said Pharaoh and the Egyptians would "know that I, the LORD, am in this land" (8:22) and that "there is no one like me in all the earth" (9:14). The plagues confronted and discredited specific Egyptian gods. By showing the Egyptians who the true God was and discrediting their gods, God extended an invitation for them to believe in *him*. Apparently some of the Egyptians did believe since Scripture says when the Israelites left Egypt, "Many other people went up with them" (12:38).

The process of deliverance, however, was also for the benefit of the Israelites. Speaking about the day on which the Israelites were released from Egyptian slavery, God said, "This is a day you are to commemorate; for the generations to come ..." (12:14). The story of God's mighty hand using ten plagues to deliver his people has been told for many centuries as a reminder of his power, mercy, judgment and care for his children.

There is significance not only in what God does but also in how he does it. In using the ten plagues, God demonstrated his mercy, delivered an invitation and designed a memorial.

THE ULTIMATE BLUSH

The LORD knows the thoughts of man; / he knows that they are futile.
(Psalm 94:11)

I was a freshman in high school, a fourteen-year-old male replete with girl interest. Gloria Laramore was a seventeen-year-old senior, the most beautiful creature I'd ever seen. I'd only admired her from afar, and I'm sure she was completely unaware of my pining existence. One fateful day, a teacher sent me on an errand, and I suddenly found myself alone in a room with Gloria and a Xerox copy machine. I felt my face and ears rapidly transform from white to pink and then to an intense, heat-emitting red. One probably could have roasted marshmallows near my blushing face. I'd have been no less inconspicuous with a screeching siren and a flashing light affixed to my head.

Unfortunately, a high school crush is just the beginning of a long list of thoughts and actions I could be embarrassed about. God knows all the bad deeds I've done and all the good deeds I've not done. The psalmist also tells us, "The LORD knows the thoughts of man." Furthermore, the day is coming when all people will be gathered before the all-knowing God, who will separate the sheep from the goats (Matthew 25:31-33). One could fear that the Day of Judgment will initiate the ultimate and eternal blush.

The good news, however, is that our Lord is compassionate and gracious, and our sins have been removed "as far as the east is from the west" (Psalm 103:12). When our inner lives are inspected on Judgment Day, that which will be seen is Jesus. His sacrificial death on the cross and his atoning blood will cover our sins. We will have no need to blush.

LONELY OR ALONE?

Very early in the morning, while it was still dark, Jesus got up, left the house and went off to a solitary place, where he prayed. (Mark 1:35)

Loneliness and intentional solitude are two distinct entities. Our culture tends to have too much of the former and not enough of the latter. We fear being alone. Yet spending time in solitude does not mean one is lonely any more than being with a group of people precludes loneliness.

Our busy lives are full of lonely persons. A significant number of the patients I see each day in my medical practice suffer from loneliness. Surprisingly, it often has little to do with the busyness or amount of interpersonal contact in their daily schedules. When loneliness descends on us, it can seem overwhelming. It's as though we have become invisible and isolated from the interactive world around us. Catholic priest and author Henri Nouwen described lonely persons: "Like lost and solitary wanderers, they stare out at a silent universe."

Being alone, however, does not need to lead to loneliness. Being alone should not be an end in itself. Being alone or feeling alone can be used as an opportunity to experience solitude with God. Time alone with God will enrich our times of fellowship with others. In fact, German pastor and theologian Dietrich Bonhoeffer said, "Let him who cannot be alone, beware of community." Those who are uncomfortable being alone often make poor companions for others. If we are unable even to be at ease with our own selves, being with others is unlikely to fix our underlying dis-ease.

While it is true that God created us to be in community, it is also true that he calls us to times of solitude with him. Quaker author and pastor Richard Foster says that inner solitude with God actually sets us free from loneliness. He says loneliness is an inner emptiness while solitude is an inner fullness—with God. As we pursue solitude with God, we leave loneliness searching for a new partner.

THE SIGHT AND SOUND OF JUDGMENT

His eyes were like blazing fire. His feet were like bronze glowing in a furnace, and his voice was like the sound of rushing waters. (Revelation 1:14b-15)

The apocalyptic description of Jesus in the first chapter of Revelation is cryptic and awesome. Scholars suggest the eyes "like blazing fire" indicate nothing can be hidden from his judging vision. The "bronze glowing in a furnace" speaks metaphorically of the purifying quality of judgment. His voice, "like the sound of rushing waters," probably also follows the theme of judgment, echoing the sound of the waters from the Flood. How do we respond to the idea of judgment?

I once heard a story about two groups of people and their different responses to hearing "the sound of rushing waters." The first group was a family out for a leisurely ride in a rowboat. They'd never done any boating before and hadn't paid the extra money to rent lifejackets. After rowing around the placid lake, they decided to explore one of the outlet streams. Suddenly, they heard the foreboding "sound of rushing waters" from the Class III rapids they were rapidly being pulled toward—their hearts were gripped with fear.

The second group included two athletic young men in a Kevlar canoe constructed to withstand the toughest rapids. They both wore helmets and streamlined lifejackets and had been training for months to tackle the toughest white water they could find. They too heard the "sound of rushing waters" around the next river bend. They smiled with anticipation as adrenaline surged through their veins.

Both groups heard the same sound. Both groups knew whitewater judgment awaited them. Yet due to the difference in preparation between the two groups, their anticipatory emotions were completely the opposite. At the final judgment, when we hear the "rushing waters," will we be fearful or excited? Are we prepared?

PEOPLE NEED THE LORD

"Not everyone who says to me, 'Lord, Lord,' will enter the kingdom of heaven, … I will tell them plainly, 'I never knew you …'" (Matthew 7:21, 23)

One of the subtle deceptions we often fall prey to is forgetting the lostness of the lost. That friendly neighbor who volunteers at the homeless shelter or that aunt who seems so happy and carefree—certainly they're not going to hell. It seems cruel even to use the "h" word, but perhaps it's crueler *not* to use it. Scripture is clear that there will be a final judgment, and not all are going to heaven. Is it truly kind and loving not to warn people about this?

Part of the source of people's misunderstanding is the intuitive belief that if there is a heaven, kind and loving acts will insure a reservation. But the Bible, which has the unique authority to define God's qualifications for heaven, says that it is *not* based on good works but on a personal relationship with Jesus Christ (John 14:6).

Yet certainly people who exhibit natural love are closer to the kingdom of God than depraved and hateful people, aren't they? C.S. Lewis said that while natural love may *lead* to God's love, "there's also something in it which makes it easier to stop at the natural and mistake it for the heavenly. Brass is mistaken for gold more often than clay is. Those who hate goodness are sometimes nearer than those who know nothing about it and think they have it already."

One day, your neighbor, your aunt, you and I will all stand before God's throne. To some he will say, "I never knew you," to others, "Well done, good and faithful servant!" (Matthew 25:21). We cannot afford to mistake brass for gold in our own lives or in the lives of those around us.

WHY AM I SO CRITICAL?

The LORD sent Nathan to David ... [Nathan] said, "... A rich man had a very large number of sheep and cattle, but the poor man had nothing except one little ewe lamb he had bought. ... Now a traveler came to the rich man, but the rich man refrained from taking one of his own sheep ... Instead, he took the ewe lamb that belonged to the poor man and prepared it for the one who had come to him." David burned with anger against the man and said to Nathan, "As surely as the LORD lives, the man who did this deserves to die! ..." Then Nathan said to David, "You are the man!"
(II Samuel 12:1-7a)

It is so much easier to see sin in someone else's life than in our own. In Matthew's gospel, Jesus notes how we try to remove a "speck of sawdust" from our brother's eye when we have an entire "plank" of wood in our own (7:3-5). It seems our visual acuity for seeing faults drops to zero when we look in a mirror. The theory seems to be that pointing out someone else's faults will somehow make us look better in comparison. Apparently our "appearance" won't stand on its own merit and requires some denigrating of the competition.

What makes it so easy to criticize others smugly? Would we feel so self-righteous if our own hidden sins were uncovered? That is exactly what happened to David. One minute he was feeling pious and judgmental. After a few illuminating words from the prophet Nathan, however, David's entire mood was transformed. He suddenly saw himself clearly, and thus he saw the value of God's mercy.

When we first see our own faults, the sorry sight will help to curb our naturally critical nature. Although there are times when the church needs to exercise judgment (Matthew 18:15-17), healthy fellowship cannot exist without a large dose of mercy. Pastor and author Rick Warren says, "We all need mercy because we all stumble and fall. Fellowship is a place of grace, where mistakes aren't rubbed in but rubbed out. Fellowship happens when mercy wins over judgment." Let's cultivate a spirit of forgiveness toward others by remembering the undeserved forgiveness God has given us.

A PAINFUL OPPORTUNITY

And we know that in all things God works for the good of those who love him, who have been called according to his purpose. (Romans 8:28)

Sandy had been a good friend of mine for years. She was now in tears. Her father had just been diagnosed with a rapidly growing cancer; and barring a miracle, he had less than six months to live. Sandy voiced the inevitable question: "Our whole family loves him so much, and we still need him. How could God let this happen?"

It is difficult to understand how life-ending cancer could be used by God to work "for the good of those who love him." Author and pastor John Piper, after having been diagnosed with cancer, reflected on the spiritual opportunities afforded by cancer. He encouraged persons similarly affected in a short article he wrote, entitled "Don't Waste Your Cancer."

Piper reminds us that what God permits, he permits for a reason. Cancer reminds us of the inconvenient truth that we all will die. The ultimate perspective of death can give meaning and direction for our lives. God may plan to use our cancer as a means to share with others about the hope we have that goes beyond the grave. Cancer may also serve to rid us of false securities, helping us to rely totally on God. As we begin to see God's purposes, our anger toward God can be transformed into a deep love for him, and our isolation from other people can turn into a deep affection and concern for them.

The apostle Paul says that in *all* things God works for the good of those who love him, who have been called according to *his* purpose. When we see pain and suffering as an opportunity, we allow God to use it for his glory, and when that happens, our "cancer" will not be wasted.

THE DARK NIGHT OF THE SOUL

The LORD is close to the brokenhearted / and saves those who are crushed in spirit. (Psalm 34:18)

As mature Christians we assume we should feel God's presence, hear his voice and know his will. Our faith should be without doubts, and we should be joyful at all times with no cracks in our spiritual or emotional lives. Interestingly, God has little to say about such perfect Christians who have no need for him. He does, however, have many words of comfort and assurance for those who are "brokenhearted" and "crushed."

John of the Cross, a sixteenth-century Spanish mystic, wrote about Christians going through a spiritual crucible in *The Dark Night of the Soul*. The dark night may be ushered in by one of life's crises, such as the death of a loved one, a diagnosis of cancer or the experience of divorce; or the dark night may arrive unexpectedly like a flash thunderstorm. In the dark night, persons often lose all feelings of God's presence and may become angry, confused and depressed, feeling hopeless and powerless. It may last from a few months to years.

The dark night, however, is not without purpose. It is a painful path that brings us into the arms of our Savior. The dark night is a means through which we encounter God, and he transforms us. John of the Cross refers to the dark night as God's gift. Since we are prone to become attached to feelings about God rather than God himself, the dark night prevents us from focusing on our feelings about God by completely removing them.

When we arrogantly (and mistakenly) claim we are perfectly intact, we are declaring we have no need for God. It is only when we acknowledge our need that God can seep in through the wounds and cracks to cause true healing and wholeness. When we experience the dark night of the soul, God is there. As we embrace the darkness as a painful path to intimacy with God, we are broken, and we can experience the divine healing balm seeping in.

A THIEF IN THE NIGHT

... for you know very well that the day of the Lord will come like a thief in the night. While people are saying, "Peace and safety," destruction will come on them suddenly, as labor pains on a pregnant woman, and they will not escape. (I Thessalonians 5:2-3)

It was a warm summer day when 52-year-old Betty Hoover came in for her routine blood pressure checkup. She and her friends were leaving the next day for a weekend vacation at the shore. She was anxious to finish her appointment so she could resume her vacation preparations. I went through my usual routine, checking her blood pressure, listening to her lungs and then her heart. As I placed my stethoscope over her heart, I realized that what had been up until then a routine office visit had now become something entirely different. Her heart rhythm was irregular, and an EKG confirmed my suspicion that she had atrial fibrillation. Atrial fibrillation is a fairly common rhythm disturbance of the heart that can cause a variety of potentially serious complications. She was having no symptoms, however, and was annoyed at what she perceived to be a nuisance that threatened her vacation.

I reviewed the possible complications she might experience and recommended hospitalization for a few days to run some tests and get her started on treatment. She refused, however, confident that if she really had a serious problem she would feel ill, and she didn't. She did agree to start some new medicine by mouth and promised to come back for a checkup the following week. Three days later I received a phone call from a hospital near the Eastern Shore. She was being admitted there after having suffered a massive stroke from which she would later die.

A disaster, like a thief, seldom comes when we expect it. The fact that we may feel fine does not mean that we are fine. Without proper preparation (a relationship with God through Jesus Christ), Scripture tells us we won't escape the day of the Lord (judgment). While this may seem to be an annoying nuisance, it is also the truth, and it would behoove us to listen.

BUCKET THEOLOGY

For out of the overflow of his heart his mouth speaks. (Luke 6:45b)

I watched as the tall, black Zambian woman drew her bucket of water from the well. She then broke off a small branch from a nearby tree, placing the sprig in her bucket of water. Then, before I could figure out how she accomplished the sleight of hand, the heavy bucket, which just seconds before was on the ground, now rested atop her head. As she left for her village, I suddenly realized the function of the floating sprig. It broke up the ripples on the water surface to keep the water from sloshing out of her bucket.

That's what I needed several nights ago. I needed a metaphoric sprig to keep what was inside me from sloshing out for all to see. I had been at a church leadership team meeting. The meeting was ambling along in its usual fashion when I suddenly realized one person on our team was talking in a critical, mean-spirited way. What was even more disconcerting was that I was that person.

Mercifully, the meeting soon came to an end, and I was left to wonder, "Where did all that bile come from?" As I went over the list of the usual suspects (lack of sleep, my parents, the phase of the moon, and the guy on the grassy knoll), I remembered what one of my former pastors had said: "When you tip a bucket, all that comes out is what is already inside." It was a humbling reminder that I am, and always will be, a sinner who falls short of the glory of God (Romans 3:23).

FINISHING WELL

And let us run with perseverance the race marked out for us. Let us fix our eyes on Jesus, the author and perfecter of our faith … (Hebrews 12:1b-2)

One of my favorite sections in *The Chronicles of Narnia* by C.S. Lewis is in *The Voyage of the Dawn Treader*. Reepicheep, a talking mouse with unsurpassed bravery and loyalty, is one of the greatest knights in all of Narnia. Reepicheep accompanies the king and a band of daring sailors on a dangerous voyage across the sea to the world's end, Aslan's country (a metaphor for heaven). When the voyage becomes difficult, many of the sailors want to abandon their journey as fear and homesickness grip their hearts. Reepicheep, however, does not waver. He says it matters not what others do; his plans are fixed. He will go as far as possible in the *Dawn Treader*, and then he'll continue the journey paddling his small boat. If his small boat gets stuck or sinks, he will swim on with all four paws until he can go no more. When his body sinks to the bottom of the sea, he will, with his last bit of strength, point his nose eastward, toward Aslan's country.

Last week I was at a weekend retreat for spiritual seekers and new believers. One of the persons helping with the retreat was Elizabeth, a frail ninety-five-year-old woman in the last days of her earthly journey. She is down to about eighty pounds, is attached to oxygen tubing 24/7, is hard of hearing, has failing vision, and needs help for even the basic activities of daily living. Yet when asked if she wanted to share anything about her faith, like a dark ember blown to life by a gust of wind, she began to glow radiantly. Directing all her energies into her testimony, she shared with passion and conviction that had been tested and proven through the experiences of her life. I leaned over to my wife and whispered, "She's stretching her nose toward Aslan's country." Tears came to my eyes as I heard her speak of the transforming power of God's amazing grace. Elizabeth is persevering in the race God has given her, with her eyes fixed on Jesus. She is finishing well, and in doing so, she challenges us to do the same.

ADVICE FOR THE PROUD

[W]isdom is found in those who take advice. (Proverbs 13:10b)

The baby was barely a week old, but he was already knocking on death's door, and I hadn't the foggiest notion why. He had been born in the village, but that circumstance was common in this remote, rural area in eastern Honduras. My wife and I had been sent there to give relief to an overworked missionary doctor couple. They were just returning from a long-overdue vacation, and I wanted to reassure them of my competence. This critically ill newborn, however, was *not* very reassuring.

The baby had been healthy and vigorous the first few days of life but then started nursing poorly, and his belly began to swell. I had put him on one of the new broad-spectrum antibiotics I'd brought with me from the States. Certainly this medicine should have been enough to persuade him to get better, if for no other reason than out of deference to the high cost of his treatment! Nonetheless, his condition continued to deteriorate, and he had now developed some ominous twitching movements. Norvelle, one of the returning doctors, took one look at the baby I had been agonizing over for several days and said, "Maybe he's got tetanus." Newborn tetanus—now why hadn't I thought of that? Maybe the thought had eluded me because there'd only been a handful of cases in the U.S. in the past twenty years. But it would have been kinder to my ego if she had pondered or hemmed and hawed a bit before making her astute diagnosis.

I was embarrassed. Rather than applaud her keen diagnosis, I found myself wanting to defend my faulty treatment plan. Nonetheless, I switched the baby over to appropriate treatment for newborn tetanus. The baby recovered more quickly than my bruised ego.

A MARRED WITNESS

"The Pharisee stood up and prayed about himself: 'God, I thank you that I am not like other men—robbers, evildoers, adulterers—or even like this tax collector.' ... But the tax collector ... beat his breast and said, 'God, have mercy on me, a sinner.'" (Luke 18:11, 13)

We Christians somehow have the idea that we should cover up sin and failure in the church to avoid marring our witness to the world. Such a stance, however, is not honest, biblical or helpful. To begin with, it's not honest because we are *all* sinners (Christians included). This sinful nature is not only our experience but also our theology (Romans 3:23). Secondly, it's not biblical to hide our sins—the biblical approach to sin and failure was full disclosure. The Bible did not whitewash David's committing adultery with Bathsheba, Moses' killing a man in a fit of anger, Thomas' doubting Jesus' resurrection, Paul and Barnabas' arguing and then parting ways over a mission trip, etc. Finally, it is not helpful because non-Christians *know* that believers are not perfect. Our attempts to protect our good names produce the opposite effect. The label Christians are most often given is "holier-than-thou hypocrites" for trying to cover up our moral failures. The *sine qua non* for the Christian is not a perfect, holy life, nor is it orthodox theology. The hallmark for the life of a Christian is love (John 13:35).

While pursuing holiness wholeheartedly, the monastics have always been well aware of personal sin. Sixth-century monks, in an attempt to pray without ceasing, often practiced "breath prayers." Breath prayers are short prayers that can be spoken in one breath. The most famous breath prayer is the "Jesus Prayer," sometimes described as an abbreviated form of the whole message of the Bible: "Lord Jesus Christ, Son of God, have mercy on me, a sinner." This is an honest and biblical prayer, and if we live our lives with this attitude, we won't have hypocrisy as a stumbling block for nonbelievers. This prayer demonstrates that the essence of Christianity is not in thinking we are extremely good (which we are not), but rather, in knowing and acknowledging that we are sinners in need of God's mercy and grace.

GOD IS OUR REFUGE

And when Jesus had cried out again in a loud voice, he gave up his spirit. At that moment the curtain of the temple was torn in two from top to bottom. (Matthew 27:50-51a)

Recently, two friends of mine unexpectedly had someone close to them die. One lost a grandson and the other her husband. I've been pondering the huge chasm between our intellectual understanding of suffering and death, and the anguished cry of our souls in despair. Platitudes about death and suffering abound, but they are inadequate. When one has been stabbed in the heart, a bandage for the mind somehow misses the mark. When one aches so deeply that all the senses are numbed and reason itself seems meaningless, an explanation is nothing more than a round peg in a square hole.

After Lazarus died, his sister Mary fell at Jesus' feet in tears (John 11:32-33). Jesus could have talked about faith or the afterlife, but instead, Scripture says Jesus was "deeply moved," and he "wept" (11:33, 35). Sometimes *that* is the God we need. We need to have the same God who inexplicably failed to intervene in our sore tragedy, cry with us in our pain. Somehow, that is more helpful than explanations that lie beyond what our minds can grasp.

Our God is not uncaring or indifferent. At the moment of his son's death, God tore the curtain that barred the entrance into the Holy of Holies. Hebrew scholars remind us that rending the curtain symbolized more than permission for everyone to have direct access to God; it also represented God's anguish over Jesus' death. When King David received word his sons had been killed, he tore his clothes (II Samuel 13:31). When Job got word of the death of his sons and daughters, he tore his robe (Job 1:20). It is no coincidence that at the moment of Jesus' death, God tore *his* garment (the curtain) as well.

It is somehow comforting to know that when we suffer with anguish too severe for words, when the very bones that were made to support us have turned to rubber, and when we may not even want God's company—he remains with us anyway. He tears his garment in shared grief, he weeps with us in sympathy that surpasses words and reason, and when we feel ready to collapse, "underneath are [his] everlasting arms" (Deuteronomy 33:27).

THE MARRIAGE COVENANT

... It is because the LORD is acting as the witness between you and the wife of your youth ... she is your partner, the wife of your marriage covenant. (Malachi 2:14)

All four of my daughters are now married. Now that the excitement and busyness of those events have passed, I find myself waxing more philosophical about the significance of the marriage covenant. Marriage, like God's other covenants, is a pledge or promise. While some biblical covenants were conditional, the promise to Noah (to never again destroy the earth by flooding) was unconditional (Genesis 9:8-17). In a similar way, my daughters and sons-in-law promised to love each other unconditionally—"in sickness and health, for richer or poorer, for better or worse." In the marriage covenant, we see that each partner shares his or her assets and debts. The sharing of assets and debts is also seen in the New Covenant instituted by Jesus (Luke 22:20). The sharing in this covenant, however, is very lopsided. Christ paid the debt for our sins on the cross, and we are also the beneficiaries of his unending assets/blessings. It's a "win-win" situation for us. He pays our debts, *and* we get his assets.

Abram's name changed to Abraham when God established his covenant with him. Similarly, in many cultures a name change occurs with the marriage covenant. Biblical covenants often had accompanying signs for remembrance. God promised Noah he would never again destroy the earth with water. The pledge was sealed by the sign of the rainbow (Genesis 9:8-17). My daughters used the traditional wedding ring as symbols to remind them of their solemn vows. In the Old Testament, covenants were often sealed with the blood of animals (Genesis 15:9-21). The New Covenant was sealed with Christ's blood. In many ancient covenants, the participants cut themselves and mingled their blood to seal the covenant. In marriage, we see the mingling of bloodlines in a unique and intimate way; children are the living symbols of the genetic mingling of the couple's bloodlines.

Marriage is unique among the covenants of Scripture, as it has been incorporated into our secular culture. Thus every marriage, whether between Christians or not, provides a natural opportunity to share with our non-Christian friends about the nature of God and his workings with us, reflected so graphically in the God-ordained covenant of marriage.

THINK ON THESE THINGS

But his delight is in the law of the LORD, / and on his law he meditates day and night. (Psalm 1:2)

In spite of Scripture's frequently mentioning meditation, many modern evangelical Christians view it with suspicion and practice it by omission. Some of the caution stems from the frequent association of meditation with Eastern religions. You no doubt have heard of the guru who had his tooth filled without Novocain; he wanted to "transcend dental medication." On a more serious note, Christian author Richard Foster points out that Eastern religions' goal is to empty the mind (detachment). Christian meditation starts by emptying one's mind (detachment from the world) but then proceeds to the goal, which is filling one's mind with God (attachment to him). The book of Psalms encourages us to meditate on God's words (119:48), his attributes (48:9), his creation (77:12) and his promises (119:148).

Paul also recognized the importance of contemplative thought. He said if anything is true, noble, right, pure, lovely, admirable, excellent or praiseworthy, we should "think on these things" (Philippians 4:8, KJV). Meditation can serve as a means for entering into God's presence. As we reflect on God, his attributes, words and deeds, we are ushered into the Holy of Holies. To be in God's presence is to be changed by him.

Brother Lawrence, a seventeenth-century cook in a French monastery, used meditation as a way to focus on God in his lifelong pursuit to "practice the presence of God." He couldn't understand how Christians could be satisfied when they didn't "live in God's presence. I keep myself there by simply paying attention and gazing lovingly at God ... [it] often gives me such happiness and joy on the inside, and sometimes on the outside, that I have to control myself so I won't look silly to others." Oh, that I would be so affected by God's presence that I would have to worry about looking silly to others! Let us take the time to "think on these things."

A FORESHADOWING
OF TRINITARIAN THEOLOGY

Therefore go and make disciples of all nations, baptizing them in the name of the Father and of the Son and of the Holy Spirit. (Matthew 28:19)

The revelation and understanding of the Trinity was not fully developed in Old Testament (OT) times. As a result, when we read about God in the OT, we tend to think of God the Father. However, since the New Testament (NT) has revealed the nature of the Trinity (the Father, the Son and the Holy Spirit), we should not forget that the God of the OT is the same triune God.

Although not clearly stated, there are provocative hints of the Trinity throughout the OT. In Genesis 1:1 we read, "In the beginning God created ..." The Hebrew word used here for God, *Elohim*, is plural. This plurality in a name can be used as a literary form of intensification, but it also allows for the plurality of the triune God. In Genesis, God said, "Let *us* make man in *our* image" (1:26a, italics mine). While the use of plural Hebrew pronouns can reflect royalty (i.e., God the Creator-King), it also allows, once again, for the involvement of the Father, the Son and the Holy Spirit in the creation of man.

The Holy Spirit is frequently spoken of in the OT. At the dawn of creation, we read that "the Spirit of God was hovering over the waters" (Genesis 1:2). We also find frequent mentions of God's Holy Spirit's coming on persons at special times and for special purposes (Exodus 31:3, Numbers 11:25, Isaiah 63:11, et al.). Perhaps even more intriguing, however, are numerous OT instances when God came in a visible form to speak to his people as the "angel of the LORD" (Genesis 16:7, Exodus 3:2, Numbers 22:22). As these passages are studied, most Christian scholars agree that the angel of the LORD is the pre-incarnate Jesus Christ.

There is only one God. Yet there are three persons who share that being with the other two. While our limited minds will always fall short of understanding the mystery of the Trinity, it is a mystery present in both the Old and New Testaments. While it is important to understand as much theology as we can, it is also important to understand that our finite minds will never be able to comprehend an infinite God. The presence of mystery with our God is a reflection of his greatness.

HEARING AND DOING

Do not merely listen to the word, and so deceive yourselves. Do what it says.
(James 1:22)

God speaks, we hear him, and all too often our behavior goes on without change. God's voice may come to us through Scripture or a friend, or it may come during prayer or worship time. It is the same voice that some time ago spoke the world into existence. In spite of the speaker's credentials, he has given us the ability to choose how we respond. We can obey God's voice, or we can let his words dissipate unheeded into the crevices of space. All too often we exercise our power option to disobey God—how's that working out for us? James says the only thing it accomplishes is that we deceive ourselves.

Does God, however, really expect us to do what he says? The few persons who have actually done that in the past were labeled radicals or extremists and defied explanation by the rest of the world. Francis Chan, in his book *Crazy Love*, says, "The world is always bewildered by its saints." When our actions cannot be explained by our personalities, our upbringing, or our potential for personal gain, however, people are likely to take note. As Christians, our lives and actions should cause others to wonder and beg the question, "Hey, what's going on here?"

Nonetheless, all too often we grasp at straws by hoping that our lives in overview will somehow add up to more than the sum of their parts. Even though I'm not really heeding God's voice today—it's no big deal—it will somehow all work out in the end. Pulitzer prize-winning author Annie Dillard reminds us that how we live our days is how we live our lives. We need to grasp this truth. How we live each day (and that includes this one) is how we live our lives. We should not deceive ourselves into thinking otherwise.

ACCOMPLISHMENTS

I tell you that in the same way there will be more rejoicing in heaven over one sinner who repents than over ninety-nine righteous persons who do not need to repent. (Luke 15:7)

Steve Jobs, co-founder and former CEO of Apple, recently died at the age of fifty-six. Jobs' accomplishments are already legend. He developed the first widely used personal computer (PC) in the world (Apple II) and the fastest selling PC ever made (iMac). He also developed the first PC to be controlled by a "mouse." He oversaw the development of the iPhone, the iPod and the iPad. He was also the owner and developer of Pixar, which produced the first computer-animated feature film, *Toy Story*. Jobs once said, "We are here to put a dent in the universe." Certainly from our perspective we would say he accomplished that goal with amazing success.

I began to wonder, however, "How does our perspective differ from that of the heavenly hosts?" This is what I envisioned: One day a heavenly host (for the purposes of our discussion, one host equals 2,000 angels) was perched on the clouds discussing the mortal realm. Michael asked, "Did anyone notice that Steve Jobs fellow and all the things he did in his lifetime?" There were nods across the crowd, and one of the angels responded, "Yeah, that was nice." Then Gabriel spoke up, "Did anyone notice Ethel Hooper?" Big smiles broke out across the entire group. Gabriel continued, "She's been praying for her troubled granddaughter for the last three years. Yesterday when Ethel was teaching her granddaughter how to bake cookies, Ethel shared with her about Jesus, and her granddaughter gave her heart to our Lord." There was a holy hush that spread across the entire host like a ripple on a pond. Then, with one accord, the angels broke out in cheers, "Hallelujah! Glory to God in the highest! Yes! Praise be to Jesus the Savior!" The cheers and praises continued for one hundred and fifty years.

THE PASTORAL LAITY

It was he who gave some to be apostles, some to be prophets, some to be evangelists, and some to be pastors and teachers, to prepare God's people for works of service. (Ephesians 4:11-12a)

I was in my early teen years and having a discussion with my father, who was also the pastor of my church. He said something that shocked me. We were talking about the importance of a vibrant healthy church, in which the sick were visited, the poor were given aid and the non-Christian co-workers and neighbors were told about the good news of Christ. It was at this point that he spoke what I feared must be heresy. "You know," he said, "those things aren't really *my* job."

"What do you mean that's not your job?" I asked. "You're the pastor, aren't you?" My dad then went on to tell me about the leadership gifts from Ephesians 4 and how the primary job of Christian leaders is to prepare and equip *God's people* to do the work of the church. We are the body of Christ, and each of us has been gifted to function in unique ways in Christ's body for the common good (I Corinthians 12).

Too often, we expect the work of the church to be done by an overburdened few. It's been said, "The church is like a football game, with fifty thousand people who are desperately in need of exercise, watching twenty-two people who are desperately in need of rest." The church, however, is not meant to be a spectator sport. Perhaps it would help to do away with the word "laity" since Scripture teaches us that we are actually all priests (I Peter 2:9). As each of us realizes our own calls to ministry, we can undo the shackles on the body of Christ to release the unused power of the church.

October

THE YEAR OF JUBILEE

"Count off seven sabbaths of years—seven times seven years ... Consecrate the fiftieth year and proclaim liberty throughout the land ... each one of you is to return to his family property ... The land must not be sold permanently, because the land is mine and you are but aliens and my tenants ... [Slaves] are to be released in the Year of Jubilee." (Leviticus 25:8, 10, 23, 54)

Every fifty years was a jubilee year for the Israelites. Land was to be restored to the family of its original owner, and the land was to rest (i.e., remain fallow) that year. Debt-slaves were to be freed during the Year of Jubilee. The Sabbath principle, of persons resting every seventh *day*, had been extended to the sabbatical *year* when the land was to rest. This was then extended to the jubilee year, which followed every seventh set of sabbatical years. God established jubilee (like the Sabbath) for humans.

The Israelites were apparently not so different from us today. They got caught up in the temporal values of their day. They needed to be reminded that the things they strove so hard to obtain and clung to so tenaciously were not really what was most important. The Year of Jubilee was a speed bump in the rat race of their lives to remind them that *God* owned all the land, that no one owned the people and that their temporal values and pursuits were often misguided.

The essence of Sabbath is the cessation of our normal pursuits. The Year of Jubilee contains the Sabbath principle but goes further since jubilee means to celebrate or rejoice. Hence, we are to *cease* clinging to possessions, power and prestige, but beyond that, we are to *celebrate* and enjoy people (not slaves), parity (not feudal land ownership) and provision from God (not from our own working of the land). Jubilee was a year of inversion, in which everything was turned upside down. Instead of humanity's perspective ruling their lives, God's perspective reigned for the entire year—a refreshing viewpoint.

ARMED WITH TRUTH

Put on the full armor of God so that you can take your stand against the devil's schemes. … Stand firm then, with the belt of truth buckled around your waist. (Ephesians 6:11, 14a)

Lawrence Richards, in his Bible Dictionary, points out that the Old Testament concept of truth emphasizes *reliability*. If something is true, one can rely on it; it is dependable. On the other hand, the New Testament concept of truth emphasizes *reality*. If something is true, it harmonizes with the reality of the world around us.

The apostle Paul speaks about truth being part of our spiritual armor. The purpose of spiritual armor is to stand against the devil's schemes. The devil is a deceiver, but deceit is disarmed with the weapon of truth. Jesus himself, when tempted in the desert, used the truth of God's Word to fend off the devil's attacks (Matthew 4:1-11).

While God's Word is truth, his Word also points us to the ultimate Truth, who is Jesus Christ (John 14:6). Jesus, as the ultimate Truth, is completely reliable *and* reveals reality. He fulfills both the Old and New Testament emphases regarding truth. Jesus' reliability is demonstrated by the fact that we can put our faith and trust in him, and he will never leave us nor forsake us (Deuteronomy 31:6). Jesus shows us reality in several ways. He demonstrates the following: 1) the reality of who God is (his heart and his ways), 2) the reality of who we are (self-centered persons in need of him), and 3) the reality of our world (seeing beyond the camouflage of culture and secularism).

As soldiers of faith, we are vulnerable without the belt of truth. However, when armed with truth, the winds of deception and the arrows of illusion will have no effect—we can truly "stand firm."

AT JESUS' FEET

*Then Mary took about a pint of pure nard, an expensive perfume; she poured
it on Jesus' feet and wiped his feet with her hair. (John 12:3a)*

Mary, Martha and Lazarus (of resurrection fame) were siblings, and
friends of Jesus, who lived in Bethany, a town just a few miles from Jerusalem. Jesus often used Bethany as a place of rest during his years of
ministry. The Bible gives us three vignettes of Mary in which she is found
"at Jesus' feet." Each story illustrates a different aspect of her devotion to
Jesus and is worthy of review.

Worshipful service (John 12:3) Judas criticized Mary for
"wasting" expensive perfume when she anointed Jesus' feet. Judas complained the money should have been given to the poor. However, Jesus
commended her devotion, reminding us that nothing is more important
than giving worshipful service to our Lord.

Waiting on his words (Luke 10:39) Martha, the consummate
hostess, thought she couldn't go wrong by busily doing good deeds. Mary,
however, sat "idly" listening at Jesus' feet. Surprisingly, Jesus rebuked
Martha and affirmed Mary. Mary realized we can be so involved with
good activities that we miss what God is saying to us. True devotion is
focused first on hearing God's words, which gives us *his* direction for our
activities.

Weeping when all seemed lost (John 11:32) Lazarus, Mary's
brother and Jesus' friend, had just died. How could Jesus have allowed
this to happen? How could life go on without Lazarus? Overwhelmed
with sorrow and questions, Mary fell at Jesus' feet. Where else could she
go when her world was crumbling around her?

Mary's devotion in each of these situations is exemplary. She
demonstrates that there is *no* greater service than to worship our Lord.
She shows us that listening to our Lord is more important than a frenzy
of good deeds. And finally, she reminds us that when our carefully cho-
reographed life disintegrates before our eyes, our response should be to
fall at the feet of Jesus.

DISCERNING SPIRITUAL ODORS

[Goliath] was over nine feet tall. ... Goliath stood and shouted ... "This day I defy the ranks of Israel! Give me a man and let us fight each other." On hearing the Philistine's words, Saul and all the Israelites were dismayed and terrified. ... David asked the men ... "Who is this uncircumcised Philistine that he should defy the armies of the living God?"
(I Samuel 17:4b, 8, 10-11, 26)

My nurse, Faith, had just put a woman and her three children in an exam room. I noticed Faith was an off shade of green and looked like she might regurgitate her breakfast. This poor family emitted an odor that was overwhelming. Nonetheless, as I walked in the room, they smiled broadly, completely oblivious to the malodorous tidal wave I was experiencing. They were the beneficiaries of a merciful physiologic phenomenon called olfactory fatigue; due to their prolonged exposure to the odor, they had lost the ability to smell it.

The Israelite army, due to their prolonged exposure to a secular, godless mindset, had lost their ability to "smell" the stench of their own faithlessness. David, however, was acutely aware of the stench on the battlefield. Calling it as he saw it, he candidly wondered, "Who is this uncircumcised Philistine [i.e., this person who doesn't even know Yahweh] that he should defy the armies of the living God?"

Similarly, when we have prolonged exposure to the secular world and its values, we risk *spiritual* olfactory fatigue—an inability to smell whether something is fresh or rancid (godly or godless). To allow our noses to regain their discriminatory ability, we need time breathing pure fresh air (studying Scripture, fellowshiping with Christians, listening to good music, praying and meditating with God). The food on our plate may be fresh and tasty, or it may be spoiled and putrid; it's prudent to make sure we can smell the difference before we eat. We need to be able to sniff out the good from the bad.

FOLLOW ME

"Come, follow me," Jesus said ... At once they left their nets and followed him. (Matthew 4:19-20)

Most persons would define religion as a set of beliefs and practices that adherents are to follow. With this definition, Christianity would not really qualify as a religion—for we are not called to follow a set of rules, moral standards or a belief system. Instead, we are called to follow a person, Jesus Christ.

While modern-day Western Christianity has fairly clearly compartmentalized one's spiritual call (to follow Jesus) and our job-related call (to a particular occupation), this division has not always been the case. The word "vocation" comes from the Latin word *vocare*, meaning "to call." One's vocation was originally seen in the context of a spiritual calling, although this meaning has largely been lost. While Christianity has historically integrated our work and spirituality, we have too often bought into our culture's way of sorting and categorizing our lives.

Our secular culture would say religion can serve a function in society by encouraging people to do good things. Whatever brings out the latent good in people, with or without the association of a god's name, can serve in some way to benefit the common good. Ethics professor Stanley Hauerwas, however, tells us that the world's way of thinking is false and assumes goodness can be present without God. With regard to our culture, he says, "Atheism is the air we breathe." I would add that secularism is the water we drink and humanism is the food we eat. The omnipresent world-think in which we are immersed is contrary to true Christian thought.

As Christians, our primary call is not to do good deeds, to help people, or even to have a positive impact on the world around us. Rather, we are called to follow Jesus. Without Jesus, doing good deeds and helping people are empty, shallow actions. Worse yet, they are misleading imitations of our true calling. In his book *The Call*, Os Guinness says that a life lived listening to the divine call is a life lived before the only audience that matters—"the Audience of One." With a simple, "Follow me," Jesus invites ordinary people into an extraordinary adventure, a relationship with the triune almighty God.

PART OF CHRIST'S BODY

So in Christ we who are many form one body, and each member belongs to all the others. (Romans 12:5)

Our local church has been struggling. We have lost three-fourths of our members in the past three years. There have been issues with leadership, unhealed wounds from the past, thoughtless gossip, ill tempers and unkind words. We have disputed our vision and our theology. We have Arminians, Calvinists, charismatics, conservatives, liberals, messianic Jews and pacifists all under one roof and, I trust, one God. Although we are the body of Christ, we are also damaged, divided, distraught and distracted. I wonder where God is in this mess and what it means to be a body of believers committed to each other when the easiest option would be to abandon ship.

In his book *The Blue Parakeet*, Scot McKnight describes the Bible as a story with a plot—creation, fall and redemption. He says we often tend to jump from the fall (Genesis 3) to redemption (the Gospels), but in so doing we skip more than seventy percent of the Bible, which lies in between. Those hundreds of intervening pages deal with the covenant community of Israel, God's chosen people. In the New Testament, God's chosen people are the covenant community, now called the church. God has always chosen primarily to relate to his people in the context of community (i.e., where persons are in relationships with others). Jewish philosopher Martin Buber, in his typically cryptic-yet-profound fashion in *I and Thou*, emphasized the importance of relationships: "I require a You to become; becoming I, I say You. All actual life is encounter." We need other people to help define who we are in the world and before God. We need others to recognize ourselves as individuals, and we need others to live life as God would have us live. God's community can provide encouragement, accountability, fellowship, discipleship, and the joy of living life in dynamic relationship with God and others.

So, although some of my church family may be about as similar to each other as *The Odd Couple*'s Felix and Oscar, we cannot fully accomplish God's purposes for us without each other. Although my present church is smaller than before, we remain one of God's covenanted communities of believers, and we need each other to be God's people. And as the Body of Christ, God has not and will not abandon us.

GOD'S ETERNAL LOVE

Give thanks to the LORD, / for he is good. / His [loving kindness] endures forever. (Psalm 136:1)

The Hebrew word *hesed* has been variably translated as "love," "mercy," "kindness," "faithful love," "steadfast love" and "covenant faithfulness." Some say "loving kindness" may best flush out its rich meaning. Psalm 136 repeats the phrase "His *hesed* (loving kindness) endures forever" twenty-six times. In the psalm, the phrase is interposed throughout a narrative history of God's creation, deliverance and judgment. On first analysis, the repetition seems overplayed and unnecessary. Perhaps, however, it is there to remind us how important it is to read between the lines of history where God's "loving kindness" *is* ever-present. Without God's "loving kindness," history (and this poetic passage) reads like an uninteresting series of accidental happenings without any point. When God's "loving kindness" is seen to permeate history, however, we see a vibrant story with God's presence and purpose written all over it.

Bible teacher Ed Miller once remarked that if we read Psalm 136 without the historical narrative portion, we are left with "God's loving kindness" over and over again. His loving kindness was present before our history began and will remain after it ends. *Our* story, which seems so important to us, is only an evanescent soap bubble in a room full of porcupines. His loving kindness, however, endures forever!

THE VALUE OF DOUBT

Consider it pure joy, my brothers, whenever you face trials of many kinds, because you know that the testing of your faith develops perseverance. (James 1:2-3)

Living in Zambia for three years, we saw hundreds of children get a severe form of malaria called cerebral malaria—many of these children died. Adult Zambians also got malaria, and although they felt quite ill and miserable for several days, they virtually never got cerebral malaria or died. Adults survived because they had weathered frequent bouts of malaria as children and had developed some protective immunity.

Timothy Keller, in *The Reason for God*, says, "A faith without some doubts is like a human body without any antibodies in it." Such a body is susceptible to overwhelming infection. Persons who deny and avoid doubts or questions, perhaps fearing that doubt is wrong or reflects a weak faith, fail to experience the benefits of a tested faith. Weathered doubt, an uncertainty that has been experienced and examined, can provide protective strength against future questions.

During college, my wife, Doreen, had her childlike faith challenged by one of her professors. He was a learned, charismatic theologian in a trusted position as a teacher in a Christian college. As he led the class down the rose path of historical criticism of the gospels, many in the class suddenly found themselves questioning all they had ever believed. Doreen could have tried to deny the existence of her doubts, or she could have embraced her doubts as being more valid than her faith. Instead, however, she chose to acknowledge her doubts, and she used them as an impetus to investigate the basis for her faith and the substance of her doubts. As she researched, she found answers to many of her questions and evidence enough to convince her to believe the Christian faith was reasonable and worth believing. Having travelled that difficult road has given her the benefits of a weathered, tested faith.

A BROTHER'S FAULTS

If your brother sins against you, go and show him his fault, just between the two of you. If he listens to you, you have won your brother over. (Matthew 18:15)

You could have pushed me over with a wet spaghetti noodle. I was stunned, aghast and embarrassed by the criticism that had just been leveled against me: "You are arrogant, and you walk around like you own the place." There was more, but that was the gist of it. The words were out, and like Chernobyl, once destructive material is released you must deal with the fallout. There were three of us in the room—a mediator, the accuser and a gelatinous replica of me about to ooze out of my chair.

I would like to tell you my first response was gratitude to him for caring enough to take time out of his busy schedule to share his concerns with me. However, my first thoughts were more along the lines of "Who asked for your opinion?" and "What about you, you're not so perfect yourself!" and "Why did I ever agree to hearing you out in the first place?" As I tried to suppress my baser responses, my brain kept trying to verify with my ears that I had actually heard what I thought I had heard. During the eternal pause that ensued, two sets of eyes remained riveted on me, making the possibility of an unnoticed escape seem unfortunately improbable.

The admonition Jesus gave in Matthew 18 as a pattern for settling disputes and addressing sins had always seemed like a good one … but that was before I was the one with the faults. And for that matter, I had also never wanted to be the one to confront someone either; both roles seemed very difficult. American author Donald Barthelme said truth is a hard apple to catch and a hard apple to throw—this seemed, however, more like trying to catch a giant pumpkin than an apple. I found myself pushing back fervently against any truth in his accusation; I wanted to drop the pumpkin, or perhaps throw it back at him. Unfortunately, I remembered when I first became a member of our church that I had said something about being willing "to give *and* receive counsel"—bummer!

October 10

A GOD FULL OF GENDER

So God created man in his own image, / in the image of God he created him; / male and female he created them. (Genesis 1:27)

One of the things about God that is both awesome and frustrating is that he is so far beyond our comprehension. Nonetheless, he has made himself known to us in numerous ways: 1. The *spoken word* (Creation). God spoke the world into existence, and his natural creation reveals him to us (Romans 1:20). 2. The *written Word* (the Bible). Scripture reveals stories about how God has worked with humans, the plan of salvation and counsel for holy living. 3. The *living Word* (Jesus Christ). The Apostle Paul tells us, "For in Christ all the fullness of the Deity lives in bodily form" (Colossians 2:9). By becoming human, Jesus gave us the fullest and clearest revelation of God.

In Genesis we see yet another revelation of God, for man and woman were created "in his own image." Though mere mortals, we can in some way reflect something of the image of our Creator. Masculinity and femininity *together* unveil an aspect of the wholeness of who God is.

When discussing masculine and feminine traits, we often argue about which attributes are better or get caught up in the nature versus nurture debate. Anthropology has shown us how the ambient culture can affect the development of different traits in men and women. Biology, on the other hand, has demonstrated the presence of innate differences between men and women based on genes, hormones and neurophysiology. Nature and nurture is clearly one of those cases of "both/and," not "either/or."

While Scripture most often portrays God as our Father (e.g., Deuteronomy 32:18), maternal imagery for God also occurs (e.g., Isaiah 49:15). Since both males and females were created "in his own image," this should not come as a surprise. Therefore, looking at both masculinity *and* femininity can reveal more of the totality of our awesome God.

OUR MATERNAL FATHER

"O Jerusalem, Jerusalem, … how often I have longed to gather your children together, as a hen gathers her chicks under her wings, but you were not willing." (Matthew 23:37)

God is spirit and is therefore neither male nor female. We've all heard that said and accepted it as truth, for the most part. However, I believe a richer vision of God is that he is *both* male and female. The union of the unique traits of men and women is a part of the wholeness of God. Our Creator encompasses the traits we call masculine and feminine yet transcends the limitations of human gender.

Scripture uses several maternal metaphors for God. A mother hen calling her chicks to safety and comfort under her wings illustrates God's care and protection for us. God nurtures us as a mother nurses her baby (Isaiah 49:15). God's "feminine" traits also include tenderness (Hosea 2:14), compassion (Exodus 34:6) and creativity of new life (Genesis 1-2). John Eldredge says, "Eve [as a symbol for all women] embodies the exquisite beauty and exotic mystery of God." God wants to be the "beauty" that we desire above all else. Eldredge says God's desire to be pursued, chosen and treasured is another part of his image imprinted on women.

God created men and women to complement each other. A man and woman's sexual union is much more than a species' method of propagation. Sexual intimacy is in some ways a reflection of God that includes openness, vulnerability, tenderness and joy. It also enables us to join hands with God in the creation of new life. Sexual union, as God desires it to be practiced, is a revelation of who God is.

God is our maternal father. Seeing God's feminine traits does not emasculate him. It shows that who he is goes *beyond* masculinity. Indeed, even the *sum* of masculinity and femininity is but one facet of the huge diamond of God's wholeness.

THE MALENESS OF GOD

[Jesus] said to them, "When you pray, say: 'Father' ... " (Luke 11:2)

Although God made man *and* woman in his own image (Genesis 1:27), the Bible usually portrays God as male. Masculine pronouns are exclusively used, and the rich metaphor of God as our father is used over two hundred times in the New Testament. And of course Jesus, the incarnation of God, was a man. So what does masculinity reveal to us about the nature of God?

John Eldredge, in *Wild at Heart*, talks about typical male and female characteristics. One masculine trait he discusses is a wild passion in the heart of every man. As I envision Jesus clearing the temple of the moneychangers and animals in John 2, I see a picture of God's untamed passion for purity and justice. God placed passion in us as a reflection of what is also a part of him.

As our Father, God is the male parent who is traditionally owed honor and respect. Although he may discipline us, he does it out of love not anger (Proverbs 3:12). Our Father also makes sure our needs are met (Matthew 6:33). In the Jewish culture, reverence and awe precluded even uttering the name of God, Yahweh. Yet Jesus said, "When you pray, say: 'Father.'" The father metaphor conveys a wonderful yet unfathomable revelation of our intimacy with God.

When we see earthly mothers (or fathers) who are left to raise children without the other parent, their parental shortcomings are often evident. God, however, is not limited by gender. As his children, we have a parent who is complete, lacking in nothing. He contains the unity of masculinity and femininity, while going beyond both. As we view this unity, we are given a tiny glimpse of the depth and breadth of God's greatness.

ATONEMENT

All this is from God, who reconciled us to himself through Christ, … not counting men's sins against them. … God made him who had no sin to be sin for us, so that in him we might become the righteousness of God.
(II Corinthians 5:18-19, 21)

The problem is clear. We are sinful creatures, whose most noble intentions are fraught with duplicity. Yet God, who desires a personal relationship with us, is holy, pure and perfect. Our sin separates us from God, and we are totally unable to do anything about it.

A middle-aged man walked into our mission clinic in rural Zambia. He complained about a rash on his arms and neck. He'd also had diarrhea for several weeks. His family said he was becoming confused. It was this last bit of information that finally caused the dim lights in my head to start flashing. This man had pellagra. Although I'd never seen the illness, I'd read about it, and it was a favorite test question in medical school. It was the disease with four "d"s—diarrhea, dermatitis (a skin rash), dementia and death. This devastating illness is caused by a deficiency of the vitamin niacin. His life-threatening problem had a simple and readily available solution.

Our separation from God, caused by sin, also has a readily available solution. The sacrifice of Jesus, the Lamb of God, has already paid the penalty for our sin. When we accept this sacrifice by faith, we are made holy in God's eyes and reconciled to him. This concept, called the atonement, has several deep, theological definitions. However, the definition I like best is more practical than theological. The "Atonement of Christ" is the answer to the question, "How can I, a sinful human being, approach a pure and holy God?"

LISTENING LOVE

Everyone should be quick to listen, slow to speak and slow to become angry.
(James 1:19b)

In medical school and residency training, one of the points frequently emphasized was the importance of getting a good history from the patient. After twenty-eight years in clinical practice, I realize now more than ever that listening to the patient's story is the most important means to ultimately diagnosing their illness. Of course examining the patient, doing blood tests and ordering x-rays can also be helpful, but these things usually just confirm the diagnosis I suspected from the history.

The importance of good listening is not restricted to the medical field. In virtually any type of relationship, good listening is fundamental. A study was once done asking persons to look at pictures of faces with different expressions to try to identify the emotions correctly. Most people could correctly identify anger, pain, joy, surprise, fear and sorrow. Interestingly, however, most were unable to distinguish between faces expressing intent listening and those showing love—they looked the same.

When we listen intently, we confer personal value on the speakers. Because we communicate that what they are saying is important, this translates into their surmising that they are also important. We show persons that we care for them when we give up our time to hear them speak. It's also the best way to get to know someone well, and often we're pleasantly surprised at what we find. But most importantly, good listening conveys *love*, and it is "by this all men will know that you are my disciples" (John 13:35). We know God listens well and loves us well. Are we sharing God's listening love with those around us?

THE GOD OF HOPE

May the God of hope fill you with all joy and peace as you trust in him.
(Romans 15:13a)

This is a presidential election year, and we have heard countless speeches glibly promising *hope* for a better future. Yet there is a palpable undercurrent of skepticism in our country about whether the possibility of a better future is really likely ever to happen. The US economy is in a slump, our divorce rate is approaching fifty percent, each day over fourteen hundred Americans lose their lives from suicide or homicide and nearly five hundred rapes occur. Approximately thirty-four percent of our high school seniors admit to illegal drug use, school shootings are becoming more commonplace, and the wars in Iraq and Afghanistan drag on. Perhaps fear and despair are appropriate responses to our present situation.

A biblical perspective on hope, however, shows that when circumstances were most dismal, hope was even more important. When David anguished over his enemies and his own mortality, he knew where to turn. "But now, Lord, what do I look for? / My hope is in *you*" (Psalm 39:7, italics mine). When persons conspired to dethrone and kill David, he understood that "[God] alone is my rock and my salvation" (Psalm 62:2). Biblical hope is not based on circumstances but on God and our relationship with him.

In the New Testament, the object of our hope was made more tangible in the person of Jesus Christ, whose resurrection gives us hope over even death (I Thessalonians 4:13). Paul says the God of hope fills us with joy and peace. This doesn't mean we will not suffer pain, sorrow and tragedy, but it does mean that in spite of any circumstances, we can look toward the future expectantly, with joy and peace, knowing our hope lies with God.

ANSWERED PRAYER

[God] answered their prayers … (I Chronicles 5:20b)

As a child, my mother told me God always answers our prayers. Sometimes he says "yes," and sometimes he says "no." Through the years, I've learned some other ways God responds to my petitions: "I have a better way." "Not now." "You do it." Or perhaps the most cryptic response, "I am God."

From our perspective, the purpose of our prayerful petitions is to get God to act in line with our desires. However, we must acknowledge that many of our prayers are misinformed, shortsighted, self-centered or some combination thereof. Our prayers may also be contradictory to what others are praying for. I'm praying for a sunny day for my daughter's outdoor wedding while my neighbor is praying for rain for his failing crops.

If God answered all our prayers as we think best, he would be no wiser than us. We often pray for life's circumstances to be easier. Yet catching a glimpse of God's perspective reminds us that hardships may be necessary to develop patience, trust and empathy. Thus, God's answers to our prayers may be other than expected. When Jacob wrestled with God and demanded a blessing, God touched his hip, causing a permanent limp (Genesis 32). When we pray for a touch from God's hand in our lives, like Jacob, we may get what we need rather than what we want.

Sometimes we may also have "boomerang prayers." As we pray, we may be convicted that "somebody really needs to do something about this." Then it boomerangs and hits us; we are somebody. C.S. Lewis goes so far as to say that God "seems to do nothing Himself which He can possibly delegate to His creatures."

Finally, however, reason and logic sometimes are found wanting. There are times when we can't figure out any possible explanation for God's lack of response to our prayers. When Job cried out to God in his agony and confusion, God's only reply seemed to be basically, "I am God" (Job 38-41). For Job, it was enough—is it enough for us?

BEAUTY IN VARIETY

[Christ] is the head of the body, the church … (Colossians 1:18)

As I've fellowshipped with different denominational groups, I've been impressed by the variety of emphases seen in different denominations. Although a *balanced* theology seems like the logical goal, I've been blessed by the diversity. I've found myself saying, "They're right to emphasize this aspect of Christianity; it's such an important part of what God wants for us." Denominational differences reveal important truths about God by highlighting them in bold type.

Quakers stress the contemplative life, listening to God in solitude. Methodists see the importance of holiness in our lives while Presbyterians are strong on God's grace and sovereignty. The Assemblies of God are open to experiencing God's Holy Spirit in all his fullness, and the Baptists revere God's Word (the Bible) and its inspired revelation to mankind. Mennonites have captured the importance of the community of believers and Christ's call to be peacemakers while the Salvation Army has stepped into the service and social justice ministry in a way that puts belief into practice.

Most of us think our own church is the only one that is properly balanced. We're critical of groups that emphasize one facet of Christianity at the expense of others. Perhaps, however, we should revel in the unique strengths each group offers. The beauty of a rainbow is magnified when the intensity of each individual color is greatest—denominations allow this to happen. The "body" language describing the church in I Corinthians 12 echoes the fact that variety can be good. While this was written with reference to gift diversity within individual churches, it may also be a truth that applies to denominational diversity in the universal church as well. "Now to each one [a different] manifestation of the Spirit is given for the common good" (12:7).

GOD AND US

"You are worthy, our Lord and God, / to receive glory and honor and power..." (Revelation 4:11)

Young children think the whole world revolves around them. They think everyone and everything exists to meet their needs. Adolescents are no better; they continue to be self-centered, believing their personal desires should be the basis for everyone's decision-making. As adults, however, we become more altruistic, putting the needs of others before our own. We also give in readily to other people's ideas and plans, realizing that being right and getting our own way are not really important ... or not?

The first sentence in Pastor Rick Warren's popular book, *The Purpose Driven Life*, is revealing: "It's not about you." I believe Rick Warren made that statement because he knows we are prone to believe the lie that it *is* about us. From childhood to adulthood, our selfish perspective doesn't really change very much—we just become more sophisticated about how we disguise it.

There is, however, hope for us. As we get a glimpse of the reality of who God is, our inflated self-image has a way of being tempered; awed by God's greatness, we are humbled. Charles Spurgeon points out, "Humility is the proper estimate of oneself." *Worship*, on the other hand, is the natural response to the proper estimate of who God is. Not only is life *not* about us, but it also *is* about God. Theologian Eugene Peterson said, "Worship is the strategy by which we interrupt our preoccupation with ourselves and attend to the presence of God." The basis for our creature/Creator relationship with God must be one of humility (because of who *we* are) and worship (because of who *he* is).

THE LONGEST WALK

Therefore shall a man leave his father and his mother, and shall cleave unto his wife ... (Genesis 2:24, KJV)

We walked on. Like Moses crossing the Red Sea with the children of Israel, we walked on dry ground between two oceans teeming with friends and relatives. My daughter's hand was wrapped around my elbow on a stroll that would forever be etched in my mind. Each step brought back a memory—warm memories that made my eyes moist.

We walked on. Had I loved my daughter well and encouraged all that God had placed within her? Had my wife and I modeled how to be good parents, how to fight fairly and forgive readily? Had I taught her how to check the car's oil and not to leave candles burning unattended? Had I stressed the importance of their always paying the credit card bills completely each month? And does she know not to run with a sharp object in her hand?

We walked on. Ahead of us stood a handsome young man. His eyes rested on his bride, my daughter. More difficult for me, however, were not *his* eyes but *her* eyes; my daughter was focused on Sir Galahad.

We walked on. I sensed more than felt her grip release my elbow as her outstretched hand melted into his. I had a brief impulse to grab her hand, pull her back and re-establish the old normalcy. However, just as one can't un-spill the milk, so also we could not return to my being the most important man in her life.

Dazed, I stopped walking and reluctantly sat down. My wife squeezed my hand, re-establishing reality. Leave and cleave—I reflected—leave and cleave. This is God's established rhythm of life. Reduced to spectator status, I managed a weak smile. And *they* walked on.

THE POWER OF SUFFERING

He then began to teach them that the Son of Man must suffer many things and be rejected ... and that he must be killed and after three days rise again. (Mark 8:31)

In 2004 Mel Gibson's movie *The Passion of the Christ* debuted. Many Protestants thought the film focused too much on Christ's suffering and death. We Protestants like to emphasize Christ's life, teachings and resurrection; that's why our crosses are empty while Jesus is still on the Catholic crucifixes. Obviously, Christ's life, teachings, suffering, death and resurrection are all important, and Mel Gibson had no argument with that. However, he wanted to focus on the passion, the suffering of Christ in the film.

I was deeply moved by the experience of viewing *The Passion of the Christ*. One of the things I still vividly remember was the awesome silence in the theater when the movie ended. As the credits rolled, everyone remained seated as though we dared not move, for we were seated on holy ground. A few sniffles could be heard through the darkness, and then slowly and reverently people began to leave, a few at a time. It seemed as though we were dumbfounded by God's love so profoundly demonstrated. Like the song title, I found myself asking, "What wondrous love is this?" A love far beyond any love I can imagine or comprehend.

Scripture tells us Christ was an example, and we are to "follow in his steps" (I Peter 2:21). Although few of us will be asked literally to lay down our lives for another, perhaps we underestimate the power of self-sacrifice in the mundane, everyday activities of life. Suffering and self-sacrifice may cause those around us to pause, sensing in some way that *they* are on holy ground. They may ponder, as I did in the theater, "What wondrous love is this?" And if they do contemplate, we can point them to Christ, the one who loved us so wondrously.

KNOWING GOD IN STILLNESS

Be still, and know that I am God. (Psalm 46:10a)

One of my patients suffered from a condition called tinnitus (ringing in the ears) for many years. He had been told there was no cure, and he had learned to live with it. Recently, however, the ringing had become worse, and he was now having difficulty sleeping at night. I'd heard about using "white noise" to replace the tinnitus and explained the idea to him. He was soon sleeping peacefully again by running a small bedside fan through the night.

Just as the ringing noise was a distraction that kept my patient from sleep, the busyness of our lives can be a distraction that keeps us from God. We suffer from cultural tinnitus, which diverts our attention from the divine. God is aware of our tendency toward distraction. In fact, for this very reason, he created the stillness of the Sabbath as a spiritual white noise to oust the diversions around us. Sabbath is not a time of silent, motionless nothingness. Instead, it is a time devoted to God. When God is our main attraction, he replaces the distraction of the daily diversions around us, like a spiritual bedside fan.

Sabbath is also a time to remind us of our nonessential role in keeping the universe aligned. We should not work hard to get everything done in six days, so we don't *need* to work on the seventh day. Rather, we should be willing to leave things undone. Resting when things remain to be done is a reminder that God, rather than you and I, is in control of our world.

The Psalmist realized the importance of a decision to be still. He didn't say, "When stillness happens to occur." Instead, he said, "*Be* still." In other words, we are to make stillness happen. And when we allow the stillness to replace the distractions of our everyday lives, we are better able to hear and know God. "Be still, and know that I am God."

FOLLOWERS OF CHRIST

As Jesus was walking beside the Sea of Galilee, he saw two brothers, Simon called Peter and his brother Andrew. They were casting a net into the lake, for they were fishermen. "Come, follow me," Jesus said, "and I will make you fishers of men." At once they left their nets and followed him.
(Matthew 4:18-20)

Although I'm not enthusiastic about labels, if I had to affix one to myself, I would say I am an evangelical, charismatic, contemplative, Anabaptist Christian. Since I've placed myself in the evangelical camp—sort of—I've given myself the right to criticize those of us who camp here. As evangelicals, we often stress the importance of *belief* at the expense of diminishing the importance of *discipleship*. We dwell on the theological significance of Jesus' birth, death and resurrection (Christmas, Good Friday and Easter) but minimize the importance of his life and teachings (no holidays here).

We are called, however, not just to be believers but also to be disciples of Christ. The New Testament call to discipleship in its simplest form is, "Follow me." Our call is not just to have faith and trust in Jesus but also to follow him. Sixteenth-century Anabaptist leader Hans Denck said, "No one can know Christ unless he follows him in life." So, to be disciples (followers) of Christ, we must live our lives as Christ lived his. Stuart Murray, in *The Naked Anabaptist*, says we should ask, "What *did* Jesus do?" instead of, "What *would* Jesus do (WWJD)?" This question takes us back to the Gospels and Jesus' life and teachings. Our faith cannot be separate from our walk. Our spiritual beliefs should be entwined with our finances, social interactions, health habits and environmental concerns. Following Jesus is not a one-time decision; it is a lifelong, all-encompassing journey.

LOVING ENOUGH TO SPEAK THE TRUTH

Instead, speaking the truth in love, we will in all things grow up into him who is the Head, that is, Christ. (Ephesians 4:15)

It was our first year of marriage. I was driving the car south along State Road 15, involved in a rapidly escalating argument with my wife. Suddenly she said, "Let me out of the car; I don't want to be with you anymore!" Deciding to call her bluff, I pulled over to the side of the road and stopped. Not willing to give in so easily, she actually got out of the car and began stomping back toward home, a twenty-mile trek. I defiantly drove onward in the opposite direction. Eventually, however, I softened, realized my stubbornness, and turned around to pick up my wife again. Although we both vividly (and with embarrassment) remember the event, neither of us can remember *what* the argument was about. Disagreements and conflicts are a part of life, and there are helpful and unhelpful ways (see above) to deal with such conflicts.

When differences arise, we can avoid them or confront them. Paul tells us we are to "speak the truth" (confront), but we are to do it "in love." David Augsburger, in his book *Caring Enough to Confront,* coined the term "care-fronting" to describe confronting in a caring way. Care-fronting, however, is not for the faint of heart. In fact, most of us prefer roundaboutness (tiptoeing through the tulips). We justify our lack of candor with a cloak of civility or as being thoughtful and kind. The Bible, however, says we are called to a "ministry of reconciliation" (II Corinthians 5:18) and are to be active "peacemakers" (Matthew 5:9). Avoiding conflict can actually be condescending if it is assuming the other person is unable to change. Evading clashes can also be dishonest when the perception of agreement may not be what either person is thinking or feeling at all.

The biblical prescription for candor and caring is somehow contrary to our natural inclinations. If we can't avoid conflict, we tend to want to fix the blame and fix the problem. The caring approach, however, is to heal the hurt and restore the relationship by speaking the truth in love.

October 24

FORGIVEN

"I, even I, am he who blots out / your transgressions ... / and remembers your sins no more." (Isaiah 43:25)

In *Girl Meets God*, Lauren Winner recounts the first time she went to confession. She spent three days composing a complete list of her sins. When she met Father Peter, her confessor, she liked him and wanted him to like her. She began mentally to delete some of the more awkward sins from her list. If she were to confess all those "awful-sounding things," she would appear very "ordinary and normal and not impressive" in Father Peter's eyes. Nonetheless, in the end she somehow managed to confess the entire list. Afterward, he absolved her: "The Lord has put away all your sins." Father Peter then took her six pages of carefully categorized sins and tore them to shreds. As they left the church, he told Lauren, "It's funny ... whenever I hear confession. After I leave the altar, I can never ... remember a single thing the penitent has said."

I was a junior in high school taking a quiz in Mr. Allen's English class. I couldn't remember one of the answers, but as my eyes fell on Nelda Beasley's paper, my memory was suddenly refreshed. Guilt must be one of the most potent of all cosmic forces since I stayed after class, face flushed from embarrassment, and confessed to my teacher. The following day, one of my classmates, who had been absent on the day of the infamous quiz, returned to school. Mr. Allen called on me, an untrustworthy convicted cheater, a ne'er-do-well if there ever was one, to go out in the hall and give her the quiz. How could he have forgotten my checkered past so quickly?

Father Peter and Mr. Allen both demonstrated a truth about how God forgives us. He remembers our sins no more. Not remembering is not the same as forgetting. God does not lack the ability to recall our sins. Instead, he *decides* not to recall them. He no longer sees us in association with our sins. They are removed "as far as the east is from the west" (Psalm 103:12).

GOD CARES

When you make a loan ... to your neighbor, do not go into his house to get what he is offering as [collateral]. Stay outside and let the man ... bring the [collateral] out to you. (Deuteronomy 24:10-11)

Like many Old Testament laws, this one seems to have no relevance for modern-day Christians. Today persons get their loans from banks, not other people, so there's no need to go to their houses to confirm adequate collateral. There may, however, be a principle here that is worth noting.

Dave Dorsey, seminary professor of Old Testament theology, says we are not bound to Old Testament laws (even the Ten Commandments) since we are under the New Covenant. Yet Paul tells us, "All Scripture is God-breathed and is useful" (II Timothy 3:16). The 613 Mosaic Laws were certainly a part of the Scripture that Paul was referring to, and therefore, these laws must reveal something important about God's heart, mind and ways.

With this perspective, Dorsey says we can look at the instructions given to the creditor in the above verse, do some reverse engineering and receive a revelation about God. Although the creditor had the upper hand, he was not to use his advantage to humiliate further the poor person in need of aid. Permitting the borrower to maintain the sanctity of his own home (not going barging in) and allowing him to bring out what was used for collateral allowed him to save face, rather than deepening his humiliation by the creditor's charging in and lording his superior position over him.

God cares so much for the poor and the powerless that he gave this law, not to protect their innate rights but just to protect their *feelings*. This divine insight has practical implications for many of our common activities such as how we do charitable giving (without demeaning the recipients), how we raise our children (with love and respect), and how we treat the waitress at the local restaurant (as a person of value providing us a service). God cares about people's feelings; we should do no less.

AN UNWAVERING STANDARD

Jesus Christ is the same yesterday and today and forever. (Hebrews 13:8)

The Age of Reason, or the Enlightenment, began in the 1600's and emphasized reason as the ultimate guide to discern truth. Rene Descartes, a leader in the movement, believed in God but still chose secular reasoning over a divine source of knowledge—described by some as putting "Descartes before the source." The fact that the latest mode of "wisdom" from secular society often opposes Christian thought is not surprising, but reason is now often left behind as well.

Contemporary philosophy tells us, "There are no absolute truths." This enlightened, tolerant, and progressive position, however, fails to address the fact that if there are *no* absolute truths, then even this statement itself cannot be an absolute truth. Therefore, absolute truth remains a possibility even by the statement that tries to dismiss it.

Western culture glorifies the wealthy, the strong, the popular and the influential. Yet a biblical perspective and Jesus' life tell us it is the poor, the weak, the meek, and the insignificant who are blessed. Capitalist America tells us that what we earn is ours to do with as we please. Yet Scripture tells us all we have and all we are is a gift entrusted to us by God, and we will be held accountable for how we use it.

Former US Secretary of Defense George Marshall wisely noted, "We must stop setting our sights by the light of each passing ship [the fluid morality of our culture]; instead, we must set our course by the stars." The authority of God's *written* word (the Bible) and the unchanging nature of the *living* word (Jesus) are our spiritual "stars" and trustworthy standards by which to set our moral course.

GOD IS WHO HE IS

"[The prophet] will turn the hearts … or else I will come and strike the land with a curse." (Malachi 4:6)

There is a popular notion that if God exists, he must be a force of pure love, without anger, dissatisfaction, judgment or punishment. It's difficult for people to believe in a loving God who is also a God of justice and judgment. In fact, however, a God who was not judgmental or angry when his creation acted in evil, self-destructive ways would be a God who didn't really care very much about us. The simplistic and erroneous picture of a God of love without judgment has led some to conclude that the picture of God in the Bible is inaccurate. Richard Dawkins, in his book *The God Delusion*, says the biblical God is the most unpleasant person imaginable: "The God of the Old Testament is a monster."

The book of Malachi begins with the powerful words, "I have loved you" (1:2)—nice God—yet ends with the ominous threat of judgment and "curse" (4:6)—mean God. However, is a God who judges justly really "mean," or is his judgment just an intrinsic outgrowth of his deep love? In the New Testament, as in the Old Testament, God reaches out to us in love (John 3:16), yet a day of judgment is coming for those who have rejected God and his ways. In the end, God will not tolerate rebellion, injustice and evil—would we want a God who did? We observe that our world is not always fair. There are people who suffer grievously at the hands of malicious persons who care for no others but themselves. Do we want a God who will ultimately set all that is wrong right? If so, we are asking for a time of judgment and meting out of justice.

God is complex, not the simple creation of our imaginations. His existence does not depend on what we might think or want him to be. He is who he is. We need to stop trying to conform him to our misconceptions and start trying to modify our understandings to the reality of his self-revelation.

THE DECEPTIVE TASTE OF SIN

When the woman saw that the fruit of the tree was good for food and pleasing to the eye ... she took some and ate it. She also gave some to her husband, ... and he ate it. (Genesis 3:6)

My patient was in his mid-forties, and he had just confided to me that he was having an affair with a woman ten years younger than him. He was married with two children but was ready to give it all up for this woman whom he truly loved and who really understood him. Although I was sure his new infatuation would give him nothing but buyer's remorse, he was sure I was wrong, and his situation was the exception to the rule.

Best-selling author Malcolm Gladwell, in his book *Blink*, analyzes how people make decisions. One of the decision processes he looked at occurred in the mid 1980's. Pepsi was challenging Coke in head-to-head taste tests and winning. Worried, Coke changed their secret formula until they could consistently beat Pepsi in taste tests. They then spent millions of dollars in marketing the New Coke, which ended up being the Edsel of the soft drink industry; they returned to the original Classic Coke. Their fallacy was that they failed to realize that a sip test of Coke and Pepsi was quite different from a take-home test (drinking an entire can). With just a sip, people favored the sweeter drink (New Coke, rather than Pepsi; or Pepsi, rather than Classic Coke). However, when drinking an entire can, people still preferred Classic Coke.

My philandering patient, like the soft drink sip tasters, found something he liked initially. However, the long-term satisfaction (take-home test) was sure to leave him disenchanted. Sin has a way of looking and tasting good in the beginning, but in the end it will always fall short of its inflated and deceptive claims.

CHILDLIKE HUMILITY

"Therefore, whoever humbles himself like this child is the greatest in the kingdom of heaven." (Matthew 18:4)

I was sixteen and had just gotten my driver's license, and the world was at my feet as I took Pat Graber out on my first official date. We went to see a movie, and all was going well until we drove away from the theater. I suddenly realized I had taken a wrong turn, and we were lost. Like all adolescent males, I hated to admit being wrong, so I didn't. Instead, I alternated right and left turns, hoping to spot a landmark I would recognize. This was probably not a navigating plan that would have impressed Lewis and Clarke, but I was desperate. I ended up turning on to a dead-end street and had to admit I was navigationally challenged (i.e., lost).

Four decades later, it is humbling to realize that neither my direction-finding skills nor my ability to admit error has improved significantly. Paul says that as Christians, we have been crucified with Christ (Galatians 2:20). Our old self was nailed to the cross to die. However, T.S. Eliot reminds us, "Nothing dies harder than the desire to think well of oneself."

It may seem easier to humble ourselves before God than to humble ourselves before others. However, if our humility before God is genuine, it will find expression through humility toward others. It's not "either/or"; it is "both/and." The sooner we confess our hopelessly lost condition, the sooner God will find us. When we humble ourselves before God, "self" reluctantly gets off the throne in our lives, and Christ takes his rightful position. Only as Christ is enthroned in our lives will we truly be able to live humbly with others.

GRACE AND WORKS

Do not merely listen to the word, and so deceive yourselves. Do what it says.
(James 1:22)

Grace is commonly defined as "unmerited favor." As Christians we realize that we have been saved by God's grace, and we are kept by that same grace. There is no amount of good works that could earn or keep our salvation. This is one of the unique aspects of Christianity among world religions; good works are not required for membership.

Just as we begin to understand the gravity of this truth about grace, along comes James telling us we should be doing good works. He expands on this theme in James 2, claiming, "Faith without deeds is useless" (v. 20). But aren't we supposed to be set free from the legalism of works? Hasn't James heard about grace?

Grace and works seem to be irreconcilable entities. Commenting on similar paradoxes in Christianity, English writer and apologist G.K. Chesterton said, "Christianity got over the difficulty of combining furious opposites, by keeping them both, and keeping them both furious." Struggling to be righteous by good works is a reversion to the futility of the law; it is a reliance on ourselves rather than the work of Christ. However, obedience as an outward expression of our personal relationship with Christ should be expected. Our good works are not "in order to" be saved, loved and accepted, but "because of" his salvation, love and acceptance.

Because of what Christ has done for us and because of his love for us, obedience is a natural response. If we are having trouble being obedient or have no desire to do good works, the deficiency is not one of willpower. Obedience and the desire to do good works are intimately linked to our relationship with Christ. Therefore, when we are lacking in obedience or the desire to do good works, we need to improve our relationship with Christ; therein lies the desire and the power.

A LIVING SANCTUARY

Moses could not enter the Tent of Meeting because the cloud had settled upon it, and the glory of the LORD filled the tabernacle. (Exodus 40:35)

The word "sanctuary" is used in the Old Testament to refer to both the tabernacle (built during the exodus from Egypt) and Solomon's Temple. The idea of a sanctuary was an area set apart to worship God. It was considered a dwelling place for the Almighty but was also a place where a holy God could meet with sinful people, usually by way of a sacrifice.

In the New Testament, we have a progression of the concept of God's dwelling place (sanctuary). The Apostle Paul tells us that as Christians, *our bodies* are temples (sanctuaries) of the Holy Spirit; God lives in us (I Corinthians 6:19). The corporate Church is also referred to as a "holy temple" where God can dwell (Ephesians 2:21). The fact that the Church is called the "body of Christ" (I Corinthians 12:27) reinforces the idea that God is pleased to dwell in us.

Moses said he couldn't enter the tabernacle because the glory of the LORD had settled on it—God's presence was there in all its glorious splendor! The fact that this magnificent, awesome God dwells in us should cause us to tremble in our seats. Since the time of Christ, *we* have become the dwelling place of the Most High. Individually, as Christians, and corporately, as the Church, *we* are the sanctuary for the Living God—what a privilege!

November

TRAINING OUR CHILDREN

Train a child in the way he should go, / and when he is old he will not turn from it. (Proverbs 22:6)

Our daughter Charis was four years old when she began to lie—not just half-truths or little white lies but blatant prevarications intent on deception. I'd previously imagined I was just as good a parent as any other self-centered, impatient father, but now I wasn't so sure. My secret fear that I was an inadequate father had now become a manifest reality, and everyone in the world would see that the emperor had no clothes. No one had ever really told my wife and me what we were getting into with raising children, and now here we were—clueless—with this larval-stage Idi Amin for a child.

"Train a child in the way [she] should go ..." Perhaps implicit in this proverb is the fact that without training, children are prone to go in directions they shouldn't go. Therefore, we should not be surprised or frightened when one of our children heads off in the wrong direction. In fact, their tendency to go in the wrong direction may be why they've been given a G.P.S. (Godly Parental Signal). Like a traffic light, parents give a green light when a child can proceed in the same direction and a yellow light when caution is needed. And when a parent turns red (especially in the face and ears), that means the child should stop and completely re-evaluate their direction.

Although proverbs are not promises or guarantees that hold true in all cases, they are descriptive principles that portray what usually happens. Accepting this principle (a trained child will tend to stay on that path of instruction), this proverb becomes an encouragement for conscientious parents and a warning for casual ones.

CONTENTMENT

I have learned the secret of being content in any and every situation, whether well fed or hungry, whether living in plenty or want. I can do everything through him who gives me strength. (Philippians 4:12b-13)

An interesting study was once done asking persons from different income levels what income they would need to be satisfied. From the lowest to the highest income levels, the answer was the same—just a little more than they were presently making. We tend to look enviously at those who have more than we have, so it's hard for us to realize that we wouldn't be satisfied even if we had just a little more. The believe-it-or-not truth of the matter is that contentment does not come from satisfying more of our desires.

Our family spent five months living with the indigenous Miskito people in Honduras. After several months of eating rice and beans on a daily basis, one of our children complained about the monotonous rice and beans. The rest of us chimed in with our "woe is me" chorus. Several days later as we sat down to eat lunch, our Miskito housekeeper Leticia passionately thanked us for the job we had given her. "Now I have enough money to buy rice and beans for my family," she beamed with her toothless smile. Our family became uncharacteristically quiet. Staring at the plate in front of me through misty eyes, I swallowed hard, hoping my gulp was not as audible to others as it seemed to me.

God taught us a simple truth that day—contentment doesn't come from fulfilling more desires but rather from changing our desires. From the youngest child to the oldest adult, no one in our family ever again complained about eating rice and beans. Our circumstances were unchanged, but God had changed our perspective. The loss of our desire for something more made us content with what we already had.

MOTIVES TRUMP ACTIONS

[King Amaziah] did what was right in the eyes of the LORD, but not whole-heartedly. (II Chronicles 25:2)

Holding freshly cut flowers behind his back as he approached our mother, my little brother Marty's eyes were beaming. He watched her face as he triumphantly presented his surprise gift, a bouquet of scarlet cannas and purple petunias harvested from the flowerbed in front of our house. I was seven years older than Marty, and I too was watching Mother's face. I was old enough to know that several decapitated cannas and a big hole in the middle of the petunia patch might not make Mom real happy. So I was a bit surprised and even a little disappointed when Mom joyously accepted his ill-gotten gift with a big smile and a hug.

Perhaps King Amaziah was also surprised when he did what was right yet fell from God's favor just because his *motives* weren't quite true. It seems God is more concerned with the person than the product, placing more importance on the attitude than the action. As God re-minded Samuel when he was selecting the second king of Israel, "Man looks at the outward appearance, but the LORD looks at the heart" (I Samuel 16:7).

Author and modern-day Trappist monk Thomas Merton spoke eloquently of God's gracious attitude toward us: "God, I have no idea where I am going. I do not see the road ahead of me ... The fact that I think I am following your will does not mean that I am actually doing so. But I believe the desire to please you does in fact please you."

Although my mother has probably long forgotten the flowers my little brother gave her on that otherwise unmemorable day years ago, I have not. She tangibly demonstrated a shadow of God's grace to my brother and me. Even today when I come to God with a bouquet behind my back, two thoughts cross my mind. First, what I may see as a won-derful gift is undoubtedly flawed by my imperfections, a realization that serves to keep me humble. But more importantly, God's grace by way of a "smile and a hug" reminds me of the unmerited benefits of being his child and the importance he places on the intention of my heart.

A TARNISHED TONGUE

A gentle answer turns away wrath, / but a harsh word stirs up anger.
(Proverbs 15:1)

It was midnight in the Dominican Republic, and I was still wide-awake. I was one of the adult chaperones for our church youth group on a short-term mission trip. I shared a small room with two teenage guys who continued to whisper despite my requests for silence. Suddenly, I found myself standing up in my underwear, yelling at these two rather surprised young men—not a pretty sight.

Needless to say, my outburst did not elicit the best response. After some heated discussion, I lay back down in a now silent room. I stared into the darkness as sanity slowly resumed control of my thoughts and feelings. Although I apologized for my harsh words, I was unable to retrieve the passionate words that were now tightly wedged into the crevices of their minds and emotions.

The tongue is so fickle; it is capable of blessing or cursing, gentle words or harsh ones. While I would like to lay the blame on my unruly tongue, Christ reminds us that the mouth speaks from the "overflow of the heart" (Matthew 12:34). The problem lies within me.

Mark Twain knew well the importance of our words. He once said, "The difference between the right word and the almost right word is like the difference between lightning and the lightning bug." Paul reminds us that our conversation should be "always full of grace, seasoned with salt" (Colossians 4:6). Because of the heart-tongue connection, we continually need to have our hearts transformed by the power of the presence of God. When that happens, our speech will be a blessing rather than a curse to those around us.

KNOWING GOD

You believe that there is one God. Good! Even the demons believe that—and shudder. (James 2:19)

We visited our daughter in Vancouver, British Columbia, during her first year of seminary at Regent College. We were fortunate to be able to sit in on a lecture from one of her professors, Bruce Hindmarsh. He pointed out something that many of us would prefer not to hear yet, nonetheless, need to know: Seminary, and the study of theology in general, can be dangerous to our faith.

One of the inherent risks of a formalized study of God is that the knowledge can become an end in itself, rather than a *means* to knowing God better. When our goal is to know more *about* God, rather than knowing God, we end up mistaking the bun for the burger.

The essential distinction is knowledge about God versus a relationship with him. I could learn a lot of information about my wife, Doreen—her favorite color, her favorite restaurant, her hobbies, her height and her hair color, without knowing her in a relational way at all. James reminds us that even the demons know *about* God, but that is not the goal. God wants us to have more than factual information about him (head knowledge); he wants us to be in an intimate relationship with him (heart knowledge).

We should learn about theology, and we should study Scripture, but each of these practices needs to be a way to knowing God better. If any of these practices becomes an end in itself, it has taken the position meant for God.

There are some parents who constantly video record each and every activity of their children. I fear if one of their children were to draw a picture of their parent it would have a video camera covering their face. Their excessive parental desire to preserve memories results in fewer memories that are made. As parents or as students of theology, we do not want to lose track of that which is most important. May our prayer echo Moses' plea: "Teach me your ways *so I may know you* ..." (Exodus 33:13, italics mine).

OUR FIRST LOVE

"You have forsaken your first love. Remember the height from which you have fallen! Repent and do the things you did at first." (Revelation 2:4b-5a)

I had the dubious distinction of having two of my daughters become engaged within six weeks of each other. I experienced some ambivalence as each of them shifted their affection and allegiance in a new direction. It was also interesting to see them inebriated with the experience of their "first love"—the first man they each gave their hearts to.

Their desire was to spend all their free time with their fiancés. When they were together, they seemed to have a joy that defied common sense. My daughters' desires were to please the special men in their lives, and those desires readily found outlet in acts of service and appreciation. When they looked into the eyes of their betrothed, their faces revealed a sense of wonder, adoration and excitement.

Our Lord criticized the church at Ephesus for having lost its "first love"; the passion was no longer there. The Ephesians were told first to *remember* "the height from which you have fallen" (cloud nine). They were then called to *repent* and *return* to "the things you did at first."

It is important for us to hear these words of admonition. We should be looking into the eyes of our Lord and Savior with joy and adoration. Jesus should be the focus of all we think and do. We should be spending time with him in spite of our busyness. As we relax in his presence, remember all he has done for us, and repent from our apathy, we will rekindle a sense of excitement and anticipation for our Beloved. It's like courtship all over again! Remember our first love …

THE GREAT VIRTUE

Be completely humble and gentle; be patient, bearing with one another in love. (Ephesians 4:2)

C.S. Lewis called pride "the great sin," so it seemed appropriate when Andrew Murray identified humility (in his book by the same name) as "the great virtue." Pride fosters a feeling of self-sufficiency that precludes a need for God. A humble self-appraisal, however, recognizes that we are needy, and this is the requisite state of the soul for approaching God.

One definition of humility is the proper appraisal of oneself in relation to God and others. The Apostle Paul speaks of humility as an integral part of "bearing with one another in love." Since humility is a part of how we demonstrate God's love, it is also a fruit of the Spirit and not of our will. Our natural self gives us pride while Christ's Spirit gives us humility. Since we are unable, by force of our wills, to make ourselves humble, what can we do? We can elevate Christ. It is as we make Christ foremost in our lives that we are made humble. The more Christ is high, the more we are low; it's a spiritual seesaw principle.

Scripture calls us to be humble: "Clothe yourselves with humility toward one another " (I Peter 5:5). Jesus also challenges us with his example: "Now that I … have washed your feet, you also should wash one another's feet" (John 13:14). But how can we have humility in us without becoming proud of its presence? Once again, it can only happen when we clearly realize it is not we, but Christ in us, who produces humility. If our lives have even the smallest trace of humility, we can rest assured *we* did not produce it. This realization should keep us humble!

WHITEWASHED TOMBS

Woe to you ... You are like whitewashed tombs, which look beautiful on the outside but on the inside are full of ... everything unclean. In the same way, on the outside you appear to people as righteous but on the inside you are full of hypocrisy and wickedness. (Matthew 23:27-28)

I was working in the outpatient clinic at Macha Hospital in the Southern Province of Zambia. The person who stood before me was a handsome, muscular man in his early thirties. He was well-dressed and spoke English, a sign of formal education. His complaint was a small dark purple nodule on his lower leg. Unfortunately, I had seen far too many of these innocuous-looking nodules while working at Macha. As I confirmed my suspicion by examining the lump, I was impressed (and depressed) by the irony of the situation. This man was in the prime of life and externally appeared to be the picture of good health. But this small nodule was not only a window into his internal health but also a window into his grim future.

The nodule was early Kaposi's sarcoma, an aggressive cancer that would literally eat away his body. The cancer, however, was a sign of a deeper problem. Virtually all the patients we saw with Kaposi's sarcoma had AIDS. The immune suppression caused by AIDS allowed the cancer to flourish. With no chemotherapy and no AIDS drugs available, his outlook was dismal. It was a sad realization to know that in spite of his external facade of good health, this young man was terminally ill.

His physical condition reminds me of our spiritual condition. We work so hard for that external, healthy, whitewashed look. Yet internally, we have a terminal case of sin that is resistant to even the most vigorous scrubbing efforts and potent medicine. The only remedy for our brokenness and sin is forgiveness by God's amazing grace. As Christians, we have accepted the gift of forgiveness, and the window into our future now looks through the cross of Jesus Christ, bestowing on us a righteousness we could never have mustered on our own.

A GOD OF EMOTIONS

He was despised and rejected by men, / a man of sorrows, and familiar with suffering. (Isaiah 53:3a)

Does God experience emotions? We might be inclined to admit he feels love but probably not much else. Surprise seems to be ruled out by his omniscience and fear by his omnipotence. But what about some other emotions like anger, sadness or happiness? Does God suffer, or does he laugh? Why does it almost seem sacrilegious to raise such questions? While God is spirit (John 4:24) and not a frail human being, we are told that we were created "in his own image" (Genesis 1:27), and emotions comprise a big part of who we are. Also, the Bible does talk about God's "anger" (e.g., Deuteronomy 7:4) and even describes him as "jealous" (e.g., Exodus 20:5).

In the New Testament, we see Jesus as one who wept when Lazarus died (John 11:35) and who lamented over Jerusalem (Luke 13:34). Yet even in the Old Testament, Yahweh grieved for his rebellious people, "Let my eyes overflow with tears" (Jeremiah 14:17). Perhaps the emotion and suffering of Jesus, which we tend to associate with his humanity, were actually part of his divinity.

Old Testament scholar Terence Fretheim says there are three ways by which God suffers: 1) *because* of people having rejected his love, 2) *with* people when they experience suffering and 3) *for* people because of their sin and its grievous consequences. Indeed, imagine a God who is unmoved in these situations. What kind of love would not grieve or be disappointed by rejection? Or what if God were uninterested and unsympathetic when we experienced tragedy, suffering or sorrow in our lives? A loving God who is detached and uncaring toward people who have rejected his Lordship and are destined to eternal separation from all that is good is difficult to envision. It seems to limit God if we say he is unable to respond emotionally to the people he loves—we have weakened him, not empowered him.

God's sovereign decision to experience emotions in response to feeble human beings does not diminish his power. In fact, biblical scholar Walter Brueggeman points out that a God free to be emotional is actually more dynamic than an unemotional God, with a greater range of responses. God's decision to be vulnerable to emotions paints a caring and powerful picture of his love. Christ's suffering and death bring that picture of love to life.

CHRISTIAN HYPOCRISY

For all have sinned and fall short of the glory of God. (Romans 3:23)

Christian hypocrisy could be defined as the difference between Christians and Christ. Unfortunately, the disparity is sometimes so great that people think it begs the question of whether or not Christianity is real. Non-Christians often seem to find great satisfaction in pointing out the latest moral failure of a televangelist or some well-known Christian figure. It's that "aha moment" that proves what they knew all along—Christianity isn't for real.

There are two problems with this chain of logic. First, they're looking at the wrong thing. They are looking at Christians instead of Christ. And secondly, they're under a false assumption; Christianity isn't a cure for sinning. We Christians too often try to project ourselves as prime examples of what Christianity is all about. But Christianity is all about Christ, not us. We should be pointing people to Jesus, not ourselves or other Christians, no matter how godly they may appear.

When non-Christians find imperfections in Christians, they believe it proves Christianity doesn't "work." As Christians, we encourage this misunderstanding by trying to hide our imperfections, fearing they will hurt our Christian witness. G.K. Chesterton, however, says that one of the strongest arguments for Christianity is the failure of Christians, thereby proving what the Bible teaches about our fallen nature. We need to remember that the primary difference between Christians and non-Christians is not that Christians sin less, but that we are forgiven.

While it's true that we are called to holy living and God is making us more holy, we have not yet arrived. We remain sinners with various degrees of residual imperfection. We need to acknowledge our persistently unholy lives and point people to Christ. He alone will never fail our trust.

HOW TO PRAY

Be joyful always; pray continually; give thanks in all circumstances, for this is God's will for you in Christ Jesus. (1 Thessalonians 5:16-18)

As Christians we are called to pray. The essence of our relationship with God, and with others, is communication; our communication with God has been given the name prayer. While there is no right or wrong way to pray, many have found using the acronym A-C-T-S useful. I would like to add an "F" at the beginning to give you the F-A-C-T-S for a helpful structure to your prayer life.

F – Face our need: This must come first because it is only as we face our inadequacy, our incompleteness and our need for God that we will see the necessity of prayer. Without this humble awareness of our need, the idea to pray won't even occur to us.

A – Adoration: Adoration involves looking at *who God is*. This is a very appropriate way to begin our prayer. As we see God in all his glory, honor and power (Revelation 4:10-11), we are reminded that he alone is worthy to receive our worship and praise.

C – Confession: Confession involves looking at *who we are* in honest terms—we are sinners. Being on our knees in confession is the appropriate posture to be in before a holy God whose forgiveness and mercy we require. Confession is important because unconfessed sin acts as a barrier between God and us, inhibiting our prayer life.

T – Thanksgiving: As we give thanks, we acknowledge what God has done in the past and is doing in the present, then praise him for it. The psalmist calls us to come into God's presence with thanksgiving (95:2), and the apostle Paul tells us to "give thanks in all circumstances."

S – Supplication: Asking God to act in response to our requests may seem arrogant, self-centered and manipulative, but it is also what Jesus tells us to do (Matthew 7:7). God's sovereignty has somehow incorporated our involvement through prayer. Petitioning God also affirms our dependency in the creature/Creator relationship.

Each of these steps in prayer should be interspersed with a period of expectant listening, for prayer is a conversation, not a monologue. This is a view of the F-A-C-T-S of prayer, as I see them.

DUST AND ASHES

"… though I am nothing but dust and ashes." (Genesis 18:27)

The Random House Dictionary defines dust as "fine dry particles of matter" and "that to which anything is ultimately reduced by disintegration and decay," and ash as "the remains after burning." Describing oneself as dust and ashes reminds us that our bodies are only a composite of the ordinary elements of the earth. Without God we are simply insignificant collections of atoms—cosmic dust.

In the cosmetic industry of the 1980's, there was a battle for the hair-color market. Preference hair-color by L'Oreal surpassed Clairol's Nice 'n Easy when the former came up with the following slogan: "I don't mind spending more for L'Oreal, because I'm worth it." This unabashed declaration of personal worth resounded with the desire of women's hearts in that era when women were struggling for equal rights. How do we reconcile this strong inner desire for significance (held by men as well as women) with the harsh reality of being dust and ashes?

When Moses approached God at the burning bush, Moses saw himself in comparison to the Almighty (Exodus 3:1-6). The façade of puffed-up pride and importance was torn away by God's presence like a toupee in a hurricane. Being in the presence of the great "I AM" (Exodus 3:14) gives a clarity of personal perspective like nothing else. When I see God as the great "I AM," I also see myself as the little "I am"—dust and ashes.

But there is an important addendum to this truth of our smallness. Scripture tells us that God formed "man from the dust of the ground and breathed into his nostrils the breath of life" (Genesis 2:7). God put something of himself into mankind to such an extent that we are created "in his own image" (Genesis 1:27). Herein lies the paradox of our identity. While we are dust and ashes, we have also been breathed into by God and are *in his image*. The value we yearn for as cosmic dust is due to his image being placed within us. The worth our souls long for can be reality if we are re-united with our Creator. Here is the source of our spiritual hope, for our value lies in what we can be if we allow ourselves to be found and loved by our Creator.

LIFE WITH PURPOSE

"For I know the plans I have for you," declares the LORD, "plans to prosper you and not to harm you, plans to give you hope and a future."
(Jeremiah 29:11)

Mrs. Stevens was thirty-eight years old and always seemed quite healthy when I examined her. Nonetheless, she seldom failed to have several complaints to address at each office visit. She would have a backache or headache, her arms were sore, she had no energy or she slept poorly. In spite of several normal x-rays and lots of normal blood tests, she was sure something was wrong—and she was right.

One day she came for her appointment, and it was immediately apparent that something was different. She was excited, energetic and smiling from ear to ear. She couldn't wait to tell me about a mission trip fundraiser she was involved in. I had to work hard to elicit any maladies that day. It turns out she had discovered the problem that I'd been unable to ferret out. Although a Christian, she hadn't understood God's plan and purpose for her life. Without purpose in her life, she had lost her joy and hope for the future. Her problems, though small, seemed intolerable.

Pastor and author Rick Warren says, "Without a purpose, life is motion without meaning, activity without direction. When life has meaning you can bear almost anything; without it, nothing is bearable. For the greatest tragedy is not death, but life without purpose." When my patient found the spiritual niche that God had designed for her, she became energized and fulfilled.

I see Mrs. Stevens less often these days. It seems she barely has time to get in for checkups. When she does come in, I now hear more about her passionate plans than her paltry problems.

November 14

FINDING THAT WHICH WAS LOST

"Rejoice with me ... For this son of mine was dead and is alive again; he was lost and is found." (Luke 15:6b, 24a)

Where could she be? Our nine-year-old daughter, Amaris, had disappeared. We were at our church's annual camp retreat in the forested hills of Pennsylvania. We had searched the lodge and asked all her friends, but no one had seen Amaris in over an hour. My heart sank as I forced myself to scan the surface of the nearby lake, which fortunately revealed nothing. Our friends noticed our frantic expressions and began to help us look in earnest. Some ran down the hiking trails calling her name while others started to organize search parties. Finally, our ears heard the words we had yearned for: "We found her!" The main lodge had a closet area where the maintenance supplies were stored. There, among the brooms, mops and cleaning agents, our beloved Amaris was reading a book, oblivious to our growing anxiety. Our whole church family joined in a collective sigh of relief followed by a wave of joyful celebration. We had found Amaris!

In Luke 15, Jesus told three parables about things that were lost. All three stories portray a strong desire for the lost to be found. With the lost sheep and the lost coin, a great effort is put forth to find that which was lost. In the case of the lost son, the father watches and waits, hopeful his son will return. The parables also depict great joy when the lost is found. When the son returns, a feast is prepared to celebrate. When the sheep and coin are found, friends and neighbors are invited to rejoice together. Jesus says that "in the same way" when a sinner repents, there will be "rejoicing in heaven" (15:7) and "rejoicing in the presence of the angels" (15:10).

As parents we love our children and desire for them to be "found" by God. However, it is comforting to know that God's heart contains that same love, though greatly magnified in quantity and quality. We experienced great joy when we found Amaris reading in the closet. How much more joy must there be in heaven when one who is spiritually lost is found—an unrestrained, joyous celebration!

THE REAL PROBLEM

Some men brought to him a paralytic, lying on a mat. When Jesus saw their faith, he said to the paralytic, "Take heart, son; your sins are forgiven." (Matthew 9:2)

Jesus saw the heart of the matter in a flash, never fooled by the glaring camouflage that blinded everyone else. Jesus was a healer, and the man brought to him was a paralytic. It doesn't take a rocket scientist to see what should have happened that day. Yet Jesus saw through the man's paralysis like a Saran Wrap vest and saw a heart crippled with sin. It was his heart that Jesus first addressed.

I used to moonlight as a doctor in the emergency department of a local hospital. We saw some unusual cases come through the doors, but I'll never forget the night when the triage nurse came running to me with fear in her eyes, "There's a crazy man here with a knife." We called for security personnel, and I got a syringe full of Haldol (an anti-psychotic medication). I hoped some big, burly security officer would sit on this guy while I gave him the shot. The scary patient, however, wasn't waiting for security people to arrive but came toward me yelling, "You have to take it out!" He was wild-eyed with blood running out of his ear, wielding what turned out to be not a knife but a fingernail file. A June bug had crawled into his ear and was unable to back out. Its burrowing activity against the man's eardrum was driving him crazy. He tried to dig it out with the fingernail file but had only succeeded in making himself bleed. Removing the beetle transformed this crazy, wild-eyed man with a bloody "knife" into a thankful, sane patient who hugged me in gratitude.

Haldol and a padded room seemed like the appropriate treatment when he first arrived, but what was really needed was a simple insect extraction. My first impression wasn't even close to being right! God is well aware of our inabilities to see true reality in life's circumstances. That's why he gave us his Holy Spirit to guide us into truth. We need to remember not to rely on our own understandings but to turn to God's wisdom (Proverbs 3:5-6). As we do this, the paralytics and the crazy people around us can be seen with God's eyes, so we can address their *real* problems.

November 16

A WEEPING WOMAN

Then the disciples went back to their homes, but Mary stood outside the tomb
crying. ... She turned around and saw Jesus standing there ...
(John 20:10-11a, 14)

Lacrimation (crying) is defined as the production of tears from the lacri-
mal gland in such quantity that they spill over the eyelid and trickle down
the cheek. Normally, tears produced to lubricate the eyes drain into the
nasolacrimal duct, which empties into the nasal cavity. That's why when
we cry, our noses run. While a few mammals will cry in response to
severe pain, crying as an emotional response to sorrow or elation appears
to be a uniquely human phenomenon.

Weeping occurs frequently in Scripture. Paul tells us, "Rejoice
with those who rejoice; mourn with those who mourn" (Romans 12:15).
Jesus affirmed the sinful woman who washed his feet with her tears
(Luke 7:36-50). Jesus himself wept as he approached Jerusalem (Luke
19:41) and when his good friend Lazarus died (John 11:32-35).

It is interesting to note that while Peter, John, and Mary Magdalene all visited the empty tomb, it was Mary whom Jesus honored with
his first post-resurrection appearance. John says the two disciples "went
back to their homes," but Mary stayed and wept. Perhaps it was not a
coincidence that Jesus appeared to the visitor who wept. Maybe her moist
eyes reflected a prepared heart.

While tears may blur our natural vision, they may sharpen our
spiritual vision. The Beatitudes declare those who weep are blessed, for
they will laugh (Luke 6:21). Israeli Prime Minister Golda Meir said,
"Those who don't know how to weep with their whole hearts, don't know
how to laugh either." I suspect Mary Magdalene, who wept with passion,
also laughed with delight in the company of her risen Lord.

JUSTICE OR MERCY

The teachers of the law and the Pharisees brought in a woman caught in adultery ... and said to Jesus, "Teacher, this woman was caught in the act of adultery. In the law Moses commanded us to stone such women. Now what do you say?" ... But Jesus bent down and started to write on the ground with his finger ... he straightened up and said to them, "If any of you is without sin, let him be the first to throw a stone at her." Again he stooped down and wrote on the ground. At this, those who heard began to go away one at a time ... until only Jesus was left, with the woman standing there. Jesus ... asked her, "Woman, where are they? Has no one condemned you?" "No one, sir," she said. "Then neither do I condemn you," Jesus declared. "Go now and leave your life of sin." (John 8:3-11)

It has been said the young demand justice, but as we age and see our own frailties more clearly, we cry out for mercy. The Pharisees initially were enthusiastic about meting out justice to this sinful woman. Jesus, however, challenged their false piety. Something he wrote in the sand changed their minds. Some think he may have written out the Ten Commandments, or perhaps he actually enumerated the Pharisees' own specific sins. In either case, when faced with the reality of their own sinfulness, they suddenly felt more compassionate. When we feel critical, how might that feeling change if *our* sins were suddenly written in the sand for all to see?

A middle-aged woman once went to a great artist to have her portrait done. When she returned to inspect the results, she was disappointed. "This portrait just doesn't do me justice," she said. The artist looked at the portrait and then the woman who stood before him. "Lady," he said, "it's not *justice* you want, but *mercy*." When we find ourselves demanding justice, we should remember this woman and be happy with God's mercy.

THE LAMB'S BLOOD

Since we have now been justified by his blood, how much more shall we be saved from God's wrath through him! (Romans 5:9)

As a young boy, I remember being surprised when my dad explained to me that no matter how hard I tried to be good, I would still be a sinner. He explained that it is not that we are sinners because we sin, but that we sin because we are sinners.

Salvation deals with both aspects of the problem of sin. Watchman Nee says the *blood* of Christ deals with the forgiveness of our sins (plural), while the *cross* of Christ deals with deliverance from the power of sin (singular) in our lives. Another way to say this is that the blood deals with what we've done (sinned), while the cross deals with who we are (sinners). While this parsing may or may not hold up to theological rigor, I find it helpful for understanding the overall picture of Christ's atoning work.

In Exodus, we read about the death plague on the firstborn of each household (12:1-30). This plague threatened the Israelites as well as the Egyptians. The only way of escape was to put the blood of a sacrificed lamb on the sides and tops of the doorframes. God said, "When I see the blood, I will pass over you" (12:13). Escape from judgment had nothing to do with the merit of the persons inside the house but was solely dependent on God's seeing the blood of the lamb.

What happened at the first Passover was a vivid foreshadowing of the ultimate salvation plan. Romans 6:23 tells us, "The wages of sin is death." John the Baptist foresaw Jesus' purpose when Jesus approached John by the Jordan River. With great spiritual insight, John the Baptist declared: "Look, the Lamb of God, who takes away the sin of the world" (John 1:29). The blood of Christ has paid our debt. We have been "justified [made just or righteous] by his blood." As Christians, when God looks at us on Judgment Day, he will see the Lamb's blood on the doorposts of our hearts, and the death sentence will also "pass over" us.

HEART DISEASE

I writhe in pain. / Oh, the agony of my heart! ... *(Jeremiah 4:19b)*

As a family practice doctor, I've heard a wide variety of complaints over the years. Nonetheless, I was surprised when this five-year-old boy told me the reason for his office visit. "My heart hurts," he explained. I quickly began to think about diagnostic possibilities. Perhaps he had a hole between the chambers of his heart or an abnormally narrowed valve—I would need to listen carefully for a telltale heart murmur. He was too young to have blockage in his arteries, but he might have a viral infection of the heart with secondary inflammation causing his pain. Or maybe he just *thought* it was his heart, but it was really his lungs causing the pain. He could have pleurisy pain from pneumonia. I certainly didn't want to miss anything in this child with heart pain.

After asking all the questions I could think of and after a thorough exam of this child, who looked healthier than me, I was perplexed. The only points of interest were that his mother reported the pain had started two months ago, and it seemed to get worse every evening around 5 PM, which was the time his father used to come home from work. I turned to his mother again, "What do you mean that his father *used to* come home from work at that time?" "Well," she said, "we've been separated for two months now, and his father no longer lives with us."

"My heart hurts." He had told me as clearly as he was able what the problem was, yet I was off on all the wrong tangents. I guess we hear what we expect to hear, straining conversations through our personal colanders. This was a poignant reminder for me to be a better listener.

BLESSED BY HARDSHIPS

"When I fed them, they were satisfied; when they were satisfied, they became proud; / then they forgot me." (Hosea 13:6)

We tend to think of blessings as health, wealth and a life free of hardships. The New Testament, however, presents a different story. In the Beatitudes, Jesus tells us the poor and the hungry, the weeping, the hated, the excluded, and the insulted are all "blessed" (Luke 6:20-22). Following a similar alien thought process, the disciple James says we should consider it "pure joy" when we face trials (James 1:2).

On January 12, 2010, Haiti experienced a devastating earthquake (7.0 on the Richter scale). Port-au-Prince was near the epicenter, and over 225,000 people were killed, 300,000 injured and more than 1,000,000 left homeless. My wife, Doreen, and I traveled to Haiti three weeks after the disaster to help provide medical care. In spite of the death and destruction, we were surprised to see many persons joyful and hopeful as they were turning to God for comfort and strength.

It is one of Christianity's paradoxes that we can experience blessings in spite of (or perhaps because of) severe suffering and trials. Christian journalist Malcolm Muggeridge notes, "Everything I have learned in my seventy-five years in this world that has truly enhanced and enlightened my existence has been through affliction and not through happiness … if it were possible to eliminate affliction from our earthly existence, the result would not be to make life delectable, but to make it too banal and trivial to be endurable."

When we are hungry, in pain or suffering, our need is obvious, and we require no prompting to turn to God. However, as Hosea notes, when we are fed and our bellies are full, we become proud (believing the illusion that we can take care of ourselves) and forget God. Perhaps this is why Jesus said, "Blessed are you who hunger …" (Luke 6:21).

ROBES

I saw the Lord seated on a throne, high and exalted, and the train of his robe
filled the temple. (Isaiah 6:1b)

While most of us know the story of Joseph and his robe of many colors,
Genesis actually tells us *three* significant stories about Joseph's robes. In
the most familiar story, Joseph's brothers stripped his robe from him,
then dipped it in goat's blood to deceive his father into believing he was
dead (37:31-32). In the second story, Potiphar's wife was left holding
nothing more than Joseph's robe when her attempt to seduce him failed.
She then used the robe to accuse Joseph falsely of trying to seduce her
(39:11-15). In the final robe vignette, Pharaoh dressed Joseph in "robes
of fine linen" (41:42), symbolic of conferring royal authority to him. In
the first two instances, the robes were *taken* from Joseph and used to do
him harm and injustice. In the last story, however, the robe was *given* to
Joseph and used to bring him honor and authority.

Joseph's story foreshadows the story of Christ. Jesus also had his
robe taken from him during a time that epitomized harm and injustice—the crucifixion (John 19:23-24). As with Joseph, however, Jesus
is later given a new robe. In Revelation, we see Jesus wearing a long,
flowing robe (1:13), symbolic of his royal authority, reigning at the right
hand of the Father.

Joseph and Jesus were disrobed to cause them *harm*, then given a
new robe to bring them *honor*. We also are given a new robe, the robe of
righteousness, to make us *holy* (Isaiah 61:10). The good deeds of our old
life are filthy rags (Isaiah 64:6), unfit attire to stand in God's presence.
We don't need our rags mended; we need a new robe, a garment of completely different material. Paul tells us that Jesus is our righteousness (I
Corinthians 1:30); he himself is our robe. It is only when we are clothed
with Jesus that we become righteous and holy.

ORDINARY MEN

When they saw the courage of Peter and John and realized that they were unschooled, ordinary men, they were astonished and they took note that these men had been with Jesus. (Acts 4:13)

When my four daughters were teenagers, my wife and I were keenly aware of the influence their friends had on them. Those with whom they spent time molded their attitudes, behavior and even speech patterns. This influential effect can also occur with spiritual matters. Being in the company of Christians can help us form good habits or break bad ones. It can also be an encouragement to our faith and provide positive role models.

When we spend time in the presence of God himself, however, a *supernatural* change occurs. In the Old Testament, after Moses had spent time with God, he had to veil his face because of the radiance with which it shone (Exodus 34). Peter and John were unschooled fishermen, yet they spoke with insight, power and authority that "astonished" the Jewish religious leaders. The explanation for these transformed fishermen was that they "had been with Jesus."

This morning I burned a big pile of dead limbs and twigs that I'd collected from the lawn after our last windstorm. When I came inside and looked in the mirror, I was surprised to see singed eyebrows and a face flushed from the heat. This afternoon everyone I met asked what had happened to my face. It was obvious something had left its mark on me. As we spend time in the presence of the triune God, we too will be notably changed. Let's dare to get so close to God that those around us will wonder what happened to us and realize "these people have been with Jesus."

November 23

WHO ELECTED WHOM?

[God] brings princes to naught / and reduces the rulers of this world to nothing. / ... no sooner do they take root in the ground, / than he blows on them and they wither, / and a whirlwind sweeps them away like chaff.
(Isaiah 40:23-24)

Today is Wednesday, November 5th, in a presidential election year. Based on the depression among some of my Christian friends today, you would think God himself had lost yesterday's election. "How could God have let this happen? Wasn't he paying attention? There's no hope for our country now."

First of all, it's important to realize that God *did* let this happen. He wasn't distracted or otherwise occupied when people entered the polling booths. Nothing occurs without passing through his hands. When we express our dismay at what God allows, we are just affirming our lack of omniscience. If we are tempted to take God to task for his action or inaction, we will have to wait in line behind Joni Eareckson Tada, Job and each parent who has ever buried their child. However, perhaps we should evaluate our own abilities to judge wisely. If we had been alive in first-century Palestine, how many of us would have thought God was unjust and had messed up badly when he let the gentle Galilean carpenter suffer death by crucifixion?

Secondly, no political party has a corner on Christianity. God is not a Republican or a Democrat; he's not even an American. Thinking we live in a Christian country is a fallacy, and if we base other conclusions on this erroneous premise, we will find ourselves in all kinds of trouble.

Finally, our response comes down to trust. When we second-guess things that happen in our world, we are presumptuously assuming we know better. Whose judgment do we trust, God's or our own?

PRIORITIES IN LIFE

Now listen, you who say, "Today or tomorrow we will go to this or that city, spend a year there, carry on business and make money." Why, you do not even know what will happen tomorrow. What is your life? You are a mist that appears for a little while and then vanishes. (James 4:13-14)

My daughter Rebekah was about twelve years old when we had a discussion about what she might be when she grew up. She mentioned several possibilities but carefully avoided the option to be a physician (my vocation). When I directly asked her if she'd considered being a doctor, her response seemed sheepish. As I pushed to hear more, she finally admitted, "I would just like to spend more time with my family."

I felt as though I had simultaneously been hit in the head with an iron skillet and stabbed in the heart with a dagger. I was stunned and wounded. I was stunned because I thought I had worked hard to spend enough time with my children, and I was wounded because I knew deep down she was right.

Her brave words helped my priorities in life come into clearer focus. Physician and best-selling author Richard Swenson says he tries to take his priorities from the one-hundred-third floor of the World Trade Center on September 11, 2001, at the moment the individuals stuck there knew they weren't going to make it. What mattered to them in those last moments when they knew death was near? Were they thinking about finances or family?

The truth of the matter is that we are all on the one-hundred-third floor of the World Trade Center—we just refuse to admit it. Our lives are "a mist that appears for a little while and then vanishes." Our relationships with God, our family and those around us are what are truly important. I thank God for using my young daughter to remind me of this truth.

THE PERSPECTIVE OF DEATH

It is better to go to a house of mourning / than to go to a house of feasting, / for death is the destiny of every man; / the living should take this to heart.
(Ecclesiastes 7:2)

In medical school, our first encounter with death was dissecting a human body. What happens when twenty-three-year-old students, who don't like being reminded of their own mortality, are confronted with a dead body? Since avoidance (not going to anatomy lab) and denial (saying it's not really a dead person) weren't viable options, humor and deperson-alization were common coping mechanisms. We nicknamed our body "Abra," as in "Abra Cadaver," as one way to avoid the serious thoughts that surround death. In addition, we dissected only one region of the body at a time, first the arm, then the leg, the abdomen, the chest and finally the head. The only portion of the body uncovered was the part being dissected, which helped to depersonalize the experience. "This is just a leg we're dissecting, and it's not *necessarily* part of a real person." Of course it was most difficult to play these Jedi mind games when it came to dissecting the face. Here we were confronted "head-on" with the reality that we were dissecting the body of a real person. This was someone who had laughed, loved and lived like us. The only physical remains of that person were this body in a plain, black, zip-up leather bag, reeking of formaldehyde.

Most of us prefer not to talk or think about death, but Solomon says it is good for us to confront the reality of death and better than going to a party. Our life on earth is a journey, and as for any trip, it is helpful to have signposts. Seeing death is an important signpost that reminds us our lives on earth do not last forever. Death is truly the destiny of each of us, and we who are living should take this to heart. For in remembering death, we are reminded how to live.

THE FOOTRACE OF OUR LIFE

Let us run with perseverance the race marked out for us. Let us fix our eyes on Jesus, the author and perfecter of our faith ... Consider him who endured such opposition from sinful men, so that you will not grow weary and lose heart. (Hebrews 12:1b-3)

The Christian life has sometimes been compared to a battle or a journey, but the writer of Hebrews refers to it metaphorically as a race. As in a real footrace, there are potential problems that can prevent us from running well.

As we race, there are distractions along the track that may tempt us to lose focus. There are billboard distractions like power, sex, money and prestige. However, there are also subtle distractions like trying to do good works, bring about positive social reforms, and make ourselves into better people. We cannot deviate onto rabbit trails we may find, however, even when they appear to be good ones. We must "fix our eyes on Jesus" so we do not veer to the right or the left. The trail that follows Jesus is the only trail that matters.

We also need to realize the Christian life is not a sprint but a long distance race. We may be tempted to give up at times because the race is long and hard. A short flurry of energy and activity, however, is inadequate. We must be committed to persevere to the end. If we begin to tire out, we are reminded to consider Jesus so that we will not grow weary.

Our life is the ultimate footrace. We cannot afford to be distracted or grow weary. The writer of Hebrews acts as a spiritual coach. His advice is essential: Jesus is the answer for running the race well. He is both our goal to focus on and our strength to rely on.

WRITTEN ON OUR HEARTS

"I will make a new covenant ... " / "I will put my law in their minds / and write it on their hearts." (Jeremiah 31:31b, 33b)

What does it mean to have the law written on our hearts instead of stone tablets? On a practical level, how is the New Covenant different than the Old Covenant? Two examples of how sins were dealt with in the Old and New Testaments may help to clarify the difference.

Moses said that those caught in adultery were to be executed (Deuteronomy 22:22). This was the law, and it meted out justice. However, in the New Testament the Pharisees brought a woman caught in the very act of adultery to Jesus. He said those free from sin could throw stones at her, and not one pebble was cast. Rather than condemning the woman, Jesus gently told her to go and sin no more (John 8:2-11).

The Old Testament law said that a rebellious, disobedient son should be taken out and stoned (Deuteronomy 21:18-21). Yet this harsh penalty lies in stark contrast to the story Jesus told of the prodigal son in Luke 15:11-32. This rebellious, disobedient son leaves home to squander his inheritance. Nonetheless, his father forgives him and welcomes him back with open arms; where's the justice here?

While the Law stressed the importance of justice, obedience and right behavior, the New Covenant is permeated with grace, mercy, and an unfathomable love. Jesus said he did not come to abolish the law but to fulfill it (Matthew 5:17). Fulfilling the law seems to go beyond following the letter of the law and reveals more of the complete nature of God. That which was written on stone was tough, and full of justice. That which is written on our hearts is gentle, and full of grace.

A PRETTY GOOD CHRISTIAN

"So, because you are lukewarm—neither hot nor cold—I am about to spit you out of my mouth." (Revelation 3:16)

How many passionate, sold-out, whole-hearted Christians have you known? My guess is that most of us couldn't fill a phone booth with them. Yet Jesus doesn't call half-hearted, part-time slackers to follow him. His call is always for the whole-hearted. Jesus said we are to love him with *all* our heart, soul and mind (Matthew 22:37). We are to deny ourselves, take up our cross and follow Jesus (Matthew 16:24). We need to count the cost (Luke 14:28), and once we have put our hand to the plow, we are not to look back (Luke 9:62). To follow Jesus, we must be willing to sell all our possessions (Matthew 19:21) and even be willing to leave our families (Matthew 19:29). Jesus' call is not for the timid but for the courageous.

When we see who God is calling and we look at those of us who have shown up, it's like a bunch of cheerleaders responded to an ad for dragon slayers. What's amazing, however, is that God can transform cheerleaders *into* dragon slayers if we are passionately, wholeheartedly sold out to him. Unfortunately, most of us don't want that much of God in our lives. We're content with a thirty, fifty or seventy percent commitment. We have enough of God, as is. While God asks us to give him *everything* (Luke 14:31-33), we've decided which parts of our lives are not included in *everything*. We've decided it's not really reasonable to be too on-fire for God (i.e., "hot"), yet we wouldn't say we are chilly or icy (i.e., "cold") toward God. We're content to be average, pretty good Christians, somewhere in the middle ("lukewarm" might describe us)—coincidentally the same temperature as spittle.

FREEDOM OF RELIGION

Having brought the apostles, they made them appear before the Sanhedrin to be questioned by the High Priest. "We gave you strict orders not to teach in this name," he said. "Yet you have filled Jerusalem with your teaching..." Peter and the other apostles replied: "We must obey God rather than men!" (Acts 5:27-29)

One of the founding principles for which our country was formed was the freedom of religion. We consider it a privilege that we can practice our religious beliefs without fear. In recent years, however, there seems to be an effort to sanitize the government and public institutions from any semblance of religious content. The goal seems not to be freedom *of* religion but freedom *from* religion. Taking "under God" out of the pledge of allegiance, prayer out of schools, and the Ten Commandments off the walls of our courthouses seems to promote the secularization of our nation more than promoting free exercise of religion.

Our Constitution states there can be no "law respecting the establishment of religion, or prohibiting the free exercise thereof." While purging any hue of religiosity from our government seems unnecessary to fulfill the intent of our Constitution, I'm still uncertain the secularization of our government causes as heinous a situation as some of my Christian friends believe. Losing some of the supporting props our culture has provided persons of faith may actually be good. Having Christian words and symbols entwined in our government can give us a false sense of security. Some wrongly believe that since we are residents of a "Christian country" (although no such thing exists), our citizenship confers a Christian status on us all.

A personal relationship with Christ cannot be obtained by governmental edict, legislative decree or political osmosis any more than marching people through a river will make them Christians via mass baptism. The decision for Christ is a personal one, not a legislative one. Even in countries with harsh, anti-Christian governments, thriving groups of Christians are found. Years ago, one of the leaders of the French Revolution told a peasant that all the churches' steeples would be pulled down so Christians would not be reminded of their old religion. The peasant replied, "But you cannot help leaving us the stars." No government can take away that which is truly necessary for Christian faith.

GRACE

We have peace with God through our Lord Jesus Christ, through whom we
have gained access by faith into this grace in which we now stand.
(Romans 5:1b-2a)

It's been said that in view of the fact that we are weak, sinful, imperfect beings wanting a relationship with an omnipotent, holy and perfect God, some adjustments are necessary. I believe these adjustments fall primarily under the heading of *grace*. Grace is God's answer to the dilemma of how to reconcile a helpless sinner with a holy God.

An understanding of God's grace requires both the brain and the heart. If our minds *comprehend* God's grace but our hearts do not, we end up feeling guilty (for our sins) and inadequate (for the gift of salvation). However, if our hearts *feel* his grace but our minds do not understand it, we are prone to be less concerned about holy living (since we are forgiven) and have a permissive conscience.

Grace is like a two-sided mirror that reflects both the nature of God and the nature of man. It shows our sin, need, and helplessness contrasted with God's love, acceptance and enabling power. It's very difficult for us to understand how one could get something for nothing. Grace seems too easy, and we're uneasy about being charity cases. Yet the reality of who we are and the nature of who God is make grace the inevitable solution.

We are unable to win God's favor in our own strength. God in his perfect love does not require us to earn that which we are incapable of earning. Instead, through Jesus' death, God, in some mysterious way beyond our comprehension, has bridged the chasm between him and us. As we put our faith in Jesus, we are covered with the "robe of righteousness" (Isaiah 61:10) and made holy. The practical result of grace is that our inadequacies no longer matter, and we can have "peace with God through our Lord Jesus Christ."

December

THE GOSPEL OF PEACE

Blessed are the peacemakers, for they will be called children of God.
(Matthew 5:9)

We are called to be peacemakers. But what does that mean, and how do we do it? As the father of four daughters, I've refereed my share of quarrels. It took me some time to realize, however, that peace in these situations involved more than just the absence of visible (or audible) conflict. If the underlying issues were not resolved, an ember remained, waiting to burst into flame at the next breeze of discontent. So even though it took more time and effort, the source of the problem had to be brought into the light of day and addressed.

Surprisingly, the origin of squabbles we address in our families and workplaces is not very different from what we see between warring countries in our global community. Worldwide, the most common source of conflict seems to be a real or perceived sense of injustice. In some cases unfair circumstances keep people in a cycle of poverty. In other situations, persons may be oppressed or have their rights overlooked. Injustice, unfairness and oppression can lead to anger, resentment and conflicts. Reinhold Niebuhr was aware of the fact that injustice is one of the major causes of war when he said that if we want *peace*, we must work for *justice*.

A practical theology of peace should not just be reactive when conflicts arise but proactive to prevent them. Peacemaking should take initiatives to alleviate pain and suffering and to promote justice, thereby often precluding conflicts. True peace is more than the absence of conflict; it is the presence of *shalom* (wholeness—not only physically, emotionally and spiritually, but also economically and socially).

When Jesus began his earthly ministry, he read from the scroll in the temple (Luke 4:16-21). He announced the scope of the gospel he was bringing. It was "good news to the poor ... freedom for the prisoners ... recovery of sight for the blind ... [and] release for the oppressed." When we see persons suffering unjustly or in pain, illness or poverty, we are called to minister to those needs. As we minister, we are not only being peacemakers but also announcing the good news of the gospel of Jesus Christ.

A BOLD BANNER

I am not ashamed of the gospel, because it is the power of God for the salvation of everyone who believes. (Romans 1:16a)

I recently heard of a young pastor from Rwanda who was martyred for his faith. Dr. Robert Moorehead tells of a letter being found on this pastor's body with these challenging words: "I am part of the fellowship of the unashamed. ... I have stepped over the line. The decision has been made—I'm a disciple of his. I won't look back, let up, slow down, back away, or be still. ... I will not flinch in the face of sacrifice, hesitate in the presence of the enemy, pander at the pool of popularity, or meander in the maze of mediocrity. ... And when [Christ] comes for his own, he will have no trouble recognizing me. My banner will be clear."

A ship's banner or flag is displayed to let others know its country of origin. As Christians, through actions and words, our banner should show that we belong to Christ's kingdom. Some of us raise our banner with great pride and fanfare. Yet we remain in our home port, tied to the dock, where the only persons who see our flag are persons flying the same flag. Others of us are out sailing the high seas, but our banner is difficult to recognize, smudged with layers of dirt from the lives we've lived. Then there are those of us who don't raise our banners at all. We fear that if others saw to whom we belong, they would launch an attack against us.

How well is our Christian banner being displayed? Do our co-workers know why we don't swear or the reason we don't laugh at off-color jokes? Do our neighbors know why we take people a meal when they're sick? If we were to be on trial for being Christians, would there be enough evidence to convict us?

Let us remember, like Paul, that we need not be ashamed of the gospel of Christ, for it is "the power of God for the salvation of everyone who believes." And let us resolve, like the young pastor from Rwanda, to be part of the "fellowship of the unashamed," boldly flying the banner of Christ.

ENSLAVED

"No one can serve two masters. ... You cannot serve both God and Money."
(Matthew 6:24)

The metaphor of money as a master seems rather melodramatic. We are all aware of the potential problems with money. Although probably blind to seeing these problems in ourselves, we have all seen them in others. Nonetheless, the concept of being enslaved by money and worshiping it as our master seems to be overstating the case ... doesn't it? Yet the basic question of our Christian faith is one of allegiance. Does our loyalty lie with God or the world? Are we focused on storing up treasures on earth or in heaven? For where our treasure is, there our heart will also be (Matthew 6:21).

Jesus doesn't say we should avoid serving two masters, he says we *cannot* serve two masters. That which controls and directs us is our master. Do we turn to God or money in times of decision? Do we take the job that has more money or the one with more ministry?

Honest answers to these questions find many of us genuflecting to the god of money. A focus on the wealth we have or the wealth we desire distracts us from what is more important. This distracted focus betrays our failure to trust in God alone. Scottish author and pastor George MacDonald reminds us to pray for returning to a godly order in our lives, in which money is our slave and Christ our Master.

DEFICIENCIES SUGGEST
SOMETHING MORE EXISTS

For I have the desire to do what is good, but I cannot carry it out. For what I do is not the good I want to do; no, the evil I do not want to do—this I keep on doing. (Romans 7:18b-19)

C. S. Lewis suggested there is a universal knowledge of right and wrong known as the Moral Law. The interesting corollary to the Moral Law is that although we know how we *ought* to behave, we do not do so. Author Donald Miller, in *Blue Like Jazz*, says we are flawed. There is something in us that is broken or at least malfunctioning. As a result of this flaw, it is easier to do bad things than good things. He says there is something about this imperfection that gives us a clue to the meaning of the universe.

My wife and I raised four children, and not one of them needed to be taught how to brag, lie or choose the biggest piece of cake. Indeed, much of parenting seemed like we were in a canoe trying to go upstream, rowing against the current of their natural tendencies. In spite of most parents rowing hard with both oars in the water, we see that even when children become adults, they still need laws, policemen, and sometimes prisons; this should tell us something. Our government's system of checks and balances is another testimony to the fact that all of us, left to our own devices, are prone to stray from what is right.

There is an inherent flaw/deficiency in each of us—we are inexorably drawn to sin. As we recognize the need for an answer to our sinful bent, we become an equation in search of a solution, a hunger craving satiety. If there were no answer to our souls' craving, our very existence would be a cruel farce. But Paul tells us, with an almost audible sigh of relief, that there is an answer; Jesus Christ has set us free from the enslaving power of sin (Romans 8:1-17). The answer itself gives freedom in our lives, and the fact that there *is* an answer suggests there are also answers to other significant questions that worry humanity.

THE TOWEL AND BASIN

Now that I, your Lord and Teacher, have washed your feet, you also should wash one another's feet. I have set you an example that you should do as I have done for you. (John 13:14-15)

I attended Goshen College, a small Christian school in northern Indiana. The college motto was "Culture for Service." The idea behind the motto was that we shouldn't spend four years of our time and a big chunk of money just to be learned. College was an investment, a training period to equip us to serve others.

If we take in Christian nurture and instruction, but service does not flow out of us, our spiritual lives will stagnate. It's like the difference between a mud puddle and a flowing stream. A stream takes in water from snow melting in the mountains and from rainfall, but it also has a continual *out*flow of water. As a result the water is clear and teeming with life. A mud puddle, on the other hand, takes in water but has no outflow; it stagnates, gets dirty and lacks the vital life found in the stream.

The disciples experienced a steady inflow of instruction during Jesus' time on earth but were sometimes slow to respond with practical service. At the Last Supper, they were sitting around taking in Jesus' teaching and enjoying the meal, yet they all had dirty, dusty feet, and no one took the servant's role of washing them. In this setting, Richard Foster says, "Jesus took a towel and basin and *redefined* greatness" (italics mine).

Being a servant may not seem glamorous, but it is part of our calling. And since we are created for service, as we serve others, we will find fulfillment. If our Christian lives seem unfulfilled, boring and stagnant, we should remember the mud puddle. An inflow without an outflow is unhealthy. To be a clean, flowing stream and experience an exciting, fulfilling life, we need to follow Christ's example. Let's pick up the towel and basin.

THOUGHTLESS THINKING

Finally, brothers, whatever is true, whatever is noble, whatever is right, whatever is pure, whatever is lovely, whatever is admirable—if anything is excellent or praiseworthy—think about such things. (Philippians 4:8)

For those of us who are parents, we understand the tendency to worry about things that could influence our children. We care about who their friends are, what they are reading, and what they are watching on TV and at the movies. We are well aware of the potential to be influenced by our environment. Ambient influences can help prevent bad behavior or promote good behavior. In fact, some studies have shown that even stimuli we are not consciously aware of can alter our behavior.

In 1996, psychologist John Bargh performed an intriguing experiment based on the concept of "priming." Participants were exposed to collections of words that they were to unscramble and form into sentences. These words were either polite words (e.g., patient, considerate, respect) or rude words (e.g., disturb, aggressive, bother). They were then unknowingly put in a situation where their politeness was tested. The subjects who had been primed with rude words became impatient much more quickly than those primed with polite words—even though they were unaware of their priming exposure!

Books with noble characters, movies that uphold right over wrong, friends who are truthful, conversations that are pure, art that is praiseworthy, and athletic events demonstrating excellence are all things we should experience, be exposed to, and participate in. All that is good ultimately comes to us from God. He has made us in such a way that being in the presence of that which is "excellent or praiseworthy" can influence us positively, even when we are unaware it is happening. Think about such things.

TIMID AND TEPID EVANGELISM

Then they called them in again and commanded them not to speak or teach at all in the name of Jesus. But Peter and John replied, "… For we cannot help speaking about what we have seen and heard." (Acts 4:18-20)

Why don't we share Peter and John's compulsive zeal for speaking of what we have seen? As I considered this question, several explanations came to mind: 1) **Conviction** – We often lack the conviction that we, the laity, should be sharing our faith. Although we are not pastors or evangelists, we are all called to be witnesses (Acts 1:8). Surprisingly, studies have shown that less than ten percent of new conversions to Christianity are the direct result of pastors and evangelists, while over eighty percent are due to friends interacting. 2) **Concern** – How much do we really care about the non-Christians around us? Love for others and the desire to bring them to Christ are two of the most important qualities for effective faith sharing. (Yes, even more important than knowing the origin of evil and being able to recite The Four Spiritual Laws while standing on one's head.) 3) **Contacts** – Many Christians lack even one close friend who is a non-Christian. Jesus had many meals and conversations with non-Christians. His interactions with Zacchaeus, the woman at the well, and Levi the tax collector were not anomalies but the pattern of his life. 4) **Courage** – Sharing a belief system that includes sin, a final judgment, and Jesus (who was God in flesh, raised from the dead and the only way to salvation) is not chic or politically correct. Donald Miller, in *Blue Like Jazz*, says when he shares his faith, it's hard not to feel like an Amway distributor trying to get new clients. He has to remind himself that Jesus is a person to encounter, not a product to buy.

We also need to remember that our responsibility is only to share the Good News. The Holy Spirit brings conviction and draws persons to Christ; the results of our sharing are God's responsibility, not ours. We are just called to share "what we have seen and heard."

WHO GOD IS

For this is what the high and lofty One says— / he who lives forever, whose name is holy: / "I live in a high and holy place, / but also with him who is contrite and lowly in spirit, / to revive the spirit of the lowly / and to revive the heart of the contrite." (Isaiah 57:15)

Many cultures have gods who are personal but not all-powerful. Westerners are more comfortable with an all-powerful God but tend to balk at a personal God. Why do we resist the *whole* picture of God described in Scripture (personal and powerful)?

An example may be helpful to understand our reservations better. I am a person with flaws. People who know me well are aware that I have this irritating tendency to think I'm always right (and I'm pretty sure I'm right about this assessment). Another of my imperfections is that I get annoyed when my wife says I watch too much TV. Her critique probably annoys me because it's accurate—so is that two or three flaws now? Anyway, you get the idea. Not only does a personal, all-knowing God know the problems that my close friends see, but he also knows the problems that I have managed to hide from my merely mortal acquaintances.

So, if this personal God (who has all this "dirt" on me) is also all-powerful and holy and declares that sin must be punished, then he has a frightening combination of attributes. It's probably becoming apparent why we are tempted to paint a revisionist portrait of a God who is *not* both personal and all-powerful. If we discover that "our God," however, is one who conveniently gives weight to sins in the same way we do—overlooking watching too much TV, for example—we have no doubt created him in our own image (i.e., he's not real). But we don't get to decide who God is or how he views sin. He has already declared, "I am who I am" (Exodus 3:14), and he has made clear his antipathy toward sin.

Isaiah understood what it meant that God was both personal and all-powerful. When God's majesty and holiness were revealed to Isaiah, he saw his own sinfulness in sharp contrast and declared, "Woe to me! ... I am a man of unclean lips" (6:5). Sometimes we recoil at the God of reality, who is personal and powerful. It's more comfortable to live with the God of our own imagination, who is apathetic or agreeable. Yet when we approach the God who *is*, with a contrite heart and a humble spirit, we find him with arms wide open. After all, God is also a God of immense love who desires nothing more than to revive our hearts and spirits (57:15b).

DOES GOD WANT OUR MONEY?

... Jesus saw the rich putting their gifts into the temple treasury. He also saw a poor widow put in two very small copper coins. "I tell you the truth," he said, "this poor widow has put in more than all the others." (Luke 21:1-3)

At the end of our three-year term of service at Macha Mission Hospital in Zambia, one of the local villages had a going-away party for our family. Though most of their meals were meatless, the villagers had butchered several valuable chickens for this celebration. We were honored and a little embarrassed to see persons who had so little give so much to us rich Americans. After the meal we enjoyed some songs and native dances. It was a beautiful evening.

As the evening was winding down, one of the older women of the village held up an old wicker basket, eliciting cheers of excitement as the children ran off to their thatched roof huts. They returned with tattered and worn Kwacha bills (Zambian currency). Smiling widely, they put them in the basket for us. These bills were worth literally only a few cents in U.S. currency, but they were very valuable to the Zambians. We wanted to say, "Thanks, but we don't really need your money; please keep it," but we knew that to refuse their gift would be arrogant and ungrateful. So, with misty eyes we graciously accepted the gift we didn't need from persons who could ill afford to give it away.

We tend to think in terms of the absolute value of our gifts and money, but God looks at our hearts and motives. He doesn't need our "two very small copper coins" any more than my wife and I needed the Kwacha in the wicker basket. God does, however, delight in a heart that finds joy in giving, which is invaluable to him.

December 10

WHO NEEDS WHOM?

When the trumpets sounded, the people shouted, and at the sound of the trumpet, when the people gave a loud shout, the wall collapsed.
(Joshua 6:20a)

Many of us have heard the story of Joshua and the battle at Jericho. It was the first battle after the Israelites entered the Promised Land of Canaan. The battle was as unusual as it was instructive. In fact, the very things that were unusual were also instructive, as God wanted the Israelites to learn *his* ways.

First of all, it's important to realize that the Israelites were poorly prepared to wage war. They were an agricultural people, not warriors like the Canaanites. To better prepare these farmers for battle, God asked Joshua to re-circumcise everyone (5:2). Now, in addition to being ill-prepared farmers, they were weakened by their recent surgery and no doubt sore with even minimal activity. Next, God told them to march around the city once daily for six days and then seven times on the seventh day—an exhausting task. So now we have poorly trained farmers, weak and sore from surgery and worn out from marching around in circles all day. It was only at this point that they were fully prepared, perhaps not for conventional warfare but fully prepared to see that the victory belonged to God and not to them.

This story is a helpful reminder for me when I start thinking I've got this or that skill that God could really use. When I become wrapped up in my own abilities, it's hard for God to use me at all. Believe it or not, God doesn't need capable people; he can knock down huge stone walls without anyone's lifting a finger. Instead of capable people, God wants people who realize their inadequacy and are reliant on him.

DOES HE HAVE YOUR ATTENTION?

"I gave you empty stomachs ... / I also withheld rain from you / ... I struck your gardens and vineyards / ... with blight and mildew. / Locusts devoured your fig and olive trees / ... I sent plagues among you / ... yet you have not returned to me," / declares the LORD. (Amos 4:6-7, 9-10)

Sometimes it seems hard to get God's attention. When going through dire, difficult situations, God often seems oblivious to our needs. How ironic that the circumstances that seem to demonstrate God's absence or apathy may actually be God's passionate attempts to get our attention. Dismal happenings may actually be God's tool to draw us to him and to arouse us from our self-absorbed stupor.

I was thirty-one years old, confident in my abilities to serve God, impatient with others, and short on empathy. That year ended up being quite eventful and transformative for me. I was hit by a car (breaking a leg that would take a year and two surgeries to heal); I was knocked unconscious once and passed out another time; I experienced depression, a panic attack and a seizure—apparently it's harder to get the attention of some of us than others. With chagrin, I admit that while God was tugging on my arm to get my attention, I was busy praying, "God, where are you? Don't you see I'm suffering with all these problems, and on top of all that, my arm hurts like someone is tugging on it?" Mercifully, God showed himself to me in spite of myself.

Perhaps someone can learn from this slow learner or from the children of Israel. The next time you have an empty stomach, locusts devour your fig trees, the land is parched and you seem plagued on all sides, instead of crying out to a God who seems to have left you, turn around, fall at his feet, and learn from him.

THE AROMA OF PERSECUTION

"To the angel of the church in Smyrna write: ... I know your afflictions ... Do not be afraid of what you are about to suffer. ... you will suffer persecution for ten days. Be faithful, even to the point of death, and I will give you the crown of life." (Revelation 2:8-10)

Smyrna means myrrh, which is an aromatic resin used as a spice or perfume. Myrrh comes from the bark of the myrrh tree when it is crushed. It was an appropriate name for this first-century church that was severely persecuted, giving off the unique fragrance of Christ himself, who, motivated by love, was also crushed by persecution.

Polycarp, bishop over the church in Smyrna, was one of the most famous early Christian martyrs. At the age of eighty-six, he was brought before the Roman authorities who demanded he renounce Christ and pledge allegiance to Caesar. Weak in body but strong in spirit, Polycarp replied, "Eighty-six years I have served the Lord Jesus. You will not change my heart. I tell you plainly that I am a Christian, even unto death." His martyrdom released the fragrant aroma of Christ.

Even our secular culture has noted that beauty can proceed from suffering. *The Thorn Birds* was a best-selling book written by Colleen McCullough in 1978. It was a poignantly sad book that showed the beauty revealed in people's lives when they went through great suffering. The title comes from a story about a certain bird that darts rapidly in among the thorn bushes. Every so often, one of these birds impales itself on a long, sharp thorn. Helpless to escape, it sings its most beautiful song as it dies, a metaphor of beauty joined with suffering.

Perhaps one of the major tasks in our spiritual journey is learning to deal with the question of why there is evil, suffering, and death. I believe that at least part of the great mystery of suffering is revealed when we see persons who suffer because of their love for others or for the sake of the gospel message. Voluntary suffering motivated by love is a transcendent experience. It points to something beyond itself. There is a beauty and a distinctly fragrant aroma revealed when persons love enough to suffer for others. This is the aroma of Christ, who was crushed and suffered for us.

HIDDEN IN PLAIN VIEW

But the LORD God called to the man, "Where are you?" [Adam] answered,
"I heard you in the garden, and I was afraid because I was naked; so I hid."
(Genesis 3:9-10)

Charis was nearly two years old, and we'd almost weaned her off her pacifier when one day she mysteriously went missing. We'd gone through the house calling her name and were frantically starting an outside search when we found her. She had hidden herself in a large suitcase in one of the main rooms of the house, feverishly sucking on her pacifier, ignoring our distraught calls.

We smile as we reminisce about her childish attempt to hide her petty offense, but are we so different? We may not *physically* try to hide, but rationalizations and denials may be the metaphoric suitcases wherein we cower when we do something wrong. Do our rationalizations appear any less juvenile than the suitcase, to a God who knows all our thoughts before we even think them?

Addressing our reluctance to be honest with God, Philip Yancey says, "Foolishly, I hide myself in fear that God will be displeased, though in fact the hiding may be what displeases God the most." We should come to God openly. It makes no sense to hide what God already sees. We should also abandon attempts to justify ourselves and our actions, first because we cannot do it and secondly because we need not do it. Jesus Christ has already justified us; he has made us holy. No reason remains to try to hide from God.

STAIRWAY TO HEAVEN

[Jacob] had a dream in which he saw a stairway resting on the earth, with its top reaching to heaven, and the angels of God were ascending and descending on it. There above it stood the LORD ... (Genesis 28:12-13)

In the Garden of Eden, God and humans were initially in intimate fellowship. Then sin entered the world and created a chasm between God and humans. Jacob's dream portrays this separation of a holy God, high in the heavens, and a sinful man, Jacob, down on earth.

The stairway, "resting on the earth, with its top reaching to heaven," represents God's efforts to bridge this great chasm. The Old Testament tells many stories of how God's love reached out to humans, attempting to restore their lost fellowship. Each story is like a step in the stairway and an example of God's relentless, reconciling love. God initiated covenant *promises* with his people. He gave *protection* and was the *provision* for their needs. At times, God even allowed a *revelation* of a portion of his glory to humans. God entered into *partnership* with humans to bring about his purposes. God also directed sacrificial offerings as a way to provide *forgiveness*, a necessity for a holy God interacting with sinful humans. Yet the abyss separating God and humans remained.

In the New Testament, Jesus made an interesting statement: "You shall see heaven open, and the angels of God ascending and descending *on the Son of Man*" (John 1:51, italics mine). Jesus is the stairway! Jesus is the ultimate promise, provision, protection, partnership, forgiveness, and revelation of God. Jesus is the final answer to the separation of a holy God and sinful humans. It is in Jesus alone that we find reconciliation with God (II Corinthians 5:18). Jesus is our stairway to heaven. The great chasm, the huge abyss, the vast gorge that had for so long separated a holy God from sinful humans, has finally and completely been bridged, by Jesus.

THE BLUSH OF GUILT

When the woman saw that the fruit of the tree was good…, she took some and ate it. She also gave some to her husband, who was with her, and he ate it. … Then the man and his wife heard the sound of the LORD God as he was walking in the garden in the cool of the day, and they hid from the LORD God among the trees of the garden. (Genesis 3:6, 8)

Guilt is not a twentieth-century invention; it's been around since the dawn of time. In recent days, however, many have tried to purge feelings of guilt as being unhealthy or prudishly Victorian. Scripture more often talks about guilt as a condition rather than a feeling. Biblical discussion of guilt tends to focus on the responsibility we have for our actions instead of focusing on our feelings.

There is an interesting physical phenomenon often associated with embarrassment—blushing. While one may feel guilt for an action unknown to anyone else, it is only at the instant of discovery that blushing occurs. Mark Twain said, "Man is the only animal that blushes, or needs to." Almost all other emotions can be concealed or contrived by voluntary control of one's facial muscles. Yet the embarrassed blushing that comes from being "found out" is unstoppable and painfully obvious for all to see.

Guilt in our spiritual lives, like blushing in our physical bodies, can serve as a "red flag." While blushing causes us to turn away from others, guilt should cause us to turn toward Christ. He is the divine solution for our sin, guilt and embarrassment. In Christ, we see that the emphasis is not on our failure, which is a given. Rather, the emphasis is on his forgiveness, which is freely available to us.

Guilt as an end in itself is *de*structive to our emotional well-being and *ob*structive to our Christian walk. But guilt can be a blessing when it causes us to turn toward Christ and receive his forgiveness. After all, we are his "blushing bride."

THE GOSPEL OF JESUS CHRIST

But let justice roll on like a river, / righteousness like a never-failing stream!
(Amos 5:24)

Many churches find themselves divided, pulling on opposite ends of a rope engaged in a theological tug-of-war between the practical and the pious. One side has the pragmatists pulling for a stronger social gospel. Jesus was anointed to "preach good news to the poor ... to proclaim freedom for the prisoners ... and to release the oppressed" (Luke 4:18). We should follow in his steps, meeting the needs of the poor and correcting the injustices in the world around us. We are called to put words into action.

Pulling in the other direction are the pious who promote a spiritual gospel. What good is it to put food in people's bellies and roofs over their heads if they are doomed to a Christless eternity? Jesus warned, "You must be born again" (John 3:7b). Spiritual needs will always trump physical/social needs.

Yet a balanced view of the gospel message and the life of Christ demonstrates an integrated perspective. Jesus promised, "Anyone who gives you a cup of water *in my name* ... will certainly not lose his reward" (Mark 9:41b, italics mine). The good news of the gospel is not just peace and social justice any more than it is just sin and salvation. Ethicist Stanley Hauerwas says, "Words like 'peace' and 'justice' are words awaiting content. The church cannot define these words apart from the life, death and resurrection of Jesus Christ."

Unfortunately, we continue to pull on our end of the rope, straining and leaning into it, confident in our bias. We need to be able to "let go." When we let go, and inevitably fall to the ground, we will find ourselves at the feet of Jesus. And this is the right place for us to be so we can cry out for forgiveness and wisdom. For it is not just a social or spiritual gospel; it is the gospel of Jesus Christ. As Jesus lived out the good news of the gospel, he showed no compartmentalization of social or spiritual needs, practicality or piety—he met *all* the people's needs.

December 17

BOUNDARIES

And [in the Garden of Eden] the LORD God commanded the man, "You are free to eat from any tree in the garden; but you must not eat from the tree of the knowledge of good and evil, for when you eat of it you will surely die."
(Genesis 2:16-17)

From the very beginning we see that God granted us freedom within boundaries. This truth applies to all aspects of our lives, including inter-personal relationships, use of money, sexual activity, stewardship of our natural world, use of our time, etc. Our natural tendency, however, is not to glory in our many freedoms but to grumble about the few boundaries "unnecessarily" imposed on us.

As a young boy in northern Indiana, one summer day found me outside playing in a large cornfield. I ran between the long rows of corn as I chased a surprised rabbit. Suddenly, I became aware of an unset-tling fact—I was lost! The corn stalks towered a foot above my head, so I couldn't see any landmarks. Panicked, I ran this way and that way to no avail. Each cornstalk looked like the next. Waxing theatrical, I flashed forward two weeks to when circling buzzards would help my grieving family find closure. As saner thoughts returned, I pondered my predica-ment. I realized that although it was a huge cornfield, if I just followed one row to its end, I would be at an edge of the field. I could then walk around the perimeter of the cornfield until I found the spot where I had entered. The fact that the field had boundaries worked out for my good.

Our omniscient, omnipotent, loving God did not whimsically decide on various boundaries to make our lives difficult. "OK, let's put one here, and oh, let's put a boundary over there too; that one should really frustrate those humans." Instead, God put boundaries in our lives for our own good. He looked at things that would harm us, called them sin and warned us to avoid them. Unfortunately, being of the same ilk as Adam and Eve, we don't notice all the trees we are free to enjoy. Instead, we see the one tree we're not supposed to eat from, and it suddenly becomes the one we desperately want. We need to remember God gives us freedoms for our enjoyment but boundaries for our protection.

PURGED FOR PURITY

... To those sanctified in Christ Jesus and called to be holy, ... Grace and
peace to you from God our Father and the Lord Jesus Christ.
(I Corinthians 1:2-3)

To be sanctified means to be set apart or to be made holy. So, we have been sanctified (made holy) in Christ Jesus, yet we are still called to *be* holy as well. Without getting into the constructs of the theological terms of "positional" and "progressive" sanctification, suffice it to say that Scripture clearly teaches that we are to move beyond merely receiving the holiness conferred by salvation, to actually experiencing holiness in our everyday lives.

The Old Testament is full of rituals and practices designed to illustrate the importance of purity, holiness, and separation from that which is unclean. The important theme of holiness continues in the New Testament. Ananias and Sapphira were struck down dead because of greed and lying (Acts 5:1-11). God clearly desires the purging of that which is unclean from our lives.

John Hull, an Australian theologian, was born with normal vision. Due to an injury, however, he lost the vision in one eye as a child. Over a period of years, he slowly lost vision in the other eye and became completely blind. He suffered from a medical condition called sympathetic ophthalmia. Because his bad eye was left in place, his body formed antibodies against the damaged tissue. Unfortunately, those antibodies attacked the good eye as well as the bad one. If the bad eye had been removed, he could have retained vision in the other eye.

In a similar way, if that which is unholy in our lives is not dealt with, it has an insidious way of damaging other areas of our lives. God's call for us to experience a pure and holy life is clear. When we are flippant about unholiness in any area of our lives, we court disaster.

MESSIANIC ANTICIPATION

... [Simeon] was waiting for the consolation of Israel, and the Holy Spirit was upon him. It had been revealed to him by the Holy Spirit that he would not die before he had seen the Lord's Christ. (Luke 2:25-26)

I once heard someone say there are three parts to an experience—anticipation, fulfillment (the experience itself) and remembrance. Simeon's lifelong anticipation was for the coming of the Messiah and the promise that he would get to see "the consolation [comfort] of Israel." Yet Simeon's expectation was just a microcosm of the groundswell of expectation (in heaven and on earth) for the watershed event of all history, Jesus' birth.

Scripture itself anticipates the coming of the Savior. After humanity first sinned in Genesis 3, God promised that the offspring of woman would one day crush the serpent's head. Isaiah, Micah and the Psalms are full of prophetic anticipation of the Messiah. In addition to the scriptural record of anticipation, Paul said in Romans that "creation has been groaning as in the pains of childbirth" (8:22). Creation, personified as a woman in the throes of labor, anxiously awaited the birth of the Christ child.

I also believe the heavenly hosts were fervently awaiting the coming of Christ, who was the word (*logos*) becoming flesh (John 1:14). In the Old Testament, angelic visits to humans were relatively few and far between. However, as we near the birth of Christ, we see a crescendo of angelic visits: to Zechariah, to Mary, to Joseph and then the multitude of angels who appeared to the shepherds. The angelic anticipation, excitement and joy are almost palpable as one reads the New Testament account.

At Christmas each year, we remember this unparalleled event. It is no less significant for us than it was for Simeon, for Adam and Eve, for the twelve disciples and no less significant than it will be for some yet unnamed person who may be born one hundred years from now. The coming of the Messiah was an occurrence that affected all who went before and all who will come after. Our remembrance should be no less passionate than Simeon's anticipation of this amazing event.

THE SOUND OF SILENCE

Be still, and know that I am God. (Psalm 46:10a)

It's been said, "Nature abhors a vacuum" (when it comes to housecleaning, I share the same loathing). Similarly, contemporary American culture seems to abhor silence. Anytime there's a space of silence, there's a rush to fill it with conversations, activities, radio shows, music, and perhaps most often, television or computer entertainment. Why are we so reluctant to have periods of silence?

Silence makes us so uncomfortable that we often engage in meaningless chatter to fill the void. In the sixties, Simon and Garfunkel popularized a song called, "The Sound of Silence." I believe their song touched on a spiritual principle, for it is only as we get away from the ambient noise of life that we are able to hear what is more important.

God commands us, "Be still, and know that I am God." This is a silence that goes beyond the absence of noise. We need to learn to practice a receptive silence that involves an absence of distracting noise and thoughts as a means to an end. Our ultimate goal is to be able to hear the deep and inner longings of our own soul and to hear the very voice of God so that we can know him better.

The Teacher of Ecclesiastes says there is "a time to be silent and a time to speak" (Ecclesiastes 3:7). Our inner beings were created with a yearning for a receptive silence where we can enter into communion with God. It is the desire of God's heart to meet that longing. Even now, as you are reading this meditation, God may be inviting you to take some time in silence with him. Be still, and wait …

PROCESS OR PRODUCT?

But with loud shouts they insistently demanded that he be crucified ... [They] led him away ... A large number of people followed him, including women who mourned and wailed for him. Jesus turned and said to them, "Daughters of Jerusalem, do not weep for me ..." (Luke 23:23a, 26-28)

Picking out a Christmas tree has become an integral part of our family's holiday ritual. Debating the shape, height and fullness of different trees, we stomp around the tree farm with our ears and noses red from the cold. It's often quite a lengthy process, so I was delighted with how fast it went this past year. The owners always have a few trees they have pre-cut and set up in the parking area. Typically, we look at them first but are unsatisfied; this year was different. My wife, daughter and I all agreed that we really liked one of the cut trees. I went ahead and told the proprietor that we wanted it and paid the bill. We put the tree in the back of our van, and we were on our way. The whole process only took fifteen minutes!

As we drove home, I was quite pleased with how efficient we'd been. I noticed, however, that my wife was ominously quiet, and then I saw my daughter in tears. Although I'm slow about these things, it began to dawn on me that something was wrong here. Unfortunately, I couldn't figure out what it was. We'd all agreed on the tree, and we'd saved so much time—someone help me out here. My wife patiently explained how there are some things more important than just getting a nice tree. The process of stomping around together, discussing the merits of each tree and making a family memory is actually more important than getting the tree itself. Being a goal-oriented male, I'd been insensitive to the importance of the process and the people along the way.

Jesus was on his way to be crucified for the redemption of all mankind, yet he stopped along the way to comfort some weeping women. He didn't let his future goal overshadow his present path. We are reminded that our lofty goals should not trivialize what we do (or don't do) along the way. As usual, Jesus is our mentor *par excellence.*

SPIRITUALLY ALIVE

'For in him [Christ] we live and move and have our being.' (Acts 17:28a)

How do we know if we are spiritually alive? Can we check our spiritual pulse or blood pressure? Can we put a mirror next to our mouths and noses to look for the telltale vapor sign from breathing? My father-in-law is 94 years old. He lives in a personal care home, where he has to hang a sign on his doorknob each morning so people know he's still alive. How do we know if we are spiritually alive?

Even our secular society intuitively knows life is meant to be more than mere existence. In the 1995 film *Braveheart*, thirteenth-century Scottish hero William Wallace is heading off into a battle he has little hope of surviving. As he leaves, he declares, "Every man dies; but not every man really lives." He knew that it is having purpose beyond oneself that turns a meager existence into truly being alive.

Christianity has the answer to our souls' yearning for a vital spiritual life. The answer begins with the knowledge that a thriving spiritual life is *not* about us. We must progress, however, to the awareness that it *is* about Christ. In the first chapter of Ephesians, the apostle Paul catalogues a long list of things that are "in Christ." The believers at Ephesus were faithful "in Christ" (1:1). Believers are chosen "in him" (1:4) and predestined for adoption "through Jesus" (1:5). We have redemption "in him" (1:7), and our purpose is revealed "in Christ" (1:9). We have hope "in Christ" (1:12), and we were marked with a seal of the Holy Spirit "in him" (1:13). And one day, everything in heaven and earth will be brought into right relationship "in Christ" (1:9-10).

Our spiritual life is all about Jesus Christ. Paradoxically, we are alive spiritually when we die to self and allow Christ to live in us because *he* is the source of our life (Galatians 2:20). In Christ we have spiritual life and eternal life, but it is also in Christ that we have abundant life (John 10:10)—life with peace, joy and purpose. Truly, it is *"in him* [that] we live and move and have our being" (italics mine). The sign on our door attesting to our spiritual life says, "Jesus Christ."

THE WISDOM OF GULLIBILITY

May the God of hope fill you with all joy and peace as you trust in him, so that you may overflow with hope by the power of the Holy Spirit. (Romans 15:13)

The seventeenth-century Age of Reason preceded the eighteenth-century Age of Enlightenment, when critical questioning of traditional customs, beliefs, and morals was praised. In some ways, our present Western perspective is a natural progression and could conceivably be labeled the Age of Cynicism. Cynicism is an outlook that doubts rather than believes, squelching hope, optimism, and even intimacy (since intimacy is dependent on trust, which is non-existent for a cynical person). Cynical persons tend to feel smug since they're the only ones wise enough to see that no one's motives are pure, nothing can be taken at face value, and behind every silver lining there is a cloud.

In I Samuel 17, we read the story of David and Goliath. David's father Jesse sent young David to the battle lines to check on his older brothers. When David arrived, he was surprised to find Goliath, the giant Philistine champion, taunting and defying the armies of God. When David criticized and challenged the heathen champion, David's older brother Eliab "burned with anger" (v. 28). Eliab thought he could see through David's façade and concluded he was "conceited" and "wicked" and had just come for the excitement of being able to "watch the battle." Eliab's cynicism blinded him to the reality of his younger brother's courage and faith.

In *The Abolition of Man*, C. S. Lewis points out that to "see through" everything is really to see nothing at all. Some things, some persons, and some beliefs are in reality just what they appear to be at first blush. We need not see something beneath the surface, behind the curtain or beyond the obvious. If we live in constant fear of being gullible, naïve, or taken advantage of, we will miss the enjoyment and excitement of creation, the meaning and mystery of intimate relationships, and the peace and purpose of faith in God.

If you've ever been hurt in a relationship or deceived by someone you trusted, it has probably left you more cautious: "Once burned twice careful." However, which is the greater error, to choose to trust (aware that we may occasionally get hurt) or to assume that nothing is what it appears to be (fearfully protecting ourselves)? The Apostle Paul says the "God of hope" wants us to "overflow with hope." Having trust is fertile ground for growing hope, which allows us to receive God's blessings of joy and peace.

CHRISTMAS HOPE

Simeon, a good man, … lived in the prayerful expectancy of help for Israel …
The Holy Spirit had shown him that he would see the Messiah of God before
he died. Led by the Spirit, he entered the Temple … Simeon took [Jesus] into
his arms and blessed God: "… release me in peace as you promised … I've
seen your salvation." (Luke 2:25b-30, The Message)

Simeon was one in a long line of Jews who awaited the coming of the Messiah. Simeon, however, had been promised he would not see death before he had seen the Messiah, so he waited with expectancy, faith, and hope. We don't know how long Simeon waited, but it was probably many years and may have been most of his lifetime. I suspect there were times when Simeon had doubts. Simeon was not remembered, however, for any doubts he may have had but for his faith and hope. Being a person who experiences doubts, I find this very comforting.

Most of our lives, like Simeon's life, are spent in times between promise and fulfillment, times of waiting in faith and hope. Are we faithfully holding on to hope as Simeon did? Or do we fear embracing hope because we can't bear facing disappointment one more time? Simeon's life posture was one of looking for Jesus. Simeon lived for one thing, he waited for one thing, he hoped for one thing and he yearned for one thing—to see Jesus. And he did! His hope and waiting and yearning were all worth it.

Today is Christmas Eve, and my prayer is that what we want most will not be under the Christmas tree tomorrow morning. Rather, my prayer is that what we want more than anything else in all the world is the same thing Simeon wanted two thousand years ago—to see Jesus!

CHRISTMAS TRUTH

Truth is nowhere to be found … (Isaiah 59:15)

It is December, and for about eighty percent of Americans it's the Christmas Season. However, for those concerned about political correctness, it is only a generic "Holiday Season." This year, some conservative Christian groups have revolted against the secularization of Christmas. They have mounted a concerted effort to maintain Christmas as a *Christian* Holiday. Some Christians are boycotting stores that sell "Holiday Trees" or refuse Salvation Army bell-ringers or require their employees to say "Happy Holidays" instead of "Merry Christmas."

As I pondered the pros and cons of this ongoing debate, I became aware of a sense of sadness for those who don't view Christmas as the amazing event that I do. "In the fullness of time," God "became flesh and made his dwelling among us" (John 1:14). Because Christ came on that first Christmas, the great questions of our origin, purpose and destiny have been answered. Although I believe the answer is right in front of us, many do not see it that way.

Winston Churchill once said, "Men will occasionally stumble over the truth, but most of them will pick themselves up and hurry off as if nothing ever happened." In the brouhaha about Christmas, I fear that many people each year are stumbling over the truth of the most significant event of all time. With Christ's birth, the Creator stepped on the stage with his creation, in order to reconcile us to him. With Jesus' resurrection, he confirmed our hope for life beyond the grave. His statement, "I am the way and the truth and the life" (John 14:6), was either arrogant and delusional, or it was the key to the meaning of our very existence.

Each year at Christmas, millions stumble over the truth, pick themselves up and continue on. My hope is that some will examine that which they are stumbling over and embrace the truth of Jesus Christ as the Messiah, God in the flesh. If they do, they will find themselves set free (John 8:32), and Christmas will never be just another holiday again. Merry Christmas!

POURED OUT FOR GOD

A woman came to Jesus with an alabaster jar of very expensive perfume, which she poured on his head ... "Why this waste?" [the disciples] asked. "This perfume could have been sold at a high price and the money given to the poor." ... Jesus said to them, "Why are you bothering this woman? She has done a beautiful thing to me." (Luke 26:7-10)

The disciples' concern for the wasted perfume illustrates that even those of us who are followers of Christ still believe God needs the things we have. Psychology describes a similar self-important mindset in our secular world. Erik Erikson's classic stages of development suggest the primary focus of our lives from the age of 35 to 65 is on "Generativity vs. Stagnation." We focus on contributing whatever assets we have to society and on raising families—a contribution to the future. But, as is often the case, God's view tends to be at odds with the perspective of society and even many Christians. God is not looking to see what he can get from us.

Dr. David Dorsey, an Old Testament scholar from a nearby seminary, was a productive theologian who had written numerous scholarly works. Although only in his late fifties, he was already well-known nationwide in the academic Christian community. Unfortunately, he had contracted a painful, debilitating illness that markedly curtailed his ability to write, and he often struggled just to get through the classes he taught. One evening in class, he candidly shared with us students about how difficult it was to remember that in God's eyes his value was not dependent on his output; God did not need his book-writing abilities. God was more concerned about cultivating a deeper relationship with Dave and growing his faith than in using him as a resource.

Could it be that we are not primarily here to do and accomplish things, even good things, for God's kingdom? Is it possibly more important that we grow in our love, our dependence, and our trust in God than that we write a book or build a homeless shelter?

I recently attended Dr. Dorsey's funeral. It was hard not to think that his early death was such a waste of an amazing resource for God's kingdom. However, as people shared about his life and all the lives he had touched, I smelled the aroma of a very expensive perfume poured out for God. And I could hear God's voice saying: "Thank you, David. Your life has been a beautiful thing poured out for me."

FRAMEWORK FOR GROWTH

*... You need someone to teach you the elementary truths of God's word all over
again. You need milk, not solid food! ... But solid food is for the mature, who by
constant use have trained themselves to distinguish good from evil.*
(Hebrews 5:12, 14)

To say I wasn't an athlete in high school is kind of like saying Yul Brynner
didn't have a ponytail in the movie *The King and I*—it's true but doesn't
go far enough. I was, nonetheless, on the wrestling team during my sopho-
more year. My goal was to be a good wrestler (and to impress the girls), so
I put several disciplines in place to try to reach my goal. I worked out with
weights to put on more muscle mass, engaged in cardiovascular workouts
to increase my endurance, and practiced wrestling moves to enhance my
skills.

Most of us make plans to reach goals in different areas of our lives,
yet few of us make plans to reach our *spiritual* goals. We want to grow into
the image of Christ, but we kind of hope it will just happen apart from any
planning or discipline. This is not unlike the hope that one day I'll wake up
to discover that I mysteriously became a concert pianist overnight.

Peter Scazzero, in *Emotionally Healthy Spirituality*, encourages us
to develop a "rule of life," an intentional plan for spiritual growth. He explains that the word "rule" derives from the Greek word for "trellis." A rule
of life is a framework to encourage our spiritual growth much like a trellis
is a framework to encourage the healthy growth of a grapevine. Each one
of us can develop our own individualized rule of life based on the spiritual
practices that bring us closer to God. The idea is to practice them several
times each day, even if we only spend five minutes on them each time. This
rule of life reminds us that we belong to Christ and his kingdom. My rule
of life over the course of a week (doing one to three practices per day) includes silence, prayer, *lectio divina*, Bible study, listening to worship music,
Sabbath (rest) time, exercise, reading, building relationships, writing, and
going to church.

A rule of life is only a tool (a trellis) that God can use to nurture our
spiritual lives. Setting up the trellis is our part, but God alone can cause the
growth to occur. If you were going to develop a rule of life (assuming you
don't already have one), what practices would you include that would help
you grow in intimacy with God?

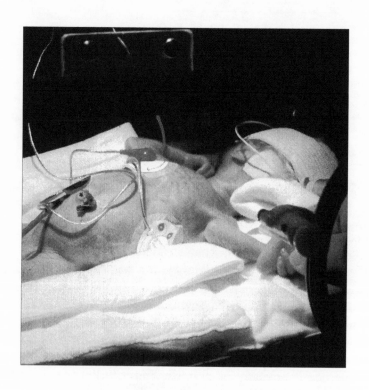

WHAT DOES PRAYER DO?

[God said], "My heart is changed within me; / all my compassion is aroused."
(Hosea 11:8b)

I gently placed my hand on the tiny head of my newborn daughter Amaris as she lay in her incubator. Born prematurely, she weighed one pound fourteen ounces. She was now depending on a ventilator to breathe, getting antibiotics for pneumonia, receiving a blood transfusion for anemia and struggling to survive. As a worried father, I prayed with a fervor and hope born out of desperation.

Are our prayers, whether fervent or flippant, heard? Doesn't God already know our situation, the desire of our heart and the outcome that is best? He certainly doesn't need our feeble prayers to allow him to intervene. How could our prayers change the mind and plans of an omniscient, omnipotent God?

Philosophically, one could make the case that our prayers do not change God's mind or the situation. If so, then perhaps prayer is primarily for *our* benefit, placing ourselves in submission to God's unchanging, perfect will. Scripturally, however, time after time we see God act in response to prayers. Angels were dispatched (Daniel 10:12), the sick were healed (James 5:15), fire fell down from heaven (I Kings 18:36-38), the Holy Spirit filled people (Acts 8:15-17), and God changed his mind about punishing Nineveh (Jonah 3:8-10).

The Bible shows us a God who clearly is influenced by prayer. Indeed, one of the *unchanging* characteristics of God is that he allows himself to be *changed* by our prayers. God holds our relationship in such high regard that he allows our talking with him (prayer) to affect him. The fact that God allows our prayers to affect him transforms our prayer time from a dutiful drudgery to a dynamic dialogue—a dialogue that demonstrates God's love, compassion, power and mercy. Amaris is now completely healthy, married and working as a family practice physician in Philadelphia.

WHO IS JESUS?

"But as I told you, you have seen me and still you do not believe." (John 6:36)

What did Jesus mean when he said that his disciples still did not believe? In the scriptural context, this was one of Jesus' most popular periods of time. The people were following him wherever he went (6:24). Some said he was a great prophet (6:14) while others thought he was a great teacher, giving him the respected title of "Rabbi" (6:25). Some persons even wanted to make him king (6:15). What more did Jesus want?

The question of Jesus' identity is a constant and recurring theme in the New Testament Gospels. Although we have a good record of many things Jesus did, the scriptural focus is not so much on what Jesus did as on who he was. The New Testament begins with Matthew recording the ancestral genealogy of Jesus—his human identity—and ends with Jesus declaring, "I am the Alpha and the Omega, the First and the Last, the Beginning and the End" (Revelation 22:13)—his eschatological (end times) identity. At the trial that ultimately led to his death, Pilate did not ask Jesus what he had done, but who he was: "Are you the king of the Jews?" (John 18:33).

In an intimate moment with his disciples, Jesus did not ask them what people were saying about his actions, but about his identity: "Who do people say [I am]?" (Matthew 16:13). The responses were strikingly similar to what we hear today. Some thought Jesus was a great teacher, a great prophet, or someone with kingly potential, but Jesus deemed all these responses inadequate. What they still did "not believe" was that he was the Messiah, the Christ, the Anointed One, and the Son of the living God!

Ultimately, the supreme question Christianity poses to each person today is the same as it was two thousand years ago. It is the question Jesus finally put to his disciples: "But what about you? ... Who do you say that I am?" (Matthew 16:15). If Scripture is true, how we answer this one question will not only affect our present lives but also determine our eternal destinies.

SQUANDERED YEARS

What the locust swarm has left the great locusts have eaten / ... Wake up,
you drunkards, and weep! / ... Rend your heart / and not your garments. /
Return to the LORD your God, / for he is gracious and compassionate, / ... "I
will repay you for the years the locusts have eaten ..." (Joel 1:4, 5, 2:13, 25)

In high school Rob paid for two of his girlfriends to get abortions, yet
he still fathered one child (that he's aware of) out of wedlock. He abused
alcohol and drugs and stole to support his habits. He ended up in prison
and then a series of rehab programs. He had the classic story of a squandered youth.

This man's life, however, was miraculously changed by a transforming encounter with Jesus Christ. He is now married with three children and pastors a church. God has indeed been "gracious and compassionate" to him. His youth was a barren wasteland devastated by the
locusts of self-gratification, yet God has led him to "green pastures" and
"quiet waters" (Psalm 23:2). In some sense, "the years the locusts have
eaten" have been redeemed through God's grace and compassion.

Nonetheless, he shared his past with tear-filled eyes. The process
of true repentance ("rending the heart") is a painful one. It involves seeing
the reality of our sin and its ramifications. For Rob that involved seeing
his former girlfriends as young women whose lives he had wounded. He
also became aware of friends and family whom he had hurt and disappointed time after time. Through the process of rending his heart, he also
came to the painful understanding that his disobedience was a spurning
of God's love. We can rejoice that we have a merciful God who forgives
us and often blesses us in spite of our heinous histories. Nonetheless,
restoring the years the locusts have eaten doesn't necessarily mean we
won't experience pain for what we've done. Even forgiven sin may have
consequences.

REMEMBER

Then Jesus asked them, "When I sent you without purse, bag or sandals, did you lack anything?" "Nothing," they answered. (Luke 22:35)

The last few days before each of our girls left for college were always packed with final words of advice. It's a big world out there with many decisions, temptations and dangers. We didn't want to neglect any final counsel that might have proven helpful.

At the Last Supper, Jesus knew he would soon be leaving his disciples, and he also had some final counsel for them. Instead of just making wise declarations of good advice to guide his disciples (which is what I tried to do with my daughters), Jesus asked them a question. He asked his disciples if they lacked anything when he had sent them out with nothing. As they thought back, a collective chandelier of light bulbs lit up in the disciples' heads (imagine their pre-Edisonian surprise!). No, they had not lacked anything; God's provision had always been present. The memory that God was faithful served as their instructive advice— God had always supplied their needs. The fact that God had met their needs in the past gave them faith that he would continue to do so in the future.

Our 27-year-old daughter, Amaris, had two life-threatening events in the past year. First, she accidentally stuck herself with a needle from an HIV-positive patient, and then several weeks ago she had a pulmonary embolism (a large blood clot that lodged in her lung). After I got over the "It's not fair. Why her again?" feelings, I was struck by a positive reality. Amaris is collecting experiences of God's faithfulness in adversity. When she encounters difficult times in the future, she will remember (as Jesus' disciples did) God's faithfulness in the past. Those memories will form a firm foundation for her faith in God for the future.

ABOUT THE AUTHOR

Myron Miller is a family practice physician in rural
Pennsylvania. He has spent several years doing medical
mission work in Zambia and Honduras. He enjoys
reading a wide variety of books and being out in the
beauty of God's creation. He is married and has four
married daughters and one granddaughter.
This is his first book.

Made in the USA
Charleston, SC
05 October 2014